EZIO PINZA

BOOKS BY ROBERT MAGIDOFF:

Rye and Nettle (Verse)

In Anger and Pity

The Kremlin vs. the People

Yehudi Menuhin

The Possessed
(A dramatization of the Dostoevsky novel)

Ezio Pinza

EZIO PINZA

An Autobiography

WITH ROBERT MAGIDOFF

Rinehart & Company, Inc.

NEW YORK   TORONTO

Grateful acknowledgment is made to Alfred A. Knopf, Inc. for permission to reprint a brief excerpt from THEME AND VARIATIONS, An Autobiography, by Bruno Walter, Copyright, 1946.

First Printing, August 1958
Second Printing, November 1958
Third Printing, February 1959

Published simultaneously in Canada by
Clarke, Irwin & Company, Ltd., Toronto

A Note from the Collaborator

ONE FEBRUARY day in 1957, I pressed the doorbell of a handsome modern house in the wooded suburbs of Stamford, Connecticut—and gave a start. Instead of the usual ring, I heard chimes play the opening bars of "Some Enchanted Evening."

I needn't have been surprised; the house was Ezio Pinza's, and my visit was in response to an invitation from the famous actor-singer to collaborate in the writing of his autobiography.

The door was opened by a maid, who invited me in, then left me face to face with the most enormous great Dane I had ever seen. Although full of instant friendliness, he scared me half out of my wits by pawing me with feet that seemed the size of boxing gloves. Then, in excess of affection, he pressed his huge bulk against me and nearly threw me to the carpet.

"Satan!" thundered a voice which matched the size of the animal. Satan instantly deserted me and bounded to the door of the living room, where he meekly subsided at the feet of his master, Ezio Pinza. It was an aging Pinza—streaks of gray in his thick brown hair, his step slow—but he was still, as the press called him, "Pinza the Magnificent": over six feet tall, with an enormous chest and broad shoulders, a splendidly shaped head and a strong, stern face. His light eyes were tired, and his movements slow and deliberate, in the manner of a man trying to conserve his strength, giving him an air of detachment, of indiffer-

v

ence almost. But once we had come to an understanding about the events in his life outside the scope of a published work, Ezio Pinza proved a frank and willing subject. Every now and then his reserve broke, his eyes would sparkle and laugh, and his voice would ring out with its old force as he relived some episodes of his life with all the intensity of youth. I particularly cherished those moments when, in talking about opera, he would sing softly by way of illustration. The beauty, the artistry of half voice filled the sun-swept living room, compelling me to forget my paper and pencil and share in the happiness that now transformed the singer's face.

From the outset Mr. Pinza insisted that his wife, Doris, participate in our talks. This she did gladly, but not before she wrested from me a promise that I would ask her to leave us alone if at any time I felt her presence curbed Pinza's style or my freedom of inquiry. That presence, I soon realized, was in fact a necessity to me. I noticed that whenever her duties as mistress of the house or the mother of three growing children compelled her to leave us for any length of time, Mr. Pinza began to lose interest and indulged in lapses of memory. When baseball games started, he turned on the television the moment Mrs. Pinza left the room. In fact, even her presence could not keep him from watching the first inning or two on the days his beloved Dodgers played. His running commentary on the game, I might add, was incomparably livelier and hardly less knowledgeable than the one by the official commentator.

Since my visits with the convalescing singer were limited by the doctor to the two hours beween four and six, and therefore often coincided with a televised game, I would force myself to suggest resuming our work after the first inning, for I, too, am a baseball fan. Then Mr. Pinza would ask his cook to keep an eye on the television set in her bedroom and instantly report each run to home plate. If she failed to appear after ten or fifteen minutes, he would raise his voice in a thunderous "Viola!" The startled Satan, lying peacefully at his feet, would rise to his gigantic height and turn his eyes on me, while Viola would come rushing in to report guiltily, "No run yet, Mr. Pinza."

In the course of the slightly more than two months we worked together, the singer's cheer deserted him only two or three times, when he complained of a stiffness in the right leg, or of a general feeling of weakness. Fearing the interview was too tiring, I would then offer to leave, but he would not hear of it.

"I'll feel weak whether you are here or not. What is worse, I'll start worrying about not being able to work again. And so, where did we leave off?" Pinza would say.

If anything can be said to have dominated Pinza's mind during those last weeks of his life, it was the thought of going back to work. It did not necessarily have to be the stage; he knew by now that never again would he be able to sustain performances night after night. But he could take part in a television show, or in a motion picture.

One day I found him particularly weak. Almost irritable. I would have left, but Mrs. Pinza had taken one of the children to Stamford and had asked me to stay on until she returned. I was about to suggest to the singer that he lie down when the telephone rang in the next room. Limping, he went to take the call. When he returned, he was a new man.

"It was an offer of work!" he exclaimed. "Two offers! No, don't worry, not right away—in the fall. I'm accepting one definitely—a show based on my first years in the opera world. Some young man will portray me and do the singing. I'll narrate the story, or something of that sort. But it's the other program that fascinates me." He paced the room slowly, but without a trace of the limp that had been so pronounced only a few minutes earlier. "What a show David Susskind has dreamed up! A spectacular built around the story of Pinocchio. Mickey Rooney would play Pinocchio, and I the old carpenter, his father. But they want me to sing, and I know what Dr. Fogel will say about that," he added gloomily.

I recalled the magic of Pinza's half voice and suggested that he could get by with it.

"Do you think I could?" He looked at me. "Well, maybe. It would suit the character."

The thought of taking part in the spectacular stayed with him until the day of the fatal stroke. He often spoke about *Pinocchio,* and when Mrs. Pinza reminded him that the doctor forbade him to make any public appearances for at least another year, he replied quietly, deliberately, as though of a decision made, "I know what he's afraid of, but I don't care. I want to die on the stage."

Ezio Pinza's thoughts were very far from death on that day of the telephone call about *Pinocchio.* When I repeated my earlier suggestion that he lie down, he chided me for being lazy. "Let's go back to work," he said. He suddenly looked at his watch, then at me, thoughtfully. "I'm glad Doris is still away. There's something I'd like you to put in the book about which she must not know

now. It must come as a surprise. I want to dedicate my life story to Doris. I want you to say in the dedication something very simple and direct, something like this:

'*To Doris, My Love, My Guardian Angel*'

Contents

A Note from the Collaborator   v

PART ONE: *The Beginnings*

   I   A Boyhood in Ravenna   3
   II In Search of a Profession   25
   III My First Steps in Music   45
   IV The War and Marriage   69

PART TWO: *Opera, My Life*

   V   Opera, My Life   93
   VI   The Metropolitan   117
   VII Salzburg: Enchantment and Tragedy   141
   VIII Figaro and Boris Godunov   162

PART THREE: *"They Dreamt Not of a Perishable Home"*

   IX My Wife Doris   183
   X   Sempre! Sempre! Sempre!   202
   XI South Pacific   229
   XII And After . . .   255

Epilogue: Ezio's Last Days by Doris Pinza   278

Operatic Repertoire   289
Index   295

PART ONE

The Beginnings

*The day may dawn when this plight
shall be sweet to remember.*

VIRGIL

CHAPTER ONE

A Boyhood in Ravenna

❦

*I*T WAS the month of May in Rome, May 28, 1892. Though I was ten days old, I still had no name, for my father had refused to register me with the police and the Church, despite Mother's repeated pleas.

"The boy must have a name, Cesare. He will live! He gets stronger every day."

But Cesare Pinza kept shaking his head. He had fathered six children in seven years of marriage, and not one of them had lived long enough to use a name. His wife was true and devoted, and came from a better family than his. The Burgarellis of Ravenna were fairly prosperous, whereas he was a poor itinerant carpenter.

Being a woman, Clelia Pinza could not understand that Fate was against their raising a family, against his having a son. Had not each poor *bambino* died shortly after its christening? Why tempt Fate again? No, he would not name his newborn son, not for a while. Even the fact of my having come into the world at all must not be discussed until he saw a sign, had a hunch that the danger had passed. When Mother pointed out that the midwife had already spread the word in the neighborhood about her seventh child, he had a reply ready. "Your midwife will do the boy no harm. When you were in labor, you didn't see the two feathers she thrust into your nostrils to make you sneeze so as to help him along. Those feathers were white for luck!"

Day after day, as Cesare Pinza walked the streets of Rome in search of work, he looked for an omen, too. Perhaps a coin would drop at his feet just as someone shouted a name. Or a song would come floating through an open window, ringing out a name suitable for a boy. Perhaps the shapes of the clouds might suggest one. But portents seemed as scarce as work, hardening his conviction that Fate was against him.

My mother fed me, sang to me, her hopes for my survival rising with every squirm and gurgle. She did not mind my crying in the middle of the night. The lustier, the better. It was a sign of life in me, of a will to live. She did not resent my father's refusal to share her joy in their son just then. She understood that he was, perhaps, more anxious for my survival than she who had brought me forth, for what is a man without a family of his own, without a son to bear his name?

But on the morning of the twenty-eighth she said, "The boy has lived ten days, Cesare. Now he must be registered with the police and the Church. This is the law."

My father nodded. Like all poor men, he feared the law more than he feared provoking Fate. Shouldering his tools, he went out into the street, determined to find a name for me before the Registry closed. Luck was with him from the start. As he approached the winding Tiber, he saw a familiar face among the repairmen working on a bridge. The friend who was in charge invited my father to help them complete the job, which meant a few days of well-paid work. Father gladly agreed, provided he could quit early that day; he had to register his newborn son. Learning that Father had not chosen a name for me, the friend exclaimed, "What a lucky day for you! Call the boy Ezio and he'll be a singer!" (The man, it appeared, had a younger brother who had received a contract only the day before to sing with La Scala.)

My father recognized the hand of Fate. "What is your brother's name?" he asked.

"Ezio! Name your boy Ezio and he'll be a singer, too. He'll be famous and rich, sing in Milan and Rome, and travel the world over like a royal prince!"

Father registered me that afternoon. Things went well and quickly with the civil authorities, but not so with the Church. The name Ezio, said the priest, had been banned for centuries, for it belonged to a pagan general who had massacred early Christians.

"But this is the name I want for my son. It's a lucky name; it will bring him good fortune!"

"If it's fortune you're seeking, then call him Fortunato."

There was no answering that. Besides, the priest was getting angry, and it was dangerous to anger a priest. But my father was a stubborn man and had his mind set on Ezio. Then the thought occurred to him: Registries were for those who knew how to read. He could not, so what difference did it make to him what was in the book? Thus

it came about that, though my name was officially in-
scribed as Fortunato, Father hastened home with the news
that their son had been duly registered, that his name was
Ezio, that he would grow up to be a singer and would
travel the world over like a royal prince!

My birth, the happy choice of a name for me and my
father's temporary job on the bridge, signified to him the
end of ill luck. I grew strong and healthy, and in time had
a little sister and a brother, Beniamina and Alfonso. Now
my father could boast of really having a family. Not a
very large one, true, but a family, nevertheless, as any self-
respecting man ought to have.

My father sorely needed something to bolster his self-
respect. Having a family helped, but it also meant more
mouths to feed, and jobs were scarce. His handsome chest-
nut hair was combed neatly as always, the mustache arrogant, but when he came home evenings, his eyes lacked
their old luster, and he was discouraged at not having
found work. He did not complain to my mother, yet she
found him more receptive to her pleas that they move
back to Ravenna. Her family lived some seven miles from
the city that had been the home of the Burgarellis for
hundreds of years. Close-knit and prosperous, they
worked the fields of a nobleman's ancient homestead, had
their own horses and cattle, bought and sold sheep, and
ran a store stocked with wine, meats, cloth, needles,
thread and other household necessities. This put them in
a class above the other farmers in the area, and their
standard of living was such as befitted their station.

Clelia Burgarelli had had no conception of poverty

when the young, handsome itinerant carpenter, Cesare, who had done some work on her father's farm, proposed to her. Even had she known poverty, she would not have hesitated, for she was in love and gave little thought to practical matters.

When Cesare told his wife one morning that he was ready to move on and fend for himself, she did not hesitate, but followed him to Rome.

Now, listening to her three children cry for food, exhausted by the yearly ordeal of childbirth, by carrying water to her home from the well in the center of town, a mile away, and wood to the open fireplace in the kitchen, Mother pleaded with Father to go back to Ravenna. He finally agreed, but he settled us in the city, instead of the Burgarelli farm, as he was too proud to be dependent on his in-laws. Moreover, encouraged by the good luck he saw in my survival, he conceived a project for selling lumber, for which Rome was too big, but which should do well in a town the size of Ravenna.

I was about three years old when I first saw Ravenna, known chiefly as the deathbed and the tomb of the Roman Empire, and Dante's last refuge. Wrapped in mist and legend, filled with churches and mausoleums, surrounded by noxious marshes and imperishable forests, Ravenna's decaying magnificence has attracted tourists as well as students of medieval Europe.

My first memories revolve around Ravenna. We took a large house with six rooms, four of which we rented, leaving the two smallest rooms for ourselves. One combined the functions of kitchen, dining and living room; the other was the bedroom for all five of us. My father had a spacious carpenter shop in the courtyard, where he worked and kept his tools and boards of different length and thickness, stacked up all the way to the ceiling. He was no longer merely a carpenter, but also a dealer in lumber and a "landlord." This new status, plus his bank loans, gave him a feeling of getting on in the world.

The rent for the whole house was one lira a day, then the equivalent of twenty cents. This may not sound like much to you, but his venture was a bold one for an illiterate carpenter without capital of his own. All the money borrowed from the bank was spent on lumber, as he collected only sixteen cents a day from the tenants. He worried himself sick trying to scrape up the additional four cents he needed to pay the day's rent.

We ate meat only on Sundays and holidays. My mother's skill in making a little meat go a long way was miraculous. She'd buy beef, for instance, always with a large bone (and all too often she bought nothing but bone), and make a broth with vegetables and noodles, which we thought more savory than anything in the finest restaurant. If times were good, Mother would grind the meat, mix it with bread crumbs and an egg, and turn out a fine potato and meatball stew.

The mainstay of the family diet was soup, three times a day. At breakfast each one of us made his own soup by mixing chunks of bread into a large bowl of coffee and milk. The midday broth was delicious—just vegetables and noodles, flavored with tomato sauce and boiled in water. In the evening we had another plate of the broth, and, on a rare occasion, a small piece of meat was added. Or there would be homemade macaroni with a piece of cheese and bread. Bread, too, was made at home, baked once a week. At Christmastime, we had a veritable feast of half a chicken and *cappelletti*. Meaning "little hats," *cappelletti* are made of two or three kinds of cheese, nutmeg and lemon rind shaped in dough to look like—little hats. The *cappelletti* are served in chicken broth. Everything, you must understand, was cooked in a big iron pot over an open fire in the fireplace. There was no stove, no running water or plumbing of any kind in the house. We always had wine with our meals, but rarely any dessert. On Christmas, though, each child found an orange and a handful of raisins in his stocking.

The fruit season brought with it a grateful change in our diet. Peaches and bread for breakfast; figs and bread for lunch; grapes, cheese and bread for supper. A friend of Father's grew fine fruits in his orchard, which he sold to us very cheaply, so we had plenty of figs, peaches and grapes for luscious combinations. To this day, my idea of a perfect meal is a plate of grapes, bread and cheese, but soup is still the mainstay of my diet. Give me a great big bowl of soup, and I don't care if anything else is served or not.

As I was always ready to eat, it was no wonder I looked forward so eagerly to the several trips we took each year to the Burgarelli farm. Every visit was timed to coincide with a holiday, for a holiday meant a feast, and a feast at the Burgarellis' meant all the food one could eat. I also loved to sleep on their homemade mattresses of corn shucks. The mattresses were very high and sank slowly beneath you, so cradling and soft you fell asleep immediately and slept until morning. Our mattresses at home were thin and hard, stuffed with the moss that hangs on tree branches.

The Burgarellis were a noisy, friendly lot, who welcomed us whenever we came, but Father did not enjoy those visits and was forever looking for excuses to cut short our stay. He never spoke about it, but I understood after I had grown up a little that his pride had suffered at his inability to provide us with the kind of luxurious living he saw at the Burgarellis'. It was also humiliating for him not to be able to entertain them in a style approximating their own.

Years later, many hard years later, I made it possible for my father to repay the Burgarellis for their hospitality. But in the meantime, he had to sweat and struggle just to make ends meet, despite the thrifty housekeeper he had in my mother and his numerous schemes for getting rich.

Or, perhaps, because of them.

My father possessed a good deal of innate intelligence. He also had a wonderful memory that enabled him to come up with quotations from wise men and poets, which he would overhear in the street or in a café; or with some odd scientific facts one hardly expected to be available to a person who could neither read nor write. He did know how to count, and could sign his name, which, to be realistic about it, was all a businessman operating on Father's scale needed. He was kind but excitable, even belligerent at times, and never ran away from a fight. He was honest and lied to no one, though he was lied to many a time and was often cheated out of his hard-won earnings. Something of a show-off, he insisted on doing things with a flourish, trying to impress people with his non-existent prosperity. Finding an extra coin in his pocket, he would hire a carriage and make sure that he was seen in it. Mother, on the other hand, would walk even when she could afford the carriage. A day might come, she argued, when there was no money for such luxury. Then people would gossip. Such reasoning angered my father. It angered me, too, I must admit. We both saw in it an invitation to bad luck.

My father's misadventures in business stemmed mainly from the fact that he fancied himself an expert on trees and on horses (the latter he needed to transport lumber); something of a misconception, to judge from the way he burned his fingers time and again, losing many hours and days of work to pay for a mistake, only to repeat it at the very next opportunity.

I remember one occasion vividly because I was with him during the transaction, which took place after school hours. The horse that was up for sale looked beautiful as he was walked before us, the coat black and glistening in the slight drizzle. I could see by Father's eyes that he liked the animal, and hesitated only because the low asking price had aroused his suspicions. It would go still further down, he knew, when the bargaining started. Therefore something must be wrong with the horse. He examined it twice from head to foot, slowly, methodically, but could find nothing to account for the low price. The horse seemed perfect. He made a ridiculously small offer —and the animal was his. Cleverly doctored, it did well for a few days, then started hobbling painfully. There was nothing to do but put the poor creature out of its misery. Many hours of work had to be sacrificed to make good the loss.

What followed was also typical of Father. He was grim and thoughtful at the dinner table that day, and all of us ate our food in silence, for we knew that his hand could be heavy on such occasions. When the meal ended, we kept our seats, subdued and quiet, looking at Father expectantly. At last he straightened his shoulders, rolled up his mustache, raised a glass of wine and proclaimed in that rich, ringing voice I loved so much, *"La vita comincia domani!"* (Life begins tomorrow!)

For us, the children, it began right then and there, as we felt free to give noisy release to the suspense and to the joy of seeing Father cheerful and energetic once more.

As a growing boy I learned many things from him, but nothing proved more comforting to me through the years than the lesson contained in that phrase, "Life begins tomorrow!" I have repeated it to my daughter Clelia and my son Pietro, and I shall repeat it again to Gloria, the baby in the family, when she is old enough to understand. I'll tell her that every day is a new day, bringing with it a new opportunity and a new hope. Still, no one will blame me, I trust, for praying that my children may never have to subject this philosophy to as many tests as my father.

The "Life begins tomorrow!" philosophy continued for Father, and there were always new ventures to tempt him. For example, trees. There was less to know about a tree than a horse, at least for my father's purposes. One can tell almost at a glance whether a given tree is good for lumber or not, especially when one is a hereditary carpenter, as Father was. His trouble lay not in a lack of knowledge of trees and lumber, but in the optimism with which he estimated the amount of workable lumber that a tree would yield. True, the mistakes he made were never too great; say, ten or fifteen feet of lumber per tree. But when all the mistakes are due to excessive optimism, and the trees are many, and the money is the bank's, with interest to be paid on every single lira, the results can be disastrous. Father would spend a day or two on a deal, a few more days and a little more money on felling and working the trees, and again on transporting and selling the lumber—and then he would come out the loser or, at the best, break even. He did meet his payments, but not always on time, and this the bank did not like. I have yet to see a bank as indulgent with the poor as with the rich. There are too many poor. In Ravenna, we were legion.

With every such defeat, my father's dark mood lasted longer, and the spankings he gave me were more painful; but each time he managed to come through with his toast to tomorrow. The older I grew, the more clearly I became aware of the special way he had of looking at his wife and the children when making that toast, too proud to translate the look into words. But Mother understood, and so did I, the eldest. His look pleaded for support and a continued faith. These we gave without reservation. Mother, because she loved him; I, because of boundless admiration. True, he used to spank me, and when he did, it hurt; but somehow I never held it against him. I must have instinctively understood that he did it in a fit of ill temper due to poverty and failure. Or because he wanted to teach me something good and useful, and knew of no other way. Although I bore him no ill will, and never cursed him even in my thoughts, I felt the injustice of the beatings, and one day when I saw him strike Mother, I vowed that I would never raise my hand against a woman or a child. I must have been nine or ten at the time, and I have kept that vow.

When not in bad humor, Father was gay, thoughtful and kind. I admired him for it, as I did for his energy and the skill of his large, callused hands. And also for his daydreams, which he shared with me alone. He could not share them with Mother, for she was a woman, and a woman cannot understand such things, and my brother Alfonso was still too young.

Father taught me many things, among them a way with tools, a knowledge of lumber and its many uses, the making of bricks and the preparing of wine and food. I was a useful helper to him, for I started working at the age of eight, and so enjoyed being with him that I did not really miss the after-school games with the other little boys. All they had to play with were marbles and buttons, whereas I swung a hammer and pulled a saw. I also used to accompany my father on buying expeditions which often necessitated long walks. These I enjoyed most, for it was then that Father regaled me with his fantasies of how easy and wonderful life would be in the future.

Probably because he was having such a miserable time providing for his family, and because he had to go on foot wherever business took him, these fantasies revolved mainly around the ways and means of making life easier and cheaper, so the poorest of the poor would be comfortable. Uppermost in his mind was, of course, food. Whereas I thought merely in terms of the next meal, seeing in my imagination a steaming bowl of soup with a large—very large—hunk of meat in it, Father conjured up visions of fantastic abundance, of food that cost hardly anything, available at all times and everywhere in concentrated form, such as, incidentally, can be found today in army rations.

As for travel, there would be nothing to it in the future, nothing at all. Simply step on a platform, press a button and roll on to your destination! No walking to do, no money to spend on trains and carriages.

Father's fantasies ran wildest on the heels of some disastrous business transaction, as though he sought compensation in the abundance and comfort of an imaginary future. There came a day, though, when he sustained a defeat so shattering that many bitter weeks were to pass before his thoughts could again turn to his utopian dreams.

Ravenna is surrounded by magnificent pine woods celebrated in songs and legends that live to this day. If you ever visit my city, someone will be bound to lead you to a clearing flanked by pines as majestic as a colonnade in a Greek temple, and assure you with pride that this is the spot where Dante wrote the last stanzas of his *Divine*

Comedy. You may accept this piece of information with a skeptical smile, as you have every right to do, but you cannot deny that Dante created a haunting image of the "celestial forest of Ravenna." Every schoolboy in Italy knows this. The poet's tomb, just a short distance from the house where I grew up, is the most venerable of the edifices in Ravenna, giving the city a sanctity and a greatness that not even its proud history as key city of medieval Rome can lend it. The children of the town are brought up on stories and legends about Dante, and even illiterate people like my father can come up with a line from the *Divine Comedy* in the midst of a conversation about the best way of laying floors or the price of milk.

The pines were guarded by keepers who lived in cottages placed every few miles along the edge of the forest. A magnificent stallion roamed the woods when I was a little boy, and a fee was charged for turning a mare loose there on the chance that she might produce a colt worthy of his sire. School children were taken to the forest once a year for a picnic which few of us enjoyed because of widespread tales about vipers swarming in the woods. I never encountered a viper, but somehow those tales struck terror in my heart and plagued my dreams. Still, like all the other children, I went to every picnic, in the hope of catching a glimpse of the stallion.

From time to time, the muncipality permitted selective cutting, to give young trees the needed air and sun. Those were great occasions for the lumber dealers of Ravenna, all of whom were asked to put in bids. Father took me to one such auction, and it was there that he sustained a crushing defeat.

Two well-dressed gentlemen—an officer of the municipality and a bank representative—were strolling leisurely among the dealers who were carefully examining the trees marked for cutting. Then, at a respectable distance from each other, the dealers worked on their respective bids. My father, who could not read or write, had learned how to deal with figures, and was struggling and sweating and scratching with a piece of chalk on a small blackboard. The other dealers used pencil and paper.

Father had good reason to take his figures seriously, and check and recheck them with the utmost caution. He had outbid all competitors at the last two auctions and got the trees, but had so overestimated the amount of useful lumber that he was now lagging in his bank payments. Absorbed as he was in the figures, Father kept a worried eye on the bank representative as the man moved from dealer to dealer, exchanging greetings and casual remarks. He was no less cordial when he walked up to us, made a few remarks about the weather and the trees, and ended up by informing my father that he would be given no more credit.

As though nothing had happened, Father continued to busy himself with the blackboard. Then, suddenly, he wiped off the chalked figures with his sleeve and walked away so fast I could hardly keep up with him.

The refusal of credit was a terrible blow, the full implications of which I understood only later: the humiliation in the presence of competitors; the bad mark against his name; his virtual end as a lumber dealer. From now on he was nothing more than a manual laborer. With the insensitivity of most children toward their parents' problems and difficulties, I was aware only of my father's withdrawal from everybody, particularly from me, the witness to his downfall. It is curious how one can be cooped up in two small rooms with four other people, and somehow not be there. Father did just that. Not wanting to be seen by anyone, he did not go out to hunt for lumber or work. He just sat in the house, thoughtful, silent, his mustache drooping, his hand refusing to lift the glass of wine for the toast all of us were so eagerly awaiting. He had become a frighteningly distant stranger.

There was no work for me to do in the shop now, and even if there were, I still could not do much without Father; so I was free for several hours every afternoon all through the period of his dejection. One might think that I would rejoice in my new freedom to play or read, but I actually did not know what to do with it. It took a little time before I learned to lose myself in games once more, and I have never been an avid reader.

To tell the truth, I was not an especially bright or diligent student, and showed no promise in any direction that my teachers were able to discern. My best subject was mathematics. I also liked to recite poetry, but unfortunately a shyness would often overcome me the moment I stood up in the classroom, making me forget the lines I had so painfully memorized. It was my good luck to have a teacher who was both kind and understanding, or I would have had no end of trouble when the time came for me to enter eighth grade. Because I was too weak in grammar to pass the examination, my teacher gave me an opportunity to make up by reciting one of the sixteen poems I had memorized. I confidently rose in my seat, but then, seeing everybody's eyes on me, I was unable to open my mouth. The teacher looked at me with kind, sad eyes.

"I know that you know," he said and gave me a passing grade.

I was also interested in natural sciences, but in their practical application rather than in the theory or the poetry of the subject.

During those restless days that followed the ill-starred auction in the Ravenna woods, my unhappiness was deepened by a little incident which, I am sure, no one but a hurt boy would remember. Loafing in the street one afternoon, I chanced upon a schoolmate of mine, Guido Portinari. He was on his way to the brick factory in the outskirts of Ravenna, where his father worked as a carpenter. I happily agreed when Guido asked me to join him, and we soon were walking alongside the narrow railroad track that ran from the ancient clay pits to the factory. A man pushing a steel wagon piled high with clay soon caught up with us, and asked Guido, whom he knew, to lend him a hand. Forgetting all about me, Guido ran to the man. Shouting and laughing, they soon disappeared in the distance. I nearly burst into tears at being left out of the adventure of pushing a wagon along railroad tracks. I turned back and trudged homeward.

There was some kind of a holiday several days later, and this meant a family visit with the Burgarellis. My clearest memories go back to their enormous kitchen, which served also as a living and dining room, the walls hung with pots and pans, cheeses and herbs. Its vast fire-place was the largest I have ever seen, and the great table in the middle of the room, always laden with fruits in season, is still the very symbol of hospitality to me.

After the first noisy greetings, my mother went to the kitchen where the women were busily preparing the feast, while Father joined the men, who were killing time by putting up a brick wall. I circled around them, eager to show off the skill with which I could fit brick to brick, but no one paid attention to me, least of all my father, who had taught me the trade. Miserable, I was about to run away from them when a tall, handsome young man, my uncle Gino, asked me to help him get some melons out of the well, which was the Burgarelli icebox. I ran ahead of him excitedly, lowered the bucket and started fishing for the melons. This is not as easy as it may sound, but I quickly got the knack of doing it, and I became so carried away that I would have fished every single melon out of the well had Gino not stopped me.

Maybe it was no accident that Gino was the one adult to befriend me. We had something in common. The Bur-garellis and the Pinzas were all short and dark, except for one person in each generation of each family, who was taller and darker than the rest. I was the tallest and darkest in mine, and Gino in his. At the time, of course, I was not aware of that curious bond between us. I was simply overflowing with gratitude toward him for treat-ing me as an equal. Whatever it was that drew him to me, we quickly became friends, as much as a grown-up man and a hero-worshiping boy of ten can be. He was my private saint, and remained so to the last day of his life, fifty-odd years later. He, in turn, was devoted to me with a completeness of which few people are capable. In 1950, when he was eighty-five years old, his daughter wrote to me in the United States, urging me to hasten my plans for visiting Italy because Gino, sick and feeble, kept saying that he was trying to stay alive so that he could see me again. I went to Italy, bringing a record player and a complete set of my recordings with me as a gift for him and his wife. He died quietly in his sleep two months after my departure from Italy.

It was Gino who had the idea during the visit memorable for the watermelon-fishing expedition that I should spend my summers on the Burgarelli farm. My parents readily agreed, for they thought that farm life would be good for me, and one less mouth to feed was something to take into account. As in most Italian farm dwellings, the lower part of Gino's hut was given over to the cattle. There were also horses, sheep, rabbits, chickens and one ugly fat pig. It took me a little time to get used to the smell, but I did not really mind. It was easy to watch over the livestock when they were literally under your feet. In the winter, Gino told me, the animals kept the house quite warm.

Gino and I shared a bedroom upstairs, sleeping in Gino's enormous, comfortable bed, the only one in the room. When he got married the next summer, we found the bed large enough for the three of us, Gino sleeping in the middle. The newlyweds were so natural and warm-hearted that it occurred neither to them nor to me that I might look elsewhere for a place to sleep. All I remember of their wedding night is the magnificent soup, the turkey (the rarest of all delicacies for me at the time, prepared as turkey ought to be—boiled, then browned in a pan, with no stuffing whatsoever) and the wine. I was so full and sleepy that I went to bed long before the banquet was over, and dropped off the moment I was out of my clothes. When I woke up the next morning, I found the newly-weds in bed with me, sleeping peacefully in each other's arms.

Gino's wife, Adele, was petite and delicate, about half the size of her husky husband, but she worked as hard as he did, tending the livestock and preparing our meals.

You have gathered, of course, that I was not a house guest in the sense in which the term is used in this country. I more than earned my keep, working from dawn to dusk along with all the Burgarellis, but for the first time in my life I ate as much as I wanted. Most of all I enjoyed the Friday pilgrimages with Gino to the market place in a nearby village to sell our produce. On occasion we sold two or three full-grown cows, then purchased several calves to raise on the farm. Each market day Gino gave me the equivalent of five cents, and I spent it on a loaf of crunchy fresh bread, which I ate on the spot. That was my greatest pleasure, for we had fresh bread on the farm only once a week, just as at home in Ravenna.

Treading grapes in the *tino* was a source of pride and satisfaction to me that first summer. By way of re-ward, huge clusters of grapes and caskets filled with wine were sent to my family whenever the Burgarelli cart went to Ravenna.

The hardest work was performed and the gayest time was had during harvest, when a number of families banded together for greater speed and efficiency. The family whose crop was being gathered on a given day provided the food and wine for all, each hostess trying to outdo the other in the variety and richness of food. The corn harvest was most interesting in the evenings, when the women and girls came for the yearly shuck with which to refill mattresses. The young unmarried men strutted about, serenading the girls, with a bold line or two smuggled into the traditional verses of the songs.

Those were wonderful summers at the Burgarellis', the happiest in my life. I so loved being there, and became so attached to Adele and Gino, that I hated to leave for Ravenna when the time came to return to school. The Burgarellis taught me more than how to work on the land and handle livestock: they showed me that there can be fun and joy in the hardest toil. The difference lay in security. Though my father's natural disposition was as happy as anybody's, the fact that he operated on a shoestring and was harassed by his miscalculations gave an air of desperation to his work and business deals. The Burgarellis, on the other hand, were relaxed and happy-go-lucky, but somehow things got done—the fields were cleared; the eggs gathered; the animals and chickens fed; the cows milked; the storerooms filled with hams, meats, wines, cloth and thread for sale. I soon learned the routine of the chores, and remember to this day my surprise at the realization that what had the appearance of disorder was actually based on method, unconscious and uncontrived, to be sure, yet rooted in the experience of many generations, and absorbed with the mother's milk, so to speak.

CHAPTER TWO

In Search of a Profession

MY BOYHOOD drifted along through the untroubled years before the First World War. Food was cheap and plentiful, yet only the large number of saints in the Christian calendar kept our family from hunger. Ravenna was divided into many parishes, each with its patron saint, and a saint's day meant a feast when neighbors and strangers alike were generous with their food and wine. We observed holidays and Sundays along with everybody else, although my parents were not churchgoers. "A prayer from the house is heard as well," my father used to say and left it at that.

He was unorthodox in politics, too, having proclaimed himself a republican; but those were idyllic times, when no one was hounded or arrested for political views, just as no priest ever came with stern words of reproach to the homes of those who did not attend church. So far as I knew, the republicans of Ravenna limited their activities to flying their flag now and then from the top of a Lombardy poplar so tall it could be seen from almost any point in the town. After a day or two, somebody would wake up and call for the *carabinieri*. To the delight of us youngsters, one of the soldiers would climb to the top of the tree to remove the offensive piece of cloth, while the rest shouted merry warnings to the poor fellow about rips in the seat of his pants.

Sunday was the most festive day of the week, the day of the one big meal, followed by a walk to the square, where a military band played and people promenaded in their Sunday best. In the evening, Father and I used to watch a lottery in which each player, prompted by hunches, dreams and lucky signs, selected his numbers, writing them down in duplicate to avoid misunderstandings. The game set, a little girl—all lace and ruffles—picked a number from a drum revolving to the accompaniment of a blaring trumpet. After a moment of tense silence, a man solemnly announced the winning number, and then there was great shouting and excitement. The grand prize was four hundred liras, or eighty dollars, a real fortune. I never won, nor did my father. In fact, we rarely played.

But one day I did win something. Not in a lottery and not money, either, but it was very exciting, just the same. We had been told at school that an Exposition devoted to science, agriculture and the arts was soon to open at the Rotondo in Ravenna. I was twelve at the time and had recently begun to frequent the Rotondo in the early evenings, learning to ride a bicycle on machines borrowed from their proud owners. I became so good at it that I sometimes gave my little sister Beniamina a ride on the handle bar. A penmanship contest was announced, the winner of which would be given a free pass to the Exposition, and his paper displayed in the Calligraphy Booth.

I won and was at the gates long before they opened, the free ticket in my hand. Most of the exhibits were familiar—animals, vegetables, grains, minerals and agricultural machines—so I was beginning to feel disappointed when I saw IT: an engine that looked like a locomotive without wheels. IT could be harnessed to anything, and could even thresh wheat. When dusk fell, IT did something much more amazing: powered a dynamo and lit the glass bulbs strung about all over the Rotondo—the first electric lamps ever used in Ravenna. That moment was the high light of the Exposition for everyone, and would have been for me, too; but just then the doors of the theater opened, and I saw my first opera, Berlioz' *The Damnation of Faust.*

I wish I could honestly say that my first opera was that great revelation which inspired me to become a singer. Alas, what really impressed me most that evening was IT again, illuminating the theater (until then, gaslight had been used, as in the streets) and creating the magical lighting effects for Mephisto's "Song of the Roses," with angels soaring amidst showers of crepe-paper flowers. IT likewise generated power for the red fires of hell behind the sinister figure of Mephistopheles. I could feel the heat coming from that terrifying place, and I could see paper snakes writhing out of the mouth of hell as I imagined vipers did—those vipers I had never encountered in the Ravenna pine woods, but saw in my nightmares. Steam, reflected the color of blood by red electric bulbs, rose all around, menacing and evil. Now I knew what hell looked like.

I had asked Mother, Father and Gino about hell, but they had laughed it off. There was no hell, they said; but here it was before my very eyes, so real, so much more horrifying than any nightmare, that the hell of my first opera haunted me for long afterward. I wanted to ask Father about it again, but just then he was preoccupied with a new venture and had no time for philosophical discussions.

The new venture was the watermelon business.

My father had somehow managed to raise enough cash to buy a great big field of ripening melons. To guard them against thieves, he and I took turns at sleeping in a little hut in the middle of the field. As on so many other occasions, Father made a miscalculation: first he bought the field, then started looking for buyers, only to discover that pretty nearly everyone else was raising watermelons, and that the nearest good market for them was the great port of Trieste, which then belonged to Austria. Trieste, of course! He would sell them there. Father decided this without a moment's hestitation, miraculously raised another loan, and chartered a cargo sailboat with a captain and four sailors. Off we went to Trieste, Father and I, sleeping on the canvas thrown over the watermelons in the hold.

We anchored in the canal after inspection by health officials, had a meal of watermelon and then, a sample melon on his shoulder, Father went into the town to find a buyer for the whole load while I remained to stand guard over the boat. Father returned hours later, toward dusk, the same watermelon on his shoulder. We ate it for supper in silence. Then he told me that no merchant offered a price big enough even to make good the original investment. No one wanted our melons, or could afford to buy them, the merchants said. This my father could not understand, for he saw crowds of well-dressed people on the streets and glittering displays of wares in shop windows, and buildings going up, a sight to thrill an unemployed carpenter from Ravenna. He had to unload the melons by next morning and release the boat for some other cargo. Still a boy, I could not fully share my father's despair, but I must admit that I was beginning to get sick of our watermelon diet. There was hardly enough money for a bowl of soup in a cheap restaurant.

A thief came to Father's rescue.

As we were talking, I saw a crouching figure slink off with one of our melons, and started to give chase, but Father ordered me back.

"He's stealing our watermelon!" I protested.

"Let him keep it as payment for the idea he gave me. If a man is willing to risk arrest for one melon, there must be people in Trieste willing to pay for the others."

With this, he unloaded a batch onto the quay. True enough, passers-by stopped one by one and, because our prices were far cheaper than those in the shops, we soon had a crowd around us, shouting, laughing, bargaining. Again I caught sight of a man stealing a melon, and lunged after him. Someone tripped me, and down I went into the dirty waters of the canal. Father quickly threw a rope in my direction and helped me back to the shore, where I was greeted with laughter and applause. The sun had set and a cool breeze was blowing, but there was no time to change clothes even if I had had a spare outfit.

Fortunately, business soon quieted down. Father rubbed my shoulders and gave me a few coins for a roll and coffee. No other meal has ever tasted as good to me as that, shivering as I was with cold, and bloated with watermelon. With the help of two hired men, we worked through most of the night, unloading our cargo onto the quay, where it formed a bright-green mountain that attracted customers all the next day. Three days later, we were on a train bound for Italy, not a single watermelon left unsold!

I returned to Trieste many years later to sing in an opera, and visited the canal on the day of my arrival. It pleased me to imagine that I found the exact spot where I sold melons and fell into the water.

Although Father had made very little profit through the venture, he was talkative and cheerful on the train. Why not? There is always a tomorrow for profit. In the meantime, look at the disaster that was averted because of a heaven-sent thief! I, too, was happy; happy to have shared the adventure with my father, and happier still at the feeling that the old bond between us was re-established. Here was my chance, I thought, to tell him about the hell I had seen at the opera, and the nightmares that tormented me.

Father laughed. "The only hell there is, is inside us, Ezio." Apparently sensing that those words meant little to a twelve-year-old, he went on, "Hell is inside every one of us, and so is heaven. If you're honest and hurt no one, it's the same as being in heaven. If you're wicked and do evil, a hell-fire burns inside you."

This I could understand. I also understood why I

loved my father. There was something wonderfully honest
and good about him, despite his temper. As to the philosophical truth of what he said, how should I know? As a
boy, I believed his words to be true. Now that I am older
and wiser, I am not so certain. But right or wrong, his
words had a magical effect. From that day on, neither
nightmares nor thoughts of hell tormented me again.

On our return, I regaled my little brother and sister,
and Adele and Gino, with stories of my Trieste adventure.
Mother listened to very few of them; she had no time for
stories. Tiny as she was, she worked harder than anyone
I have ever known. The first to rise, Mother was the last
to go to bed, her chores never done. I rarely helped her,
for I worked in Father's shop, while Beniamina and
Alfonso were too young for housework. Mother's tasks
were countless and had to be started all over again almost
the moment they were finished. She gathered wood for
the fireplace, brought water from the well in the center
of town, made bread and pasta for the five of us, sewed,
knitted and patched our clothes. All the laundry was done
by her at the river, with rocks for a scrubbing board, and
the ashes from our fireplace for a bleach. Spread out on
the green grass, the laundry dried too quickly in the hot
sun to give her more than a few moments of relaxation.

One spring day, shortly before I turned thirteen, I
came home from school and saw her standing in the
kitchen, idly staring into space, while all around her were
chores still to be done: an empty water pail, dirty dishes,
a bundle of clothes to be washed. In the midst of it Mother
stood perfectly still, a sight so unusual that I shouted,
"What happened?"

She did not turn to look at me, but she answered my question, recounting in a slow, tense voice all of my father's failures, and finally came to the immediate cause of her despair. The bank had tired of waiting for payments and sequestered all lumber in the shop. As there was not enough of it to liquidate the debt, our furniture would be seized as well, to be auctioned off with the lumber. The unfamiliar, sinister word "bankruptcy" kept cropping up in Mother's story, like the tolling of a bell.

I listened without trying to silence her. What could a boy say? But, finally, I did quiet her. While she was still talking, I raised my hand and stroked her head, which was covered with the kerchief she always wore. In the Italy of my boyhood, only the wives of poor men covered their heads with kerchiefs. The others wore hats.

Mother stopped talking when she felt my hand on her head, and gave me a questioning look.

"Someday," I said, "you will wear a hat."

A few days later, our lumber and furniture were gone. Once more Father wandered the streets in search of work, but bankruptcy had put a black mark against his name and few people were willing to trust him. What hurt Father most was the gossip spread by some neighbors and acquaintances, which made it seem that he had gone into voluntary bankruptcy to avoid paying his debts, although he had plenty of money hidden away somewhere. Otherwise, how could he afford the big house for his family? These people must have known that most of it was occupied by tenants with their own furniture, whereas our two small rooms now had nothing but bare

walls. As for his debts, Father finally managed to pay
them all except one. The method by which he contrived
to pay the last altered the entire course of my life.

Though it was only a small sum he owed Guido Portinari's father, his meager earnings could not be stretched
to make even token payment. Portinari did not press for
the money, although he was none too prosperous himself,
as became clear to my parents when I came home one day
with the news that Guido had quit school to help his
father lay floors in a new extension at the brick factory.
That same evening, Father arranged for Portinari to take
me on as an additional helper and withhold my wages
until the debt was paid in full. It was in this manner that
my formal education came to an end, for I never went
back to school. I cannot say that I resented such a solu-
tion of my father's problem. At thirteen, I was old enough,
and knew enough about business, to understand that a
debt must be paid. I was also young enough to experience
a sense of relief at not having to blush and stutter any
more when reciting poetry before the class. There was
also that little matter of grammar and writing composi-
tions.

I was much happier and handier with carpenter's
tools than with a pen. I understood them better. As for
Mr. Portinari, he was as good a carpenter as my father;
and he never laid his hands on me. We worked long hours,
starting at six in the morning, and by eight we were so
hungry that we took time off for a full meal. And what a
meal it was! Lamb chops almost every day, broiled in the
carpentry fireplace. We would eat them with tomato
paste, a large piece of bread and a glass of wine. I had

not eaten that well even on the farm, and soon gained weight despite the long hours and the heavy work. To my great regret, the floors were finished quickly, at about the time my father's debt to Mr. Portinari was paid, and I had to leave him.

Instead of going back to school, I found a job as the only carpenter in another brick factory. This meant that I had no one like Mr. Portinari to turn to with the many problems that came up every day. I could lay a floor as skilfully as anyone, but since no extensions were planned as yet, I had to cope with things like smashed windows, unhinged doors and broken wheelbarrows. I can say with pride that I managed the task, but the weight of responsibility proved too much for me, especially where wheelbarrows were concerned. Each time I sent one out of the repair shop I had visions of it collapsing under its load, damaging every brick or tile in it, or breaking somebody's leg. In the end I quit.

The next job was none too easy, either, but at least there was little responsibility and still less nervous strain. I became a delivery boy in a bakery. Don't think it was as simple as it sounds. A baker in Italy usually has two kinds of customers: hotels, cafés, restaurants—and housewives. Things were simple with the large users of bread. They placed their orders, the bread was baked, and all that was left to do was to deliver it. But the housewives were something else again. Too thrifty or poor to buy ready-made bread, most of them prepared their own dough, so that all they paid for was the baking. This meant two trips for me. One to call for the dough, the other to deliver the bread. The wages were not high because my employer could not charge much for his services. The housewives knew that he had to keep the ovens hot for the large users of bread, and exploited the knowledge in their dealings with him. This was hard on my employer, but meant the difference between a full and meager meal in many a home, including mine—that is, before I became a baker's delivery boy. My pay was four large rolls a day, enough for our family needs, plus forty cents a week in cash. The thing I liked most about my new job was the walking I did in the open air, and the endless climbing of stairs, which strengthened my lungs and legs against the time when I could buy a bicycle. On the other hand, the weight of the dough and bread I carried on a wooden plank affected my posture, for the load was heavy and young bones are pliable. To this day my left shoulder is higher than the right.

I was not aware of that minor deformity at the time, and doubt whether I would have cared, had I known. There was something I disliked about my job, however, and this I did intensely, much more than I had any task before or since: the emptying of the "empty" flour sacks in the back room. This meant shaking the sacks and beating them against the wall. No sack, I discovered, ever yields all the flour in it. The pile finished, I swept the flour dust from the walls and floor, brushed my hair and clothing, then ran the gathered flour through the sifter, so that it could be used in the baking of bread for some hotel or restaurant.

The one thing that stands out, as I recall my adolescence, is the joy I took in feeling my body grow and gain strength through hard work. There was also the anticipa-

tion of owning a bicycle. Since a large part of my earnings went to Mother, I saved penny by penny, denying
myself the normal pleasures of boyhood, even a ticket to
Buffalo Bill's Wild West Show when it came to Ravenna.
It is incomprehensible to me now how I found the will to
resist those gaudy posters, showing cowboys on rearing
horses, and lady sharpshooters in leather costumes, all
against the background of Indians aiming arrows into
empty space with deadly intent.

Busy as I was with bread deliveries, I managed to
meet the special Buffalo Bill train and watch the men put
up tents, driving the stakes with heavy sledge hammers
to the rhythm of songs in a language I had never heard.
I was the envy of all the delivery boys of Ravenna because my employer supplied bread and rolls for the entire
company, which I delivered to the cook's tent. Once I
caught a glimpse of Buffalo Bill himself, driving off in a
carriage drawn by four horses. That was all I saw of the
Americans, about whose land I knew nothing except that
I must, if I ever got there, visit Niagara Falls. I have often
wondered how the idea of seeing the Falls ever got into
my head, for even the idea of my going to America was
a pretty remote possibility at that time of my life. I was
then too preoccupied with other things: hatred of
"empty" flour bags, dreams of a bicycle and the pangs of
first love.

The bags you know about. The bicycle was still beyond my reach, so I shall tell you about my first love.

I must have been fifteen at the time and already
aware that not all girls were alike. Some went by like so

many shadows. Others had music in them, compelling you to stop short when they crossed your path. But every once in a while, a girl would come along, and there would be nothing but music, a music that drew you and filled you until all else ceased to exist. I was carrying a load of bread to the Hotel Byron when I came across the first girl who had this effect on me.

The hotel played an important role in awakening the man in me. Or possibly it was Lord Byron himself, for Ravenna has been full of stories about his amorous adventures ever since June 10, 1819, the day he arrived there, according to the plaque on the hotel's outer wall. The poet came, it seems, in response to the pleas of Countess Guiccioli, his mistress, who threatened to end her life if he refused. Her husband, the count, proved as gallantly co-operative as Byron himself, having placed an entire floor of his palace at the lord's disposal, and discreetly retired to a faraway estate.

The stories of Byron's encounters with the police, of his abduction of a young girl from a convent, and of the countess' jealousy and passion, were kept alive and embellished in Ravenna with great ardor and admiration. Each bread delivery I made to the hotel was a reminder of the legends. The resplendent cavaliers I saw coming and going with their young ladies in horse-drawn carriages all looked to me like so many Lord Byrons—reckless, romantic and gay.

I used to pass a shoe factory on my way to the hotel, and see girls and women bent over their work. One day, a girl sitting close to a window raised her head as I was passing by. Our eyes met, we smiled at each other—and the load no longer seemed heavy, the skies were higher, the sun brighter and there was music everywhere.

It is remarkable how much you can know about a girl after seeing her for no more than three or four seconds. She came from a poor family; otherwise she would not be working at so early an age. She had a ready smile, a sure sign that she was sweet, good-natured, not spoiled. Her features were irregular but their combination had charm.

We only smiled at each other during the first few times I went by. Then I began to linger outside the window, talking to her with the help of gestures and mimicry. Her name, I thus learned, was Licia, and soon I also knew where she lived. One evening I went to see her.

A working girl was guarded against the dangers of love almost as carefully as the daughter of a well-to-do family. Licia's mother, for instance, walked with her to the factory every morning, and called for her at the end of work. The only way for me to spend some time with Licia was to call at her home, but that was not my idea of being with the girl, the very sight of whom made my heart leap.

Except for her father, who was usually in a café with his friends, the entire family was crowded into one room when I first called on Licia. The mother sat in her chair, knitting. The other children, all younger than Licia, were bent over their homework, stealing inquisitive little glances at us as we sat awkwardly on an old couch. But just being with Licia was not enough for me. I wanted to talk to her, to dance with her, spend hours with her—alone.

My father listened gravely when I poured my troubles out to him. After a long silence he asked, "Have you heard of the Condotti Dance Club and their annual ball?"

Of course I had. The ball had been held not long before, and was still the talk of the town.

"Join the club," Father urged me. "You're so tall, you'll pass for eighteen."

"But the next dance is a year from now!"

"Licia will need all that time to make her dress. You can't let your girl be at a disadvantage."

It was a good thing my father advised me not to delay. It took some time to be accepted by the club, where there was some suspicion about my right age. This accomplished, I invited Licia and her mother. After a proper show of reluctance, they accepted, and immediately plunged into an animated discussion of Licia's dress. I was completely forgotten and soon took leave, hoping she would at least see me to the outer door, so that I could snatch a kiss of reward, but all she did was to join her mother in waving me good-bye. I was a confused and not altogether happy young man that night. There was the dance to look forward to, yes, but also the long wait and the payment of one lira each month to the club treasury.

A girl had to be invited a year ahead of the dance because tradition required that she appear in an elaborate dress. All the women in her family took part in its creation, going about it with the thoroughness of a general staff preparing a military campaign. First came the major strategic decisions on the style of the dress, the hairdo, the shoes. Then followed tactical operations: the gathering of the various materials involved, each aunt and cousin contributing something to the outfit; the sewing; the fittings. So numerous were the fittings, which took place after work hours, that Licia hardly had any free time for me, and our communications were generally limited to the pantomime through the factory window. Finally, as time wore on, there were the petty skirmishes of the clean-up operations: the selection of stockings, ornaments, ribbons and laces.

My expenses were not limited to the twelve liras for membership. I had to pay my share for the orchestra, hire a carriage for the three of us, and come to the ball with some ready cash in my pocket, to be spent at the bar on grenadine or some other refreshment for my two ladies and myself. I had to dig deep into my savings toward a bicycle.

The big night arrived at last, and there I was, calling for Licia and her mother in the first carriage I ever hired. How stunning Licia was in her resplendent gown! How stunning—and suddenly so grown up, so much like a young lady ready to be courted and taken in marriage. It had never occurred to me that she might be older than I, but now I knew, and felt like the awkward young boy I was, the more confused when she surreptitiously pressed a small doll into my hand, whispering, "For good luck!" She had made the doll herself, stealing hours from sleep; the miniature dress was fashioned out of leftover scraps from her own, to make the doll a replica of herself. I ought to have been touched, but my first reaction was one of discomfort and annoyance with what seemed a tactless stress on my youth. But for good luck I have kept the doll—or more specifically, its successor; for, several years ago, when I was traveling from San Francisco to New York, the original doll got smashed beyond repair. All that was intact was one small portion of a foot. My wife, Doris, made me another doll, however: a little boy dressed in corduroy trousers. I still carry the doll in the original box. We were expecting our first child then and were hoping for a boy.

I was timid with Licia, but the music and the dancing worked their magic and I grew less timid. When I began whispering tender words to her, Licia was kind, gracious and not a little amused at me. Gradually I, too, sensed that ours would never develop into true romance.

I continued to call on Licia after that night, with the changed relationship understood and accepted. That is, it was understood by Licia and myself, but not by her mother. All she noticed was the flight of my old eagerness and the increasing brevity of my visits. Suspecting that I planned to desert her daughter, she began to press me for a formal acknowledgment of my visits as courting calls. Not knowing what to do or say, I mumbled innocuous excuses, which Licia's mother understood as an admission of guilt. Since the girl herself did nothing about my predicament, obviously enjoying it, her mother decided to take matters into her own hands, and looked up my father. He was flabbergasted.

"How old is your daughter?" he demanded.

"Eighteen."

"What do you want with a sixteen-year-old boy?"

"He said he was eighteen . . .!"

And she fled.

Father gave me the most painful beating of my life,

demanding a promise that I would never see Licia again. I was much bigger and stronger than he, but took the blows meekly and made the promise. Then I added, "This is the last time I'm letting you touch me."

And it was.

Many months went by, and all that was left to remind me of Licia was her pretty little doll. Like most young men of my station in life, I began to make payments for the use of a razor, soap, bowl and towel in a barbershop. I would have preferred my own shaving equipment, but I was about to purchase a Pegeo racing bicycle and needed every lira I could save.

Riding bicycles borrowed from the boys who raced at the Rotondo, I had become one of the fastest cyclists in Ravenna, and had no difficulty in finding a sponsor the moment I bought my Pegeo. Instead of delivering bread, I now represented a large store in the races, its name emblazoned across my back. My great ambition was to be a champion cyclist and enjoy the fame and riches that went with the title. The biggest money was paid to the world champion, of course, but for the time being I was ready to settle for victories in less important places. My own town of Ravenna, for instance. Once I won the title there, I would be eligible for contests in the big cities and, with luck, would land on the payroll of a great national concern. It did not take me long to find out that it was not so easy to become champion, even in Ravenna. The fault certainly did not lie in any lack of encouragement from the public. On the contrary, whenever I raced, there were thunderous shouts: "Pinza! There goes Ezio Pinza!"

In keeping with my temperament, I forced the pace from the very start, attracting attention and bringing out loud cheers. But, alas, no victories. Lightning-like in sprints, and ahead of everybody else in the first laps, I would eventually fall behind to come in third or fourth. On one momentous occasion I came in second.

There is a story often told about me, so charming that I almost wish it were true. Having won second place, so runs the story, I stood under a shower at the track, singing "*O Sole Mio*" at the top of my voice. A professional singer happened to be passing by and, overwhelmed by the power and beauty of my voice, started me out on my opera career. What actually took place was more prosaic but, in a way, much more remarkable.

My father, you will recall, was a superstitious man. He was also stubborn. It was this combination that led me to my opera career. He *knew* from the time I was ten days old that Fate meant me to be a singer, and he was not one to defy Fate. Hampered as he was by the task of making a living, he was merely waiting for Fate to do its own work. Whenever he heard a flattering remark about my voice (usually from my fellow racers, who heard me in the shower), he would shrug his shoulders. "Of course, Ezio will be a singer," he would say. "But since the boy is still young, and there is no money . . . what is the hurry . . .?"

However, on the day I won second place, showing that I may have had the stuff of a real champion in me, a bicycle manufacturer approached me with a long-term contract. As I was nearly eighteen, its acceptance would inevitably postpone my voice training until it might be too late for me to sing in opera. To sign the contract would be to defy Fate, something my father would not do. And I certainly would not defy Father.

The next morning Father and I were on a train bound for Bologna, the home of voice teachers who were renowned in all Italy.

CHAPTER THREE

My First Steps in Music

*I*T MAY sound strange to you that a young man of eighteen, on the threshold of a longed-for career as a bicycle racer, should suddenly turn his back on the golden chance merely because of his father's superstition. You may even think that I say this just for dramatic effect; that I actually had music in my bones and jumped with glee at the opportunity my father's wish had created. Well, I did have music in my bones and opera in my heart, but then, show me an Italian who hasn't. Opera is the great national pastime in my homeland, where nearly everyone hums and sings arias, just as practically every American boy swings a baseball bat and tries to pitch mean curves. Poor as we were, we somehow managed tickets to the peanut gallery at opera performances. Most everyone else in town did, too. Nor was there anything exceptional in my singing under a shower, or while riding a bicycle along a quiet road. That was merely the joy in life coming out of me. You'll have to take my word for it that I gave up my ambition of becoming a champion cyclist for no other reason than Father's trust in Fate. Yes, and because I, too, was superstitious and believed in omens.

I still do, although not all signs necessarily mean the same to me as to you or to my father. I believe, for instance, that Friday the thirteenth is my lucky day for starting a project, and I have tried to act accordingly. To toss or place a hat on a bed is a sign of bad luck, and so is meeting a hunchbacked woman in the street. But it is different when the hunchback is a man; he brings good luck. To give you another example, most artists will move mountains to get certain coveted roles, the ones best suited to show off their voices and acting skill. But, for me, to request a role is to put a jinx on it. Having known me to accept lesser parts without a murmur after I had become a leading opera star, some friends reproached me for being too shy or modest, whereas I was merely trying not to court failure. Another of my superstitions is the little doll which I always carry with me. It was my good-luck talisman, for which a place of honor was reserved on my dressing-room table alongside the make-up kit. Time and travel combined to reduce the doll's gay dress to faded rags, but this made no difference; the doll still radiated good luck.

Yes, it was natural for me to believe, like my father, that Fate had decreed me to be a singer, especially since singing promised much greater rewards than bicycle riding. After all, in Italy, opera stars earn greater fame and fortune than champion cyclists. So in taking the trip to Bologna in search of a voice teacher, I was only co-operating with Father and Fate.

Before leaving the subject of superstition, I must tell you of the one time I ignored an omen despite my father's warning, and how I was punished for it.

It happened in 1931. I was a well-established member of the Metropolitan Opera Company by that time, and a celebrated citizen of my home town of Ravenna. I was spending a brief vacation with my parents and had my own car with me. Father was almost as proud of the car as of his son, and loved nothing more than driving with me through the streets of Ravenna or Bologna, smiling benevolently at the plain mortals trudging along on their own feet.

The high light of my visit was a trip to the *Palio* in Siena. The *Palio* is the most famous horse race in Italy, so named after the rectangular piece of material (*palio*) given the winner as a symbol of victory. In the Middle Ages, the victor won a fortune as well as laurels, but the event has long since evolved into a pageant rather than a race, in which the seventeen *contrade* (districts of Siena) compete with their bands, costumes, banners and floats as well as with horses. It is a boisterous, colorful spectacle, dear to the hearts of foreign tourists, dearer still to Italians, and an inalienable part of the life of every person born in Siena.

We were gay and noisy on the way to the *palio*, the car crowded with passengers, food and wine. We had almost reached the outskirts of Siena when my father suddenly put his hand on my arm and exclaimed with great urgency, "Turn around and go back!"

He sounded so alarmed that I jammed on the brakes.

"What happened?" I asked him.

"You see that priest on a bicycle coming toward us? It's a sign of bad luck!"

"For God's sake!"

"It's a bad sign, I tell you. Turn back!"

I was so angry I did not reply, but drove on. Soon we met another priest on a bicycle. My father turned pale but did not dare to say a word.

And then, things started happening!

The crowd in Siena was so great that we had to leave the car far from the Piazza del Campo in the heart of the city, where the *palio* was to be held, and proceed on foot. We stopped at every hotel along the way to reserve rooms for the night, but there was not a room to be had. "No matter," I said, trying to sound cheerful, "we'll drive back and spend the night in our own beds. Now we had better hurry to the Piazza." We did—and reached it from the wrong end, and had to walk clear across the track, which was paved with bricks five centuries old. We were less than halfway across it when it started to rain. Then it began to pour. We kept forging ahead through the warm torrent until an announcement stopped us: the parade of the *contrade* was called off! We tried to turn back, but that was easier said than done, for we were compelled to wait for the thousands who had a head start on us. Tired, wet and hungry, we finally reached the car, which was blissfully dry inside, and had food and wine aplenty. All that was needed to restore our spirits was to get away from the bedraggled, careless crowds, who paid no attention to the impressive horn of my car. Driving out of that place was a nightmare, but we finally did get away.

And then came the crack and the hiss of a tire going flat.

The only person in the car who did not look wretched was my father. On the contrary, the expression on his face was positively triumphant in that I-told-you-so way. But I did not resent it. He had warned me, after all. And he helped me to change the tire.

The train trip to Bologna in search of a voice teacher was short and uneventful. Father knew the city quite well and directed our steps straight to the home of Alessandro Vezzani, the great Maestro of the Bologna Conservatory, and the most renowned of the city's voice teachers. I had one question on my mind, but dared not ask it: Since Vezzani was so great and famous a teacher, he surely must be also among the most expensive. How would my tuition be paid for? Gay and confident, Father seemed not to be troubled by this problem or any other. He simply asked for Maestro Vezzani to receive us, and soon we were led to an immense, gloomy studio, in a corner of which stood a piano. Leaning against it, the Maestro looked at me with tired black eyes, plucking at his eyelids in an absent-minded way. I had the strange impression that he was about to fall asleep standing up, with his eyes open, hand glued to his eyelid. But no, his lips began to move! All he said was, "Sing."

I did the baritone aria from Verdi's *Ernani*, which I had picked up in cafés and in the locker rooms where cyclists change their clothes. If I sang the correct notes for Vezzani, it was sheer accident, for I had no way of checking the different variations I had heard; the only sheets of music I had seen were at the distance that separates the audience from the conductor's stand. But faithfulness to Verdi did not seem to interest the Maestro that morning. At least, he made no mention of it. His only comment concerned itself with something altogether different.

"The voice is white. The voice is very white!" he said. Then louder, with finality, "This boy has no voice!"

I had not realized until that moment how much the visit to Vezzani had meant to me. I felt dull and empty, the way I had when Mother told me of Father's bankruptcy.

My father, too, must have been crushed by Vezzani's reaction, because he said nothing, bowed and left. But the moment we were in the street, he exclaimed, "This man knows nothing about voice!"

The next teacher we called on was Maestro Ruzza, for whom I sang the same aria.

"This boy has strained his voice," declared the Maestro. "Do no singing for six months, not a note. Then come again."

My father did not argue this time, either. Fate, it seemed, would not be hurried, and he agreed to bring me back in six months. I wondered about Ruzza's command not to sing, because I had not sung much. What had happened, he later explained, was that I had not known about proper placement and strained my voice with even a little singing. We returned home, and, as you can imagine, Father saw to it that my voice got a good rest for the next six months. Times were better now and he had enough work to keep us both busy in his carpentry shop, where he also was able to keep a watchful eye on me.

When we called on Maestro Ruzza again, he found my voice completely rested and agreed to give me two lessons a week, for which I was to travel to Bologna by train.

Ruzza proved an excellent teacher, who took his work seriously, but for weeks I made little progress. First, I was struck down by typhoid fever, my only major illness until much later in life. No sooner was I back on my feet than I met a woman eleven years my senior, who so attracted me that I neglected my studies and even managed on a few occasions to "miss" the train to Bologna and disappear for several hours to an unknown destination. That is, I imagined it to be unknown. No secret can be buried for long in a small town.

My father invited me to a café one evening, his face so grave that I knew at once what was on his mind. I was terribly ashamed of myself, and of the fact that my father knew about my escapades. To my surprise and relief, he asked no questions and spoke no words of reproach. He simply told me what I was to do, and in a way that permitted no argument.

"Tomorrow you are going to Bologna, to remain there and fend for yourself. All I ask is that you find a job and continue your studies with Maestro Ruzza."

That was the last major decision Father was to make for me, and I accepted it because it was a good and sensible one. I found myself a carpentering job in a factory, and a tiny room in the house of a railroad-station porter, where I also had all my meals. Maestro Ruzza forgave my absences and soon I began to make very good progress, especially in voice placement, on which he concentrated. Each person's throat, the Maestro explained to me, is as unique as the person's fingerprint, and has to be given individual attention. This is why good singers do not necessarily make good teachers, for most of them tend to apply to every student the same methods that have served them well. Ruzza would send me away from him, across the room, then hit a note on the piano and demand that I sing the note in as many different ways as I could devise. When I sounded just right to him, he would stop me and have me repeat the sound, time and time again, until I learned to produce it without thinking. In this way, I myself found the proper placement for my voice.

My happiness with Maestro Ruzza was not destined to last long, however, for something strange and disquieting was beginning to happen to him. Because I knew nothing about insanity, I kept blaming myself for his fits of irritation with me and my voice, and for the abrupt, frightening withdrawals into himself, during which I ceased to exist for him, however well I sang. Doubts began to assail me. If my teacher, whose job it was to listen to me, was not interested enough, then how could I expect to hold the attention of audiences? His illness suddenly took a serious turn, and my good teacher soon died in an insane asylum.

Once more I knocked at the gate of Maestro Vezzani's dreary palace, and once more he looked at me with tired, uninterested eyes, still plucking at his eyelids. He did not recognize me, thank the Lord. After a long, uncomfortable silence, he mumbled that one word, "Sing."

This time I did a piece I had studied with Ruzza, an aria from Verdi's *Simon Boccanegra,* every note of which I adored. The Maestro became so absorbed that he stopped plucking at his eyelids.

"You need more than just singing lessons from me," he said. "Apply for admission to the Conservatory, and I'll see to it that you are accepted."

This was impossible, I replied. I had a job to hold on to.

"When Maestro Vezzani is interested in a pupil," he said wearily, "nothing is impossible. Come back in three days."

When I returned, he told me everything was arranged. The Conservatory had agreed to accept me. As for money, an old lady he knew, a patroness of deserving young singers, had agreed to give me a stipend for one year—the sum of forty liras each month. Vezzani had also persuaded the Mayor of Ravenna to grant me an additional modest scholarship out of city funds, so that I could devote my entire time to studies. The Maestro did not tell me how he had accomplished the miracle with the Mayor of our impoverished city, but the word soon spread all over Ravenna that he had made this prediction:

"This young man will bring glory to your town. He is an investment worth making."

I soon learned how deeply he believed in his own words. After we had worked together for a few weeks, Vezzani was impressed enough by my progress and my diligence to reveal the identity of my mysterious patron who gave me forty liras a month: "she" was none other than the Maestro himself. He had dreamed up the anonymous benefactor in order not to embarrass me, had our work together not been satisfactory. He had no more doubts now, he said, adding that he expected me to pay him back down to the last lira, after I had succeeded on the opera stage.

Such an arrangement suited me better than nursing a feeling of gratitude to some mysterious, wealthy patroness for the rest of my life. It was a business deal I could understand and undertake. Within a few years after the First World War, when my opera career had started in earnest, I repaid Vezzani every lira I had received from him and, in addition, compensated him handsomely for the instruction he had given me. I was also tireless in singing his praises as a voice teacher. This, unfortunately, did him very little good; in a fit of jealousy, he shot his wife, wounding her, then turned the gun on himself and died instantly.

Maestro Vezzani was indeed a great teacher, although, watching him during a lesson, one would hardly think so. He would sit absently, dressed in a morning coat, plucking away at his eyelids and saying very little. But when he did speak, his words were to the point and stayed with you. The method he used did not require much talking, because he believed students should learn from example and comparison rather than from explanations. Thus, he provided us with free tickets to the opera so that we could learn from established artists and memorize scores with greater ease. I was very shy and insecure in the company of the other Conservatory students, most of whom had the advantage of an education. In their youthful recklessness, they were overcritical of others.

They particularly delighted in tearing down well-known singers, a delight I did not share because I enjoyed the singers, from whom I was learning. My sympathies were with the Maestro whenever he stopped a student's tirade against a performer to say, "Let us see if we can do better or, at least, as well."

Vezzani used the system of teaching two students simultaneously, so that they could learn from each other's mistakes and strong points. I was exceedingly fortunate in my natural endowments, except in one vital detail— the correct placement for high notes. True to his method, the Maestro brought me together with a fellow baritone from another class, to whom the placement of high notes was as natural as breathing. At first, the young man confidently plunged into an explanation of what he was doing and how, but soon found that, as Ruzza had told me, no throat is constructed like another, and gave up. But we continued to have our lessons at the same time and to take long walks together. Singing and listening to each other, we strode along, pausing when necessary, then trying again. Whenever we wanted to concentrate on a phrase or a note, we would stop under the stone arch of some gateway and strain for the sounds until windows would start opening and angry voices would yell at us to go away. Or a caretaker would rush out with a stick. Or a policeman would appear.

I cannot say exactly when or how I discovered the secret of placement of high notes, nor am I able to elaborate on its nature; yet, probably because that was the only aspect of voice control over which I had to sweat blood, I was always apprehensive about high notes even during my best years. Practically all singers are, as a matter of fact, and you can easily see why. If a man can lift a maximum of, say, three hundred pounds, add one pound and that is the end of him. If a singer reaches out beyond a certain note, his voice will break. A terrifying thought! I was luckier than most of my fellow worriers on the opera stage. While they were afflicted with headaches and stomach-aches, I paid the lighter penalty of simple nervous tension.

Maestro Vezzani, with whom I studied operas and individual roles and arias, was pleased with my rapid progress. I did well at the Conservatory, too, in dramatics, make-up and the history of music. One subject, though, proved immensely difficult: *solfeggio,* or the singing of notes, scales and intervals from the printed page. At the time I entered the Conservatory, I could not identify a single note on paper, and to this day I cannot sight-read. I would have learned, I am sure, had I remained at the Conservatory for the full three-year course, but Maestro Vezzani advised me against it. Satisfied with the rapid development of my voice and the speed with which I was mastering roles under his guidance, he persuaded me to leave the Conservatory after the first year to concentrate only on the roles suited for my voice. He may have known that my family was in need of financial aid from me; he may have been anxious to launch me on a stage career so that I could start returning his investment; or he may have hoped that I would absorb technical knowledge of music as I studied my repertoire. If the latter were the case, he was due for a disappointment. Not a scholar by nature, I was further handicapped by the abrupt end of my general education at the age of thirteen. This had prevented me from developing efficient learning habits, with the result that sight-reading is still difficult for me, complicating in the extreme my work as a professional singer.

By way of illustration, let me tell you about the time, shortly after *South Pacific*, when I made my guest appearance on Bing Crosby's radio show.

I had spent hours studying a popular ballad he and I were to sing as a duet. Some fifteen minutes before the broadcast, someone showed Crosby a sheet of music he had not seen before. He ran through it once, then again, his eyes aglow with enthusiasm.

"Say, Maestro!" he exclaimed. "What about us harmonizing on this? It's so much better than the number we've got!"

The "Maestro" had to confess he did not have the technical equipment with which to accomplish the modest feat.

When given a role, an aria or even a simple song to learn, I first ask someone to play it for me, to get the feel of the music. Then I memorize it, working alone, picking out each note on the piano with one finger. The chore over, I draw on the assistance of my friend and accompanist, Gibner King, a splendid musician who is actually both accompanist and coach. Only after we have completed our work do I consider myself ready for the stage manager and the conductor.

This system, forced upon me by the gap in my musical education, is cumbersome and time-consuming, and is not to be recommended. The fact that I have been singing for more than four decades since my Conservatory days, whereas not one of my former classmates has lasted or made a name for himself, is pure coincidence. The system worked in my case, but I had to sweat blood to make it work.

Though my single year at the Conservatory had not given me the solid foundation necessary for a career in the opera world, it gave me something else, something I value almost as much: the friendship of my classmates, the good times with a group of gay, music-loving young men and girls my own age. It was not very easy for me at first. As a fellow student, I was generously accepted by everyone, without reservations and on equal terms. All the reserve was on my side, but this had nothing to do with snobbishness, as you can easily understand.

Though I really wanted the other students' companionship, I tended to shy away from them because of my poverty and self-consciousness. How could I have developed any of the social graces, when my only companions up to that time had been my father, Uncle Gino and Mr. Portinari—wonderful teachers and guides, but certainly not models of social deportment?

Gradually, the ice of my reserve with fellow students began to melt in the warmth of their friendship, of my admiration for their true, golden voices, and of their larks and escapades. With the speed of which only youth is capable, I emulated their ways and became one of them. The mutual acceptance was complete after I spent one Christmas eve in jail because, on a dare, I had serenaded a lovely soprano student; the awakened neighbors had been unappreciative enough to call the police.

We went to operas in groups, and sat in cafés for hours on end, drinking wine, arguing about scores and singers, exchanging trade gossip or just sitting, listening with our mind's ear to the music which our youth made.

Like most student groups, ours was a closed fraternity, which rarely tolerated the intrusion of the many outsiders who tried to befriend us, seeing in us the future stars and prima donnas of the opera stage. One of the few who successfully became part of our circle was an immaculately dressed bank teller whose love for music was matched by the generosity with which he treated us to drinks in the café.

This young man, whose name I cannot recall, was destined to play a vital part in my life because he introduced me to Augusta and Alessandra Cassinelli. There were nine other children in their family, but my contact was naturally with the two sisters who were about my own age. Relationships with them were complicated from the very start, and for the same unaccountable reasons that constitute the secret of all friendships, affections and attachments. Both sisters were equally friendly and attractive, but I preferred the company of the younger, Alessandra. She, in turn, reserved her affections for the bank teller, who was madly in love with her, while Augusta of the beautiful eyes and plump figure seemed to have taken to me.

What saved the situation from becoming troublesome was that we were all young and carefree, and that I was able to restrain myself in my attention to Alessandra. The bank teller had known her first, after all, and his intentions were most serious. I could have no intentions whatsoever, if for no other reason than that the Cassinellis led the life of the wealthy and belonged to a segment of society closed to a carpenter on leave for study at the Conservatory. True, I was invited to the spacious Cassinelli house in town, and to their villa in the country, but only because I was a student, and because Augusta, who was herself taking singing lessons, insisted on my being invited. Soon, I knew, my year at the Conservatory would end, and with it the stipend from the city of Ravenna. Between concentrated study with Vezzani, odd carpentry jobs, and bicycle riding for relaxation, I would have little time for social life.

The second year of my studies with Vezzani was drawing to an end.

"You are ready for the stage," my teacher told me one day. "Your destination is Milan, the opera capital of Italy" —he paused, then added—"and of the world."

The Maestro sent me off in a most proper manner, with letters of introduction to some managers and two hundred and fifty liras to tide me over until a job came along. He also arranged for me to room and board with a conductor's widow, the opera singer, Madame Zinetti. Maestro Vezzani, I have already had occasion to mention, was a tired and gloomy man, but when he spoke of Madame Zinetti he was all smiles.

"The rent is cheap, and the food in her home is good and plentiful. Conductors and singers call on her frequently, so you will always have tips on available jobs in the opera. Best of all, she has three daughters to inspire you."

I called on Madame Zinetti, all set to be inspired, only to discover that her daughters were very small children. I had no regrets, though, for I have loved children all my life, and these three were adorable. Moreover, their mother was a great lady, temporarily in need of money. She had stayed away from the opera because of her husband's death. The day was not too far off when Madame Zinetti was to return to the stage, to become one of Italy's best and most popular Carmens. She knew just where and when to send me to look for work after the brush-off I received from agents to whom Vezzani had directed me.

The first place Madame Zinetti mentioned was, of course, the Galleria, that conglomeration of restaurants, stores and offices near La Scala, about which I had heard at the Conservatory. The Galleria is Italy's most famous rendezvous of musicians, the country's market place of operatic talent. For the price of a glass of wine or a cup of coffee, one can spend hours in a Galleria café or restaurant, exchanging information on jobs, discussing roles and gossiping about established artists. We who frequented the place were always quick to learn of the arrival of some impresario about to form a company for a provincial city or a foreign tour, although it was the wonderful eating places on the Galleria that attracted the impresarios, rather than the presence of singers on the lookout for a job. Singers were a dime a dozen at the agencies.

I found my first job on the opera stage through an agency to which Madame Zinetti directed me—to sing the only basso role in Bellini's *Norma*, that of the Archdruid, the heroine's father.

To avoid confusion in the mind of the reader, who may remember my having spoken of myself as a baritone, let me explain that I am the lucky possessor of a voice known as *basso cantante*, a "singing" lyric bass, with a range of more than two octaves. This means that I am able to wander far afield and am at home in roles intended for a *basso profondo* (deep bass), like Sarastro in *The Magic Flute*, as well as in those written for a *basso buffo* (comic bass), like Don Basilio in *The Barber of Seville*, or King Dodon in *The Golden Cockerel*. Moreover, I have been able to trespass on the baritone field for the coveted roles of Don Giovanni and the toreador in *Carmen*.

Such a range is something to be thankful for, but I have never allowed myself to forget that it is as much a gift as a personal achievement, and that the gift is not altogether unique. Caruso, for instance, the most golden tenor of them all, could easily take on a part scored for a baritone. More remarkably, on one occasion he stepped into the shoes of a bass and did beautifully. It happened accidentally, as so many things do on the opera stage. Caruso was performing in *La Bohème* with the bass, Andrès de Segurola. To his horror the bass discovered, shortly before the curtain was due to go up on the last act, that he was too hoarse to do justice to his great aria, the "Coat Song." Caruso saved the situation by singing the aria from the wings while Segurola mouthed the words. No one in the audience noticed the difference, but the men in the orchestra were choking with laughter and could hardly play, while the conductor, Maestro Polacco, nearly had a fit.

My debut took place in Soncino, a small town near

Milan, where I sang in *Norma* for six nights at eleven liras (about two dollars and twenty cents) a performance, my first money earned as a professional singer, a fact of which I lost no time in letting my father know. Fate was having its way, at last.

It was a very auspicious beginning. Though nearly everyone in the company lacked experience, we made up for it in thorough preparation, enthusiasm and the self-confidence of youth. The audience was generous to us all, giving me my first taste of applause, and I loved it.

No sooner did I return to Milan than an offer came through for me to sing in two operas at Prato, a city in Tuscany. I accepted and naturally began to congratulate myself on being a real professional. So all the talk about how tough it is to break into the opera field is nonsense! Or is it that talent opens all doors? The answer came all too soon.

The operas were Verdi's *Ernani* and Puccini's *Manon Lescaut*. The bass roles in the two operas are so different from each other in conception and demands upon the singer that only an experienced and versatile artist could do justice to both. The impresario should have engaged two basses, but to save money he hired only one—me, and I agreed to the arrangement because I did not know any better. Verdi's Grandee of Spain, a part well suited to my physique and voice, came off beautifully. The more miserable was my failure as the old satyr and buffoon, Geronte, in *Manon Lescaut!* At the time, I could have given any number of reasons for my poor performance: all too few rehearsals, lack of sympathy with the role, a young man's disdain for the part of an old buffoon. The truth is that I underestimated the art that goes into the creation of a comic role, and that I was still too immature an actor to do it justice. Instead of taking the trouble to analyze the reasons for my failure, the impresario simply fired me. Never again did I look down upon an opera buffoon! Then and there I discarded my vanity and began to watch and learn, so that when the time came for me to portray that immortal buffoon, King Dodon in Rimsky-Korsakov's *Golden Cockerel*, I was ready. But that time was very, very far away.

The experience in Tuscany so discouraged me that I decided to stay away from Milan. Everyone there, I imagined, was talking about nothing but my failure, and no agency or impresario would consider me for another job. Even the gracious Madame Zinetti and her cherubic daughters, I was sure, would turn their backs on me. I went to lick my wounds in the home of my parents, who had, in the meantime, moved to Bologna. The opera season was in full swing there, and I soon found myself substituting for an ailing bass in Bellini's *La Sonnambula*. I was happy at the sight of my parents in the audience, and gave a good account of myself. The reception accorded me was kind. We were full of hopes. Day after day passed in waiting for an invitation from the opera company, but the bass recovered his health and there were no more openings.

The year was 1914. There was much talk of war, and young men were being called to the colors. This meant plenty of work—in carpentry, bricklaying, munitions factories. I even had an offer of work on the railroad, tempting because it meant travel—the fascination and wonder of which I had already discovered.

I was sitting in a café one afternoon, trying to decide what to do, when a stranger introduced himself, saying he was an entrepreneur and had an offer to make. Then he began to boast of the big operatic tours he had managed. Names of cities and famous singers rolled off his lips with the greatest ease, and before I knew it he was calling me Ezio, the great opera star of tomorrow, his own prize discovery. All that was left to do was to carry off a spectacular coup, one stupendous enterprise to draw the attention of the world to me; and what could be more effective than a grand debut in Ravenna, where everyone still remembered the baker's errand boy turned bicycle racer turned opera singer? He, the impresario, would engage a small company and star me in an opera carefully selected for the purpose. All I had to do was to sing and, of course, put up the guarantees.

After a few minutes of work with paper and pencil, I said no, thank you, I do not have that kind of money to risk. That was the end of it, I thought; but the impresario must have heard about my father's addiction to business projects, for he went straight to him, and Father reacted with great enthusiasm and induced me to agree. We hired the Ravenna opera house and a cast and presented Donizetti's *La Favorita* before a good-sized audience. The net loss was five hundred liras. The old story with the horses and the trees had repeated itself: all the estimates were made on the basis of a sold-out house, and this the former errand boy and cyclist could not attract. The great coup ended with my father punching the entrepreneur in the nose, and with my accepting a job on the railroad.

But the cloud that hung over the ruins was not without its silver lining. That night, while I was still in the costume and make-up of Baldassare, a young man with a round head and a gay, pleasant face came rushing backstage, embraced me, and said in a voice choking with excitement, "You're going to be a great artist, Ezio! Have patience!"

He was a former schoolmate of mine, Otello Ceroni, of whom I was very fond. To cheer me up, Otello took me to a café where we drank to our friendship and vowed never to lose sight of each other as long as we lived. The very next morning I went off to become a flagman on freight trains, while he remained in Ravenna to study piano and the French horn. When we met again ten years later, we renewed the vow and have kept it always.

The other providential result of the Ravenna failure was the end of whatever dreams my father may have entertained of becoming the manager of a successful opera star. I shudder at the thought of that wonderful, honest, illiterate man, with no business sense whatsoever, in the exacting role of manager. For each fortune made he would have lost a dozen!

I earned good money and had a wonderful time working on the railroad, enjoying the sights of my native land and the comradeship of the men in the train crew. The freight trains were loaded and unloaded with something less than American efficiency, which gave me time and leisure to develop the habit of wandering through the streets of unfamiliar towns, picking up information and bits of history, striking up conversations and in general making myself at home wherever I might be. The experiences of the flagman made the opera star more appreciative of people and places in his world travels many years later.

I enjoyed the leisurely life on the railroad so much that I responded with the greatest reluctance to a wire from my Milan agent, offering me a job with the Palermo Opera House. After innumerable toasts in the flagmen's caboose, I said good-bye to my fellow railway men and went off to Palermo. If I failed on the stage, they assured me, I could always come back to the trains.

I almost did fail, on the very day of my arrival in Palermo. When the manager, named Cavallaro, asked me to sing something for him, I could produce not a single note. A phlegm had accumulated in my throat, possibly due to engine smoke, and this required about two weeks of rest and treatment. But Cavallaro proved generous; he paid my salary until my throat was well, while the only other bass in the company pinch-hit for me. We performed successfully all over southern Italy and then started north. At last I was launched on my opera career with a steady job in an established opera company.

At this point world events caught up with me: the war broke out and I received orders to report to army quarters at Bologna. I passed the physical examination with flying colors and was assigned for training in the south.

My last act before departure was to buy Mother a hat, in fulfilment of the promise I had made her as a boy. I expected her to rush to the mirror and look at herself, when I placed the hat on her head, but instead, she turned to Father, seeking his approval, her face flushed with delight and embarrassment. He nodded slowly and solemnly, as befitted such a momentous occasion. My father would have been more effusive, perhaps, were it not for the fact that I was leaving the stage for God knew how long, to take part in events about which he had the most desperate forebodings. I would be assigned to an Alpine unit, he prophesied in a tone of despair, where snow and ice multiply the dangers of combat a hundredfold.

When my training period was over, I found myself en route to the Dolomites, with orders to join a unit of mountain troops.

CHAPTER FOUR

The War and Marriage

❧

*M*Y WAR YEARS were years of hard work, heavy monotony, little fighting and absolutely no singing. Literally and figuratively, my voice was put on ice until after the end of hostilities. The sector of the front to which I was assigned lay high up in the Dolomites amid bare, steep, sharp-edged cliffs, covered with snow both summer and winter. Fortunately, the enemy we faced were the Austrians, who, as soldiers, are no more ambitious than Italians. This released us all for the struggle with a common foe—nature—which we fought with greater doggedness and ferocity than we ever fought each other. Which is as it should be, I think.

My unit arrived at its destination, a mountain called Punta Riva, on July 29, 1915, at the very height of the summer, and was greeted by a heavy snowfall that made each path a dangerous trap. No quarters had been prepared for us, so we had to camp in the open, an experience which inspired us the next morning, when we awoke covered with snow, to most energetic efforts at barracks building. The assignment for my unit was to install and man an artillery battery aimed at the Austrians across the cliffs, but we gave little thought to guns; the cold compelled us all to turn carpenter. As you can well imagine, my experience in Father's shop and with Mr. Portinari gave me such prestige that it appeared at times that I was the unit's commanding officer. My advice was wanted everywhere, and this I gave with the authority of a field marshal, which increased my enthusiasm for carpentry, if not for a military career.

While waiting for the barracks to be completed, we lived in chalets which were generally used in summertime by goat herders and forest watchmen. This meant we had a roof over our heads but no heat or other comforts, such as beds, for instance. No one missed the beds—not after a full day's work under the blasts of icy winds—but we did worry about keeping warm, for there were strict orders forbidding us to cut trees for firewood. Those orders, however, said nothing about the shingles of the chalet roofs. Our conscience made flexible by the freezing weather, we stole shingles from the few unoccupied chalets and kept them burning in empty gasoline cans with the tops cut off. The shingles burned beautifully and gave us warmth, and we would have been perfectly comfortable if only the chalets had been provided with chimneys. In no time at all smoke filled the rooms but, being lighter than air, did not settle too thickly near the floor. This meant that we had to eat in reclining positions. As for sleeping, smoke or no smoke, we had to sleep on the floor, anyway. The only inconvenience came from rats, fearless in their hunger and numerical superiority. But man's genius knows no bounds. Instead of sleeping in all our clothes, we took off our leather boots at bedtime, greased them liberally and piled them along the walls of the chalet. Attracted by the tantalizing aroma of the grease, the rats concentrated on the boots, without doing much damage to the rough leather. We were left to sleep in peace, except for a sensitive soul or two among us who, kept awake by the noise, would from time to time go after the rats with a club. I never did.

About the time the barracks were completed, beds and all, the forest guards discovered that we had been stealing their shingles and hastily marked some trees for us to fell for firewood. Now we had all the fuel we needed for our barrack stoves and we could safely sleep on straw-matted wooden beds. Soon the battery was installed, as well, and a busy routine was established on our sector of the front, which, though quiet, required vigilance, drill, standing guard and the performance of various chores that were detailed among the men.

In the course of a routine interrogation, the two officers in command of our battery learned that I was a singer. Being Italians, they immediately pricked up their ears. Where had I studied? Where did I sing? What roles? As I answered their questions, I could not help thinking: What if one of these officers proves to be my Major Nagliati? Every music student in Italy, every Caruso admirer—and who was not?—knew the story of Major Nagliati, the tenor's superior officer, who had engineered his release from the army, and found a first-class musician to teach the young unknown tenor free of charge.

Well, I found no Nagliati in the Dolomites; still, my

officers did make some efforts on my behalf. Their first signs of interest in me were limited to a bit of fatherly advice: to take care of myself and not catch cold.

A cold was the easiest thing for a private to acquire in the Dolomites, because the hard work made us sweat a great deal, and the weather was freezing most of the time. The light summer uniforms we had been issued must have been selected by someone in army headquarters who had excellent knowledge of the calendar, and none whatever of climatic conditions on our front.

The advice not to catch cold was followed several days later by an order assigning me to duties that required responsibility but were light: those of the *Guarda Batteria,* which meant that I was entrusted with the keys to our munitions dump, and was responsible for keeping our guns clean. In addition, I was the postman and had to deliver our outgoing mail to the headquarters in the valley below, and bring back the letters for the men in my unit. My work as errand boy in the bakery and my bicycle training had prepared me beautifully for the job of mailman, which, in turn, still further developed my breath power for whatever future I was to have on the opera stage.

I learned to climb rocks with the skill and speed of an Alpinist, and enjoyed every trip so much that I felt my superior officers had done nobly by me. But apparently they thought there was still more to be done, for one day they called me in to suggest that I enroll in an officers' training school located not far from our camp.

Traditionally, only men born into the officers' caste were given an opportunity to command troops, but army ranks grew with such speed after the outbreak of the war that the number of uniformed aristocrats lagged far behind the needs. Officers' training schools were opened in the vicinity of every large troop concentration, and energetic and capable soldiers were assigned to them irrespective of their origin. I was selected, I am sure, partly because of the skill I had displayed in supervising the construction of our barracks, and partly because my commanding officers felt that, by easing my lot, they were making a contribution to the exalted art of the opera. Disappointment was written all over their faces when I said no, thank you. I had no ambitions for a military career whatsoever and preferred to remain a private. I felt more at home among my kind. They did not insist, but one of them, a captain, returned to the subject in a few days, this time using a little pressure. I thought quickly and added another reason: I had had no schooling to speak of. It would be useless for me to try to fill my head with the knowledge of map reading, map making and all sorts of regulations and various other bits of knowledge that would be of no use to me after the war. Besides, I would never make it, I was sure, and would be flunked out.

"Suppose you were," the captain replied. "All they can do is send you back to my unit, where I shall appoint you postman and guard again. The winter is coming on, anyway, and you will find the climb down to the valley and back not so pleasant. In the meantime you'll be spending the worst months indoors and—who knows?—you might enjoy being indoors with books and maps. And let me tell you this: there's more to an officer's life than just map reading."

As you can easily guess, the captain had his way. I saw that he was determined to send me to the officers' school, and I thought it would be best to obey his wishes gracefully. Besides, there was good sense in what he was saying. Much to my regret, I have forgotten the captain's name, for I should like to find him and tell him that he was right and that I feel nothing but gratitude for his insistence.

School proved to be not so difficult, after all. My natural aptitude for mathematics enabled me to keep up with the class, while the howling storms and sub-zero temperatures made diligent students out of us all, just as the captain said it would. Something else he had said proved to be true, and the realization of it came to me as a pleasant surprise one very, very cold morning.

As soon as I completed the course and passed the final examination, I was given the rank of lieutenant and a brief leave to visit my parents and order an officer's uniform. It took me a full day of crawling down slippery, dangerous paths to reach the little town at the foot of the mountain. I was too cold and tired to reflect on the fact that a whole room in a private home was assigned to me alone, and that the great big bed had a soft mattress and clean white sheets. I simply took off my clothes, lay down and was soon dead to the world.

As I was emerging from sleep in the morning, I became aware of someone's presence in the room, of someone walking about with careful, quiet steps. I opened my eyes and saw the back of a private who was carrying an armload of split logs to the fireplace. He noiselessly eased the wood onto the hearth, arranged the logs in the fireplace and got the fire started. By the time the burning wood began to crackle, he was out of the room, leaving it without once looking in my direction, as though fearing that the glance might awaken me.

"There is more to an officer's life than just map reading," my captain had said to me, and only now was I beginning to understand the implications of those words as I lay in the clean, warm bed, my head resting against the sparkling white of the pillowcase, the air in the room getting warmer with each passing minute. I *was* an officer, I suddenly realized, and a soldier had been given orders to make life more pleasant and comfortable for me. Not that I felt superior to him on that momentous morning— or to anyone else, then or ever. The gods have been kind in not adding to my shortcomings a feeling of superiority. If anything, I felt equal rather than superior—the equal of my commanding officers, of the bank teller with his immaculate clothes, of the Cassinellis with their generous hospitality. Yes, the Cassinellis! The lovely Alessandra. The singer Augusta of the beautiful, worshiping eyes. The whole gay, noisy bunch of them! I had hardly thought of them in the mountains, and now I suddenly longed to see them again. But no, not before I don my officer's uniform, not before my father and mother see me in it!

My effort in the mountain school had been worth making, if for no other reason than to watch my parents' joy at the sight of their son in officer's uniform. I was six foot one and weighed a hundred and eighty pounds. They beamed on me triumphantly, especially my father, who had found new omens that augured well for his oldest son's future, so that all his old forebodings were forgotten.

He walked beside me wherever I went in Bologna, inventing possible and impossible excuses to show me off to his friends and acquaintances, even to the strangers for whom he did odd carpentry jobs. I cannot say that I minded it very much, for I found immense pleasure in his happiness, but I did balk when he came up with a plan for the two of us to take a trip to Ravenna so that everyone there who had seen our poverty and witnessed Father's humiliation as a bankrupt could lay eyes on his son in the uniform of the King's commissioned officer.

My leave was soon coming to an end, and I had not yet seen the Cassinellis. It had not occurred to me to write them, telling them that I would be briefly on leave in Bologna, and to wait for their invitation. Every day was open house with them; so early one evening I simply walked in unannounced. The brightly lighted salon was crowded with officers, all of them, it seemed, superior in rank to me. There was a great deal of chatter and laughter, and on every table or window ledge stood empty or half-filled wineglasses. In spite of my resplendent new uniform, no one paid the slightest attention to me, until Augusta suddenly caught sight of me and came toward me, her eyes brimming with happiness. She and her brothers and sisters—you remember, there were eleven Cassinelli children—were all going to a dance with their respective boy and girl friends. She beseeched me to come along with them, but I coolly told her I was not a party crasher. I would see them some other evening.

"Be sure and come back," Augusta entreated from the doorway as I left. But I did not. Somehow I preferred to stay at home with my parents. Perhaps it was pride that kept me away from the Cassinellis. I do not know. Soon I left for the front.

My very first assignment as a commissioned officer showed me that, while I was to be spared manual labor, I would have responsibility to shoulder, and I often wondered which was preferable. My first task was to supervise the transport of a section of 210-millimeter howitzer guns to a mountaintop near a place called Pasubio in the Dolomites. We had no mechanized equipment for the job, no animals trained for such work—only manpower, and not enough of that, either.

To solve the problem, someone higher up drafted the privates who were resting in a nearby health camp after horrible months of trench fighting. The men, some two hundred of them, reported to me every morning at eight, to work like mules until five in the afternoon. All they were given in return were speeches about the glory of the sacrifice they were making for their fatherland, and a hot meal in the middle of the afternoon. This did not seem enough to compensate them for the loss of the rest they so badly needed and had earned so well. There was no laughter, no singing and very little progress despite the great show they put on at hauling and pulling. After a very short while I realized that I was losing favor in the eyes of my superiors, losing face in the eyes of the men, losing confidence in myself and, above all, not delivering the guns where they were needed. The Austrians had had their batteries installed on the opposite peak and were in complete command of the position. Something had to be done, and it was up to me to do it.

The arrival of a caterpillar truck which I had requested the moment I received the assignment helped a great deal; the guns could be started on their way upward with the help of mechanized power. The truck did most of the work until the guns reached the snow-covered heights. From there on we used sleighs which my men built under my supervision. The soldiers respected my knowledge and were grateful for the innovation and for my efforts to conserve their strength, but that was not enough to spur them on to real effort. Speed was the concern of the strategists in staff headquarters, not theirs. What concerned them was the rest they were losing every single day. It took them two hours to report to work and get back to their living quarters at the end of the long pull. With the instinct of the day laborer and the private I had been in the not-too-distant past, I realized that something other than the mere shouting of an order was needed to rouse them.

What I proceeded to do may have been poor military discipline, but I was after results. Instead of issuing another futile order to keep pulling this or that gun upward, I did a little climbing myself to study the terrain, and a little figuring, and then told the men, "This gun has to be moved to that point over there, and it has to be done today. No one will leave until we do it, even if we have to keep at it through the night. But the moment the gun is where I want it, the day's work is finished and you can go back to the camp."

My father and Mr. Portinari would have been proud of me, I am sure. The men fastened their lines to the gun with a speed they had never displayed before, pulled with an effort and with method, and accomplished the task an hour or so after their midday meal. They bade me a friendly farewell for the first time, and laughed and sang as they marched off to the camp. The next morning I was ready for them with a new target to aim for, which they again reached long before the official quitting time of five P.M.

The men were now giving me not only of their brawn. The thought of returning early to the warmth and comfort of their quarters stimulated them to feats of improvisation and ingenuity that challenged mine. I should like to describe some of their contributions, but unfortunately all I can now recall is one of my own, the one I was most proud of at the time. It was devilishly hard to pull a gun up close to a mountain peak, but to get it to the very top seemed utterly impossible; the winds were so fierce that they blew the rocks bare, thus rendering our sleighs useless. In pondering the problem, I recalled that whenever Father had difficulty in transporting wood across ditches, he would improvise a bridge by filling the ditch with straw, tree branches and any logs he could sacrifice. Why not build an ice bridge for the guns? I immediately ordered the men to haul up pails of water and spray the barren rock. The freezing wind did the rest and soon we had an ice "bridge" over which we could bring a gun on a sleigh.

Subsequently I introduced this method in other sectors, but not before a tense incident took place, which threatened me with punishment instead of recognition.

We were making such rapid progress with the guns that, when a general visited our sector while on a tour of inspection, he was taken to watch my men at work. Knowing that a high officer had his eye on them, they gave an even better account of themselves than normally. In fact, an all-too-good account of themselves. The impressed general lingered on, asking questions about our improvised methods, taking notes and making me feel that ours was a real contribution to the art of mountain warfare. The lunch hour had come and gone, but he was still with us, moving upward with the men and the gun. I liked him because he knew his business, was interested in our job and talked to me and to the soldiers without either condescension or unnatural familiarity. But I could not help wishing he would leave, for the men had outdone themselves that day and reached their target some three hours before official quitting time. I could not fail them, not if I wanted to keep their respect, so I dismissed them and remained alone with the general to face the music I knew was bound to come. I did not have to wait long. The general took out his watch, looked at it and then at me, questioningly. It was no use beating about the bush with the kind of man he was, and I told him of the bargain I had made with the resting soldiers.

"But this is a violation of military discipline!" he exploded. "I'll have you demoted for this!" The general turned around and left.

Demoted? *Ma che!* I was soon ordered to go to other sectors to take charge of gun moving, whenever it had to be done in a hurry. It was, of course, a source of satisfaction to me to be recognized as something of an expert, and then again, I was meeting new people all the time and seeing new sights. The trips themselves were nowhere as pleasant and leisurely as those I had taken while working on the railroad, but they were more exciting, and my officer's pay was higher, with no expenses to speak of. In addition to food and lodging, the army gave us cigarettes, coffee and chocolate.

By this time you have probably realized that I was not much of a rebel by nature. I did violate military discipline in making a private arrangement with the gun-moving soldiers, but I did so without ever thinking of my action as a violation of discipline. I had been given a job to do, and I had gone about it in the best way my common sense dictated. But common sense and army discipline do not always go hand in hand, and the day came when I was actually arrested for insubordination because I had persisted in my preference for common sense.

This happened many months after the incident with the inspecting general. The placement of the guns had been completed, and I was assigned to an observation post high among the mountain peaks. As you may know, most of the artillery fire in the mountains has to be indirect, for the simple reason that few of the targets can be seen. You make your calculations according to distance, elevation and other factors, and then you shoot, hoping that your figures are not wrong. One can almost always find a point or two from which the target may be seen, and the results of the shooting can be telephoned to the battery along with the needed corrections. My observation platform was on just such a point; it presented a magnificent panorama of the mountains, as well as a view of the target. The Austrians had the range of our observation points, as we did of theirs, and had their guns trained on us day and night. Fortunately, my observation platform was so situated that the enemy could shoot at it from one gun only. While I was busy observing and telephoning, the soldier who was with me on the platform kept a steady eye on that one gun. The moment he saw it spit fire, he would shout "Flame!" Then we would jump into a tunnel blasted in the rocks for that purpose. Spurred on by the danger, our reflexes were lightning fast, and our encounters with the enemy gun were almost in the nature of a game.

I was not always calm and collected under fire, I assure you. I shall never forget my excitement and fright the first time I heard the order, "Fire!" during my days as *Guarda Batteria*, when it had been my duty to distribute ammunition to the men. To reach the dump, I had to run across a stretch of ground exposed to enemy snipers, and I ran it so fast that I was out of breath, as well as plain frightened. My hand was shaking so, I could not get the key into the keyhole, and the other privates kept shouting and swearing. Then one of them cracked a joke about my poor aim, and they all roared with laughter. That made me angry, of course, and I found the keyhole in no time and unlocked the door.

To get back to the observation platform. The action on our front was limited chiefly to artillery duels, which often took place at night, without involving the infantrymen in nearby trenches; their greatest concern was to sleep through the racket. They had to be there at all times, however, for one never knew when orders might come to launch or meet an offensive. To prevent a possible calamity, the observation points were equipped with sirens that were to be set off as a warning of an enemy attack.

One day, a colonel came on a visit of inspection. Unlike the general I have told you about, he seemed to know little about mountain warfare, and was angered at the sight of the sleeping soldiers and the general lack of preparedness, although he had been told that the previous night's artillery duel had been exceptionally lively.

I happened to be awake when he got to my platform, but the soldier with me was snoring the snore of a giant. Ignoring my salute, the colonel asked in a voice choked with fury, "Suppose the enemy attacked this very minute?"

"It would take them at least an hour to crawl down their side of the slope and climb up ours, sir. My men, now resting after a sleepless night, would destroy them with rifles and hand grenades. In addition, I would set off the siren to get the whole battery in action."

Far from being calmed by my explanation, the colonel ordered me to assemble my men.

Sleepy, disheveled, half dressed, their cartridge belts upside down, their rifles dragging behind them, the men presented a sorry sight. The colonel upbraided me loudly in front of them, then suddenly issued an order: "Blow the siren!"

"If I do," I said, "our guns will go into instant action. The Austrians will answer the fire. Lives will be lost. The responsibility is too great for me to take. Give me a written order, and I'll blow the siren."

My words had a sobering effect on the colonel.

Instead of writing out the order, he had me arrested for insubordination and left our battery, never to be seen by us again. I was released from the guardhouse almost immediately, to return to my observation platform, but formally I remained under arrest. This meant a blot on my record and suspension of pay. While I did not mind the blot, for I was right, I resented the suspension of pay and protested to the commanding officer, a captain. He sympathized with my point of view, but could not pass official judgment on an incident involving a higher officer and a violation of military discipline.

"Make a formal complaint," he advised.

I did—and I was cleared, and all the money due me was paid to the last lira!

Please do not think that the poverty I knew as a boy and adolescent had made me a miser. True, I was saving diligently all through the war, but for a good reason: I wanted to return to the opera stage, and there, I knew, anyone's career is precarious; the impresarios and agents are hardheaded; the audiences fickle; the standards exceedingly high. And I was not even certain that I remembered the parts I had learned; or, indeed, that I still had a voice. As I have already mentioned, my voice was "on ice" all through the years I spent on glaciers and in mountain passes. I hardly ever sang and had absolutely no idea of what was happening to the instrument in my throat.

And then—I was thinking of marriage. I had a feeling that the war would soon end, and that I'd come out of it safe and sound. I was nearly twenty-six now, and had a natural desire to have a family, a wife I loved, children

I could raise and play with—a carload of children.

The money I had saved up gave me a feeling of security and confidence, while my modest accomplishments had pulled me out of the rank of private and earned me four decorations. I was lucky not to have been involved in any of the engagements that were so disastrous to the Italian army and to our national pride. The few narrow escapes I had were more in the nature of sport than of the terrible game of war: to jump into the tunnel before a shell exploded over my observation point; to crawl back to my path after having lost it through a misstep on slippery ice; to keep from freezing or falling into a crevasse when stranded overnight on a seemingly endless glacier.

Such experiences, and the daily rubbing of elbows with men and officers from all parts of my country, helped to build up my character. I was healthier, more vigorous and self-confident at the end of the war than when I was drafted into the army. I had grown to think of myself as the equal of anyone except royalty and titled nobility, but then, these did not exist for me as real people, and I gave them little thought.

The Cassinellis, on the other hand, were very real to me, and I gave them a great deal of thought. It was not only that I preferred Alessandra and Augusta to all the other girls I had known. There was that, too, of course. The Cassinelli sisters were attractive, charming, gay, and had an elegance that I have always so admired in women. Even as a baker's errand boy, I was strongly attracted by the sight of a woman who combined a proud bearing with graciousness and lack of affectation. This, to me, is the essence of elegance. Alessandra and Augusta had it. They had something else as well, something that meant to me at least as much—they were part of a great big family, gay and noisy in the good-natured way that comes from a sense of well-being and security, not unlike the sense of security which made work on the Burgarelli farm a pleasure instead of a chore.

I had no precise idea of the Cassinelli family's financial circumstances. It really did not matter, for I was determined to make my own way in life. Yet their obvious prosperity could not but appeal to a young man with my background. They moved in a circle of well-to-do people, for whom dinner parties, dances, and boxes at the opera were a normal part of life. The girls wore fashionable clothes, used perfume and moved about with an ease and naturalness that seemed to be a Cassinelli trademark. The thought occurred to me then, and I still believe it to be true, that money helps one to acquire grace and charm almost as surely as it puts food on one's table.

Despite the fiasco of my first leave, during the subsequent furloughs I spent most of my time with the Cassinellis. So, unfortunately, did the bank teller who had a prior claim on Alessandra's affections, and I was left more and more in Augusta's company. During what proved to be my last leave before the end of the war, she invited me to a dance party at the palace of a family friend. Before the party was over, we were engaged to be married.

To this day I do not know exactly what moved me to make that commitment. It may have been that Augusta was sweet and alluring beyond resistance that night; it

may have been the impetuousness of a young officer longing to forget the icy breath of glaciers; or a subconscious
desire to share in the elegance and gaiety that permeated
the life of the Cassinellis.

During that leave, I did not indulge in any such analysis. I was a happy young man engaged to be married,
and I thought and behaved accordingly. Augusta was
radiant beyond words. Her huge black eyes were more
beautiful than ever, and her voice vibrated with joyous-
ness. Like Licia after my invitation to the Condotti ball,
she was now busy making a dress for a great occasion, but
there the similarity between them ended: Augusta gave
me every minute of the time I could be with her prior to
my return to the front.

Not long thereafter, the war came to an end. My
unit was transferred to garrison duty in Naples, where I
often joined my fellow officers on their strolls along the
Via Toledo, flirting with the girls and watching the automobiles go by. Just as with the bicycle years ago, I was
now dreaming of owning an automobile. I was also thinking of the responsibility of marriage, and wrote to my
agent, saying that I should soon be free for the opera stage
once more.

A happy misunderstanding occurred at this point.
Accepting my letter as an indication that I had been discharged from the army, the agent went to work right
away, and since few men had as yet returned to civilian
life, he found an opening almost immediately. You can
imagine my surprise when I received a wire from him
requesting me to report for an audition at the Opera
House of Rome, the Teatro Constanzi, later renamed

Teatro Reale dell'Opera. The wire reached me on a Sunday. Without giving thought to the risks I was taking, I barged in on my commanding officer at his home, telegram in hand. Luckily, he was an opera fan. As there was no official stationery in the house, he scribbled on his calling card the permission to go to Rome—a forty-hour pass.

In reporting for the audition, I took another chance. I had done no serious singing for over four years and had no idea of what had happened to my voice. On the rare occasions when I joined my men in song, my voice sounded good to me. But singing a marching tune or a folk ballad with fellow soldiers is a far cry from portraying pride, rage, love or hatred on the exacting opera stage. Yet I took the chance without a moment's hesitation. I had checked my memory while riding on the train and found that I could recall at will any of the roles I had studied. All that remained was to decide which aria to sing for the judges in Rome, and that was no problem whatever. It had to be the aria from *Simon Boccanegra,* my good-luck aria that had gained me entrance to the Vezzani studio and into the good graces of the impresarios for whom I had auditioned before the war.

Even as I sang for the Teatro Constanzi officials, I noticed that something very important had happened to my voice. It was the same aria and the same man singing it, but the sounds were more powerful, more resonant and warm than any I had ever been able to produce before. Could I be deceiving myself? But no! Watching my small audience, I sensed that upsurge of enthusiasm and joy of which every auditioning artist dreams. No sooner did I finish than I was offered a two-year contract, to begin the

day after my release from the army. That was also to be
the day of my marriage to Augusta.

On September 19, 1919, I was given the rank of captain and honorably discharged from the army. The wedding took place on the twentieth.

The Cassinellis gave us a showy wedding at which
everyone had a wonderful time except my parents, who
were ill at ease in the glittering company, and uncomfortable in the new clothes bought for the occasion. There
were too many people, too much noise, and too much food
and wine being wasted to suit their frugal ways. But they
tried to appear merry and gave us their loving blessings.

I remember myself as being gay and happy at the
wedding, singing and joking with the guests all the way
to the station. (We were taking the train for Rimini, where
the Cassinellis had lent us their villa for the honeymoon.)
Then came the farewells, the last shouted words, the last
sight of familiar faces. Standing at the window, my arm
around Augusta's waist, I turned to embrace her.

"Now you are all mine!" she said.

Those are words of endearment, natural to one in
love, but the triumph in her voice, the look of fierce, implacable possessiveness in her eyes so startled me that I
involuntarily withdrew my arm. What followed was like
a nightmare. Augusta screamed at me, spilling out a torrent of words that made me realize suddenly how deeply
she had been wounded by my attraction to Alessandra,
by my attachment to my parents, by every glance of mine
in the direction of any other girl or woman. Now all that,
she gave me to understand, was a thing of the past. I was
hers, hers alone—today, tomorrow and forever!

PART TWO

Opera, My Life

At every step Fame gathers strength.
VIRGIL

CHAPTER FIVE

Opera, My Life

*T*WO SEASONS of hard, steady work at the Teatro Constanzi in Rome were a godsend to me. From our very
wedding day, my life with Augusta had been so unhappy
that I began to understand the solace some men find in
drink or drugs. I found mine in music—a solace, a release,
and also a channel into which I could direct my energies
and dreams.

The long, silent years I had spent in the Dolomites
had improved the resonance and range of my voice, but
my growth as a singing actor had stopped. Were I a tenor,
I would not have worried much about it. Tenors, as a rule,
portray handsome young lovers and noble knights without fear or reproach; it is for them that composers write
their most brilliant and melodic music. In other words, a
tenor's role contains a wonderful built-in appeal to the
audience. It rarely demands that he portray a subtle
character or communicate complicated emotional states;
whereas, more often than not, the basso plays the part of
a social outcast, a lascivious old man, a grotesque charac-

ter, or even the very devil himself! To be effective, the basso must be able to act as well as sing. Of course, theoretically, this applies to everyone on the opera stage, but in practice tenors can and do get away with a lot by merely lifting up that golden voice.

Because of the kind of roles I was given in Rome, I had to learn how to mask my own personality. Sometimes, to achieve the required illusion, I, who was tall and athletically built, had to stand and move like a hunchback, or a silly old man, or one of royal bearing; or a master schemer, a lowly villain, an insane father. I had to hide my youth and strength behind painted wrinkles, a trembling voice, a wobbly walk.

Many people have praised me for the skill with which I do my make-up. I accept the compliment with pride, for that skill, unlike a beautiful voice or fine physique, is not a free gift but the result of painstaking work and study. I learned a great deal from my colleagues by watching them in their dressing rooms as they transformed themselves before a mirror, and by asking them innumerable questions. Generous toward a young singer, they answered freely—all of them except Chaliapin, that incomparable master of make-up who so jealously guarded his secrets. Although he was polite and appeared eager to help, he nevertheless responded to concrete questions in a vague and lazy fashion, invariably straying off into anecdotes, usually of his amorous adventures. The stories were so magnificently told that I never resented his leaving my questions unanswered.

The person from whom I learned most about the art of make-up was a Pole, Sigizmund Zaleski, the leading basso at the Teatro Constanzi and an ideal colleague. On some nights, when I was singing and he was free, he would come down to the theater for the sole purpose of helping me with my make-up, accompanying his work with explanations, practical hints and instructive advice. It was Zaleski, by the way, who showed me how to convert myself into a striking Mephistopheles.

Once Zaleski's unselfish devotion caused me unwittingly to steal the show from him. We were both appearing in the minor roles of Samuel and Tom, the scheming enemies of the Governor of Boston in Verdi's *Un Ballo in Maschera* (The Masked Ball). The sympathies of the audience do not lie with the conspirators, but when I made my entrance on the stage, the public was moved to prolonged applause, while Zaleski's own entrance went utterly unnoticed. The reason for the enthusiasm was the excellence of my make-up, executed by Zaleski; it made me look like a Rembrandt painting come to life.

The creation of a character begins with make-up but does not end there. All too often one can see a singer or even an actor attain by his make-up a perfect illusion, only to shatter it the moment he moves or opens his mouth, as though some evil genius had played a trick on the poor man. To achieve perfect likeness, one must retain the illusion whether standing or moving, talking or singing, laughing or just standing still. In other words, one must attain an inner as well as an external likeness of the character. This is why, in preparing a new role, I try to learn more than just the music and the words that go with my part, and to read more than just the description of my man contained in the libretto. If he is a historical person, I visit museums and libraries, read memoirs and biographies, and study photographs of the man I am to depict. The historical epoch and the kind of music interest me only insofar as they help me understand the character of the man I am to incarnate on the stage. The only time I went further than that was when I studied the role of the tragic Tsar in *Boris Godunov,* an opera that immersed me in a time, land and music so alien to me that, in order to understand what was taking place on the stage, I found myself searching for material on Russian history, geography and music. But of this later.

Make-up, costumes, the poses and the shrug of the shoulders are all externalities, essential and effective when well done, but externalities just the same. The real and the great art in acting lies in the projection from within—an art which the singer, as a rule, tends to neglect, because uppermost in his mind is the voice. And for good reason: however great an actor the singer is, he loses his place on the opera stage the moment he begins to lose his voice. By the same token, however poor his acting, he is assured of a well-paying job and of rapturous bravos if he is able to pour out those beautiful sounds.

Acting held a challenge and a fascination for me. It seems I was able eventually to achieve naturalness on the stage, which often misled audiences and even critics into an unawareness of the many hours of labor I had put in to accomplish a truthful portrayal. Once more I found Zaleski's example and instruction the most valuable and inspiring. The best advice he ever gave was: Keep your self-control.

"Try to absorb your character so totally," he used to

say, "that you can live him on the stage, but do not permit him to run away with you. Watch and control your every word and gesture, make a conscious effort to do it, so that you can discard the character the moment you leave the stage. Otherwise you will not last long."

To drive the point home, Zaleski was fond of quoting Constantine Stanislavsky, that great Russian *régisseur* who insisted that an actor be fired the moment he thought he *was* the character whom he portrayed on the stage.

There was little danger that I would forget my identity off stage. My biggest problem was to memorize the words and music and to understand my character. This took time, work and thought. Once I had mastered a role, having taken into consideration every word of criticism and advice; once I was satisfied that I understood and had assimilated the character of the person, I ceased to worry about the right or wrong of my interpretation and became completely immersed in the person I was re-creating. I actually lived him on the stage, unmindful of what the critics might say, and forgetful of a man named Ezio Pinza. Therein lay the secret of my security on the stage.

It goes without saying that, to be an actor, one must have a natural gift, a talent; and this is something that cannot be acquired. But talent alone is not enough. It is like vitamins: without them, you lack something crucially vital to your system; with them, you still need daily nourishment to sustain you. To an actor, that daily nourishment is work. Very few people can produce the illusion of doing an honest job without putting in an honest effort, and I do not belong to those few. Nor do I regret it. I have found rewards in work: the joy of accomplishment and the knowledge that I earned the pay and the applause given me.

As a singer, a musician, I learned very little while at the Constanzi in Rome, where, somehow, no conductor made any impact on me. It was probably not their fault. The place was too big and the artists too numerous for the average conductor to bother with a young and compliant bass who was doing sufficiently well not to detract attention from the tenors and sopranos, the terror of most conductors. After two seasons I became restive and started looking for an opening either with a distinguished conductor who would give me more of himself, or in a smaller opera company where I would have opportunities to appear in major bass roles. Both conditions were met simultaneously when Maestro Tullio Serafin, one of the finest opera conductors I have ever worked with, engaged me as the leading basso for the Royal Theatre in Turino.

There Augusta and I settled down for one year. The Maestro wanted me to sign for another season, and I liked the idea myself, but some vague hunch prompted me to postpone the decision until after a brief vacation in Bologna with my parents. Fate now proceeded to work through the completely accidental fact that the opera season is shorter in smaller cities than in the larger centers. We had to change trains at Milan, and decided to make a holiday of it by staying over for two or three days to take in some operas at the Teatro alla Scala, where Arturo Toscanini was making opera history. As is the practice among artists, I called at the office to see whether any free tickets were available.

"Ezio! *Caro!* The very man I've been thinking about!" Thus I was greeted by La Scala's secretary, who had until recently worked at the Teatro Constanzi in Rome. "How would you like to work with Toscanini, Ezio?"

Maestro Toscanini was a hard taskmaster, but there was not a singer in Italy, or in the whole world, I imagine, who would not have given his eyeteeth for the privilege of sweating blood under the whip of that music-mad conductor. As for La Scala, it was, and still is, the shrine of the opera, Italy's most important music center and the magnet that attracted the Carusos and the Chaliapins!

Catching the gleam in my eyes, the secretary came out with certain sobering facts. "Toscanini is at present rehearsing *Die Meistersinger,*" he told me, "and every day he makes the discovery that Wagner is not for Italians, so every day more heads roll. For some reason, the Maestro has been having more trouble finding a good Pogner than filling all the other parts. This week alone, he turned down two bassos, but you will make it, I think."

My face fell. "No, I won't make it. I've never seen the opera and I don't know the role."

"There are still twenty-five days before the performance. You are the man, Ezio; I know you are. Here's the score."

"No use," I said. "You've forgotten I can't even read music."

But he had not forgotten. Neither, fortunately, had he forgotten my capacity for work. That very evening he assigned La Scala's two best coaches to me, Calusio and Votto, whom singers respected and feared almost as much as they did the Maestro himself. In fact, Calusio was the

Toscanini of the coaches: tyrannical to a degree which only unselfish devotion to a cause makes possible. His cause was the opera.

After seven hellish days which I shall never forget, my two mentors agreed that I was ready for Toscanini. Instead of a routine audition, I was to take part in a rehearsal with the other singers, who had already worked with the Maestro for about a month. Along with everyone else, I reported ten minutes ahead of time, and was awed by the hush in the vast room, as though Toscanini were already there. He appeared exactly on time, looking much smaller than I had expected, but instantly filling the hall with his presence. Everyone rose with military precision, like soldiers greeting a general. Without a nod, a smile or a word of salutation, Toscanini announced, "We will begin with the entrance of the *Meistersinger*."

That meant he was starting with me. In fact, the major part of that rehearsal revolved around my role. I concentrated on what I was doing with such single-mindedness that I could form no idea of Toscanini's reaction, and impatiently waited for the rehearsal to end; then the Maestro would surely pronounce his verdict. He did nothing of the kind. Without as much as a glance in my direction, he said, "Rehearsal tomorrow at the same time."

And he left the room.

One of the baritones patted me on the shoulder. "Congratulations, Pinza, you're in!"

"But the Maestro said nothing!" I remonstrated.

"You can always tell by his face. Didn't you see it?"

Of course I did. Especially the eyes, those stern,

piercing brown eyes, but to me they expressed nothing except that they demanded, commanded, willed.

My colleague was right. I did get to sing Pogner—my first Wagner, my first performance with Toscanini, my first appearance at La Scala!

I realized that I was on the threshold of a new and a promising stage in my career. Money, fame and everything that goes with them could now be only a matter of time—if I made good use of the opportunity to learn from Arturo Toscanini, the perfectionist who was also a willing slave—and who instilled in us complete devotion to the men who had created great music.

I was one of the Maestro's most willing slaves. Unlike some singers, especially stars, I have always thought of the conductor as being more than merely chief of the accompanists. He is the man who molds and guides our voices, temperaments and intuitions, and welds them together with the orchestra and all the other ingredients that go into that complex work of art called opera. The conductor must have knowledge, artistry, sensitivity, authority and, above all, the integrity that allows him to carry out the composer's intentions in all their many-sidedness.

I saw those qualities in Toscanini to a degree rare in the history of opera. Hence my obedience, which I was to give as willingly to one other man only—Bruno Walter. I shall speak of him later, but let me mention here that no two conductors of equal stature could be more different. Bruno Walter's urbanity and tolerance left no room for intimidation. With him, men responded to wisdom and high musical standards rather than to high musical standards and the autocratic command. True, as I occasionally watched Toscanini wrestle with some singer, the splendor of whose voice was matched only by his vanity, I could not help wondering whether the severe Maestro was not right, after all. Like the violinist who holds on to a gorgeous tone until he cripples the composer's intentions, such a singer is so enamored of the sounds he produces that he holds on to them until the relationship between word and music is distorted. The greater the natural beauty of the voice, I have noticed, the more irresistible the temptation to exploit it to the hilt.

Unlike some of the other singers, I did not resent Toscanini's interest in me as a music maker rather than as the bearer of a voice, which, perhaps, explains why he was so patient with me and gave me so generously of his time. In fact, he was friendly, as friendly as his forbidding, lonely nature allowed.

It is impossible to describe Toscanini's contribution to my development as an artist without going into the technicalities of singing, the relationship between orchestra and voice, and between music and words. Therefore I shall not attempt it. Suffice it to say that he taught me most of what I know about style in operatic singing. I found Toscanini so wonderful a pedagogue that I regret the popular conception of him, which is limited chiefly to his greatness as a conductor. He was that, of course, but no greater a conductor than he was a teacher—a teacher by the grace of God. As for his own graciousness, there was little of it in his treatment of singers and musicians, whether public idols or humble beginners. Everyone in the world of music remembers Toscanini's response when Geraldine Farrar demanded that he show more courtesy to the stars.

"The only stars I know are in the Heavens."

To him, music and music making were the sole *raison d'être* of opera companies, orchestras, conductors and even soloists.

During my three seasons with La Scala, I sang under Toscanini's direction in *Lucia di Lammermoor, Aïda, Tristan und Isolde, Louise, Boris Godunov, Deborah and Jael* and *Nerone*, as well as in Beethoven's Ninth Symphony and Verdi's Requiem. (There were also *Lohengrin, La Bohème* and *La Sonnambula* with Maestro Guarnieri, and two Wagner operas with my good friend Tullio Serafin at the Théâtre des Champs Élysées in Paris, my first engagement outside of Italy.)

I emphasize the operas I sang with Toscanini because he helped me to shape my roles in them, and I retained those interpretations for the rest of my life. He was inspiring, but—a man of few words—he had practically none for praise. As a rule, he spoke only to make a demand or to upbraid an erring artist. The only compliment I ever received from him was given at a private rehearsal, with the coach Calusio at the piano. We were going over Pimenn's part in *Boris Godunov* (Zaleski had the title role) when, after a particularly well-executed phrase, Toscanini exclaimed, "At last, we have a singer who can really sing!"

The other two men from whom I learned much at La Scala were Zaleski, who joined that opera house at about the same time I did, and the wonderful French bass-baritone, Marcel Journet. Both were great artists, so much older and more experienced than I that only secondary roles were assigned to me—a situation I did not altogether resent, for so much was still left for me to learn. I thought myself lucky to be able to watch two such splendid craftsmen and artists in the roles which I hoped, sooner or later, I would sing.

Whereas Zaleski was always ready with criticism and advice, Journet taught me only by example. He was one of those rare persons who never stop growing as artists. Even his voice kept improving with age, reaching the heights of power, beauty and flexibility after he had passed his fortieth year. I have never heard anyone go from high notes to low ones with the ease and sonority of the middle-aged Journet. He left La Scala during my second season there, covered with glory, particularly for his two greatest portrayals: the Father in *Louise* and Hans Sachs in *Die Meistersinger,* roles for which my voice was well suited and which I, naturally, desired. But I would not ask for them. I had made it a rule to request no part, however coveted, for I believed that a role given me under pressure would be jinxed and that I would surely fail in it. With one exception, of which I will speak later, I always waited for a role to come to me. By way of reward, I have been given the opportunity to appear in nearly one hundred operatic roles, which just about cover the entire field available to a bass-baritone.

Shortly after Journet's departure, I was assigned his part in *Louise*. Toscanini went over it with me so thoroughly that I was soon ready for the dress rehearsal. Unfortunately, I was exhausted from practice, as well as nervous about stepping into the shoes of the great Journet.

I did well until the Father's first aria in the fourth act,
which contains a high G, sung unaccompanied. Realizing
the difficulty of producing that dramatic high note, the
composer made the G optional, allowing the artist to
decide whether to attempt it or to stay on E. As it happened, Toscanini, who normally disliked high notes, demanded the G in this case, and I had produced it for him
at all previous rehearsals. Since he knew I could do it,
and since I was tired and nervous, I did not, at the dress
rehearsal, make the extra effort, but settled for the E. The
Maestro did not stop the show, but I had already learned
to read his face and therefore was not surprised when he
appeared in my dressing room after the rehearsal, demanding, "Why no G?"

"I was too tired, Maestro."

"See the doctor at once," he ordered. "And rest over
the weekend. I want that note on Monday night!"

I did not think I needed the attention of a physician,
but I dared not ignore a command by Toscanini. The
La Scala doctor found nothing wrong with me, and assured me that I would be in perfect form after a good
night's sleep. Furthermore, he gave me permission to go
to the races on Sunday, provided Toscanini knew nothing
about it.

It was a beautiful performance that Monday night!
The Maestro's face was glowing with happiness—that is,
until the moment he reduced the orchestra to complete
silence just before my high G. Then he looked at me with a
kind of plea and despair—and buried his face in his hands.
It was strange, the magic of that man. I was facing some

of the most exacting music critics on the Continent, and La Scala's perceptive and knowledgeable audience, which was still haunted by Journet's portrayal of the Father. Yet all that existed for me that moment was just one little man, the relentless master named Toscanini, who now looked so helpless, so childishly touching, that I smiled inwardly and gave him the most beautiful high G of my entire career.

He came into my dressing room after the performance, shook my hand and said, "Soon I shall be working with you on Hans Sachs."

Then a week went by, a month, the whole season. Toscanini seemed to have forgotten his promise. At the beginning of the new season, my third with La Scala, I reminded him of it. He was too busy just then, he said, but there was still time; we'd get around to Hans Sachs one day. The season was about over, and that day had yet to come, so I tried to force his hand. When I was asked to renew my contract in the early summer of 1924—all La Scala contracts are on an annual basis—I demanded a written assurance that I would be assigned the role of Hans Sachs. I believed that I was not doing violence to my superstition, because that part had already been promised me by Toscanini of his own accord. Whatever the reasons for his change of heart, the management refused to give me a written guarantee and I, having inherited my father's stubborn streak, refused to renew my contract.

You must realize that it required more than a disagreement over a role to embolden me take so crucial a step as parting with La Scala and Arturo Toscanini.

Yes, there were other factors. To begin with, my performances at Milan had attracted the attention of various impresarios and opera-house managers in my own country and abroad. My agent had requests for me from practically every city in Italy. There was also a highly tempting offer from Teatro Colón, the famed opera house in Buenos Aires where Serafin was now conducting. And —my agent told me this in a whisper—the Metropolitan Opera itself had shown an interest in me, but he could not conduct any concrete negotiations with its General Manager, Gatti-Casazza, because of an agreement between the Metropolitan and La Scala not to "steal" artists from each other. Since I had some savings, as well as an income from His Master's Voice, which had begun to make and distribute my recordings, I instructed my agent to sign me up for performances in various Italian cities during the forthcoming season, followed by a season in Buenos Aires.

My parting with La Scala was a friendly one, particularly with Toscanini, who, so far as one could judge from his attitude toward me, had no idea that he was in part responsible for my reckless move.

The invitation to record for HMV had been an important event in my life, boosting my income and giving me a sense of wider recognition. After all, Caruso and Chaliapin had recorded for HMV! When the music stores at the Galleria informed me of the day on which they would feature the Red Seals in their windows, I invited my wife and some friends to the Galleria's finest restaurant for lunch, without telling them of the occasion for the celebration. They were impressed when I brought in the records, certainly, but no more than I was. I sent a set of discs to my parents and to Gino.

The contract with HMV had come mostly as a result of the tremendous publicity given Toscanini's production of Arrigo Boito's *Nerone*, in which I appeared shortly before leaving La Scala. So far as I know, that was the most monumental production in the history of opera. We had rehearsed with Toscanini for a full year, but so complicated and spectacular were the scenic effects that La Scala had to be closed down for a week to prepare the theater and perfect the production. The publicity given *Nerone* was so great that every participant became a nationally known figure.

This was the first of three great high lights in my career. It also brought me in contact with the man who had suggested the lucky name of Ezio for me. Father was fond of telling the story of how he happened to choose the name, but he had lost sight of his carpenter friend and of my namesake, the singer. Having seen my photograph in his newspaper, the carpenter wrote to me from Florence, and inquired whether I was the son of Cesare and Clelia Pinza. I replied, confirming his supposition and saying that my father and I would like to visit him. The man, whose last name unfortunately escapes me, responded with an invitation and we spent several happy hours at his home in Certago, near Florence. I was sorry to learn, however, that the original Ezio had had no luck as a singer and had joined the honorable fraternity of carpenters.

The *Nerone* publicity brought me in touch with yet another figure from the past, my childhood friend Otello

Ceroni. We had lost sight of each other, you will recall, on the eve of World War I, and now I received a letter from him. Not as lucky as I had been in the war, he had been sent to an active front and had soon landed in a hospital with shell shock, as a result of which he had been forced to give up playing the French horn; each time he tried to blow it, his lips trembled uncontrollably. To stay in the opera world he loved so much, he accepted the job of prompter in Faenza, a city near Ravenna. Ceroni was the first person to greet me when I arrived there with a touring company, and we have kept in close touch with each other ever since. Although I nearly crippled him during my first performance at Faenza, where I sang the title role in Boito's *Mefistofele,* he has never held it against me.

This is how it happened. At the end of the second act, the Witches present Mefistofele with a large, shining tin globe reflecting our whole planet. Globe in hand, I sang the famous aria, *"Ecco il Mondo"* (Behold the Earth), then hurled the prop in the direction of a huge pot, out of which issued smoke and flame symbolizing the devil's kingdom. My normally excellent aim failed me. The globe hit the edge of the pot and split in two, one half falling into the orchestra pit without touching anyone, the other flying into the prompter's box and knocking Ceroni on the head. He suffered nothing more serious than a bump, which was ignored in the hilarity of the occasion. I soon made up for the unintended injury, however, by finding him a job as prompter at the Teatro Constanzi in Rome.

I cannot refrain from pausing here to relate a few

incidents connected with my father during those, my first, years as a full-fledged professional opera singer. As you can well imagine, Cesare Pinza was more vociferously proud of my modest success than I myself, if only because I have always been more reserved by nature than Father, and also because I was fully aware of the heights yet to be scaled, if scale them I ever would. My father rapidly became an opera addict, using the vernacular of the profession with the greatest ease and pronouncing judgment with the finality of a music critic.

One time during a visit in Bologna, I attended a performance of *La Favorita* with him, starring Giacomo Lauri-Volpi, who was the possessor of a wonderful tenor voice, a touchy pride and a terrible temper. As is bound to happen to all singers at one time or another, Lauri-Volpi had absolutely no success that night, and when you have no success with an Italian audience, you get plenty of hisses and catcalls. I did not envy Lauri-Volpi and hastened to leave the theater immediately after the performance, instead of calling on him in his dressing room, as I would have done under different circumstances.

The next morning my father and I went out for a stroll—and met none other than Lauri-Volpi and his wife. Without stopping, I greeted them politely, but my father suddenly buttonholed the tenor, saying without any preliminaries, "The trouble with you, *Signor Tenore,* is that you sing through your nose. What you should do is open your mouth wide and give us your full voice!"

The ground shook under my feet, and I was preparing to meet a violent assault on my father. But all

Lauri-Volpi did was to bow politely, say "*Si, signore*," and walk on.

We went back to the opera that night and saw Lauri-Volpi open his mouth wide, and heard him sing with all the splendor of his full voice. The audience gave him an ovation which out-thundered the catcalls of the night before. My father, of course, took the credit for Lauri-Volpi's triumph. As for the tenor, whenever I met him in my travels, he would inquire about Father's health, never failing to send greetings to "my favorite music critic." And this from the man who, on one occasion, punched a New York critic in the nose for giving him a bad notice.

Another time, while vacationing near Bologna with Augusta and my parents, I was nursing a cold when Father brought a stranger to our villa, introducing him as a good friend, the impresario of an opera company that was about to open its season in nearby Bagnacavallo. The man was frightfully upset, for the one basso in the company had suddenly fallen ill, with only two days left until the opening performance, Boito's ever-popular *Mefistofele*. He, the impresario, would be ruined unless I agreed to replace the basso. I firmly refused, but my father joined his pleas to those of his "dearest friend" (whom he had met only that day). Of course, as always, I could not say no to Father, but warned the impresario that I was in bad voice. The poor fellow, however, had no choice.

From the stage I could see Father sitting in the front row, all dressed up in his new suit—a well-tailored outfit which elegantly concealed the steel truss he had to wear for his double hernia. Everything was proceeding splendidly, except that Father was undergoing agony each time I opened my mouth; watching me strain for the notes, he finally understood the effort it was costing me to sing that night. Then the dreaded and expected thing happened: having reached the highest note in "*Ecco il Mondo,*" I was unable to sustain it. The note broke, but at precisely the same moment the hall was filled with the terrible report of snapping metal; my father's steel truss had burst at the crucial moment, a ridiculous miracle that saved me from catcalls!

Faced with my refusal to go on pinch-hitting for his indisposed basso, because of my own ailment, the impresario produced a country doctor who painted my throat with a medicine that worked miracles. In the next twenty-eight days I gave twenty performances and felt none the worse for it. The medicine alone more than made up for my ruined vacation, for I used it many times afterward until one day, long after I had lost track of both the doctor and the impresario, I lost the prescription, too.

As for Father, he was so embarrassed by the incident of the truss that he refused to be seen again at Bagnacavallo, despite my reassurances that the incident had actually saved the day for me.

My mother, now wearing tailored suits and hats to match, was taking the blissful change in her way of life with a quiet dignity that seemed a twin sister of her resigned patience of yesteryear. She was, at last, having a long, tranquil, well-deserved rest, but still kept an anxious eye on every one of her three children, all grown up now —even on me, the family provider and, in her eyes, the greatest opera singer of them all. Her solicitude was re-

flected in her reaction to my portrayal of tsar Boris
Godunov.

"Please don't sing Boris any more, Ezio. You suffered
so, I could not stand it."

"But I love this role. I must play it."

"I shall never go to see you do it again."

My parents were now living in a large apartment
house I had bought, which Father managed for me, keeping everything in excellent repair. They also had a maid
to help Mother with her chores. Otherwise, there was
little change in their way of life. With Father actually
doing an odd job here and there, I could support them
with little difficulty.

The Cassinelli family was the one that proved a big
drain on my finances. This, I am sure, comes to you as a
great surprise. It did to me, too; take my word for it. What
had happened, it seems, was that my father-in-law had
lost, in large-scale business projects and large-scale living,
the fortune he had inherited. Instead of adjusting himself
to realities, he broke into a trust fund left for his children
and lost that, too. From time to time he applied to me for
loans, and so did some of his offspring. I cannot say that
I resented too much the business of lending them money
and not getting it back. After all, they were my family,
the more so after my sister Beniamina married Augusta's
brother, Giuseppe, my favorite among the Cassinelli boys.
What I did resent was the inability of that family to dif-
ferentiate between sheer necessity, such as daily bread,
and a business investment—or luxury. One of Augusta's
brothers, for instance, took money from me to make pay-

ments on his automobile, whereas I could only afford to
dream about one.

What hurt me most was Augusta's attitude. Capable
of forgiving her kin everything, she forgave me nothing.
All that can go wrong with a marriage had gone wrong
with ours, and it may well have been that the hope of
achieving a happier life with Augusta in a different environment had played a major part in my decision to leave
La Scala. She may have loved me, but then what is love?
To me, love is desire, possessiveness, yes; but it is also
affection, understanding, forgiveness and respect. Augusta desired me without affection, sought to possess me
without understanding. In the atmosphere of La Scala
and under the impact of Toscanini's genius, I had reached
out for wider musical horizons, whereas she had displayed
nothing but a jealous watchfulness over me—and an interest in food.

The only artist's wife to attend rehearsals at La Scala,
she missed not a single performance in which I took part,
standing in the wings when I was on stage, and insisting
that I stay in my dressing room whenever I was not performing. Her eagle eye was on me during the curtain
calls as well. Instead of congratulating me on the applause, she would put me through a third degree. Why
did I bow to the left? Who was the lady sitting there?
The questions were the same whether I happened to bow
to the right or straight in front of me. Whatever my reply,
a scene was sure to follow. The very recollection of those
countless scenes still makes me choke with anger and
indignation. There were scenes backstage, in rehearsal
rooms, in the privacy of our home, in hotel lobbies, res-

taurants, railway stations; depriving us of the only refuge in a loveless marriage—the dignity of peace.

Augusta dreaded the very thought of bearing children because pregnancy, she knew, and the care of a baby would make it impossible for her to follow me everywhere. I used to tell her that children might bring us together and sweeten the bitter cup of our marriage, but her sole reply would be another stormy scene. There was something so reckless, so elemental in her possessiveness that I began to suspect a sickness, and finally I persuaded her to see a doctor. He found a deficiency in the functioning of her pituitary gland, which he thought accounted for her excess weight and excessive temper. The doctor recommended certain treatments, of which she did not approve, and Augusta thereupon pronounced him a fraud and refused to follow instructions. This, needless to say, subtracted nothing from the enormity of her figure or the intensity of her rages.

Our unhappy home life became the talk of the town and a major topic of backstage gossip. No wonder I wanted to leave Milan and go away as far as possible. My tour of Italian cities was hardly over when I signed the longed-for contract with the Metropolitan Opera Company for the 1926–27 season. In the meantime, in the spring of 1925, we left for Buenos Aires. There, on July twenty-seventh, Augusta gave birth to a little girl.

Even that joyous event was marred by my wife's refusal to enter a maternity hospital to bear the child, for this would have meant letting me out of her sight. Her doctor, alarmed by a fever she was running because of an infection, and by the fact that the baby was overdue, resorted to a stern warning that I would be responsible for the almost certain death of mother and child if Augusta were not removed to the hospital. Reluctantly, I gave permission to take her there by force. Once in the hospital, she would not let me leave for the Teatro Colón, where I was scheduled to sing in *Aïda* that night, leaving me with no choice but to steal my way out of the room while she slept. Throughout the ordeal I found help and understanding in our good and patient friends, the soprano Claudia Muzio and the conductor Tullio Serafin. We named our daughter Domenica Claudia—Domenica for Dr. Domingo, whose skill and firmness saved the lives of mother and child, and Claudia for the soprano whose generous friendship was matched by her beautiful voice.

CHAPTER SIX

The Metropolitan

THE TIME was October, 1926.

After a vacation in Italy, Augusta, the baby, her nurse and I were on board a ship entering New York Harbor. The sight of the skyscrapers in the clear autumn air was overwhelming. So all that talk about the fabulous city was true, I thought, and also true must be the legend of the Metropolitan Opera House, a magic place in a magic world that drew to itself the world's best singers and conductors. Having heard the stories floating about Milano's Galleria, and having been congratulated, not without envy, by my colleagues, I believed—no, I knew —that I was departing for the Mecca of the arts. The singers, the coaches, the conductors were all first-rate. As for the pay, it was the highest in the world, and in good, sound American dollars. My very first contract, although modest when compared with that given a star, had cata-pulted me overnight into an income class beyond the reach of a carpenter's son's dream.

I was so impatient to see the Metropolitan that I

rushed there the moment my family was comfortably settled at a hotel. The exterior of the opera house was so depressingly ugly that La Scala or the Colón seemed, by comparison, the height of magnificence. In time, I learned historical facts about the establishment of the Metropolitan Opera House, and I would like to believe that there is nothing more to them than malicious gossip—but facts are facts. A millionaire named William H. Vanderbilt, it seems, was hurt by the refusal of the Academy of Music (the home of New York opera) to place a box at his wife's disposal. He thereupon assembled several similarly offended *nouveaux riches* and, in 1883, caused the Metropolitan to be built around a mighty tier of boxes, showcases for their female occupants to shine and glitter in. Little effort was made to achieve any balance and attractiveness in the other parts of the house, and still less to provide it with such incidentals as comfortable dressing rooms, sufficient storage space for scenery or equipment for smooth and rapid scene shifting. As a matter of fact, the Metropolitan has been compelled to keep its scenery in warehouses many blocks away, moving it back and forth; an exceedingly costly procedure, made costlier still by the damage to the bulky sets caused by mishandling and exposure to New York's damp weather.

There has been much talk about the Lincoln Square Project, which would provide a new home for the Metropolitan Opera Company. I hope it comes through, and even more fervently do I hope that its chief architect will be a man with experience in building theaters and that he will, moreover, welcome an opera-stage director on his advisory board.

The legend of the Metropolitan was destroyed for me on that, my first, visit, even though the good American dollars and the best singers and conductors the world over were no illusion. No one seeing a young, heartbroken Italian basso wandering backstage on that October day would have guessed that he would spend the major part of his next twenty-two years in that building, and end up by becoming sentimental over the very dinginess of the place. Among my most cherished possessions is a piece of the worn-out golden curtain replaced on December 2, 1940, by one of fresh magnificence.

One of my first deep impressions in the United States was the incomprehensible, brutally frank way in which the music-loving American public insisted on neglecting and even scorning native talent in the field of serious music, particularly singers and conductors. This attitude has been changing, thank God; but when I arrived, and for years thereafter, the only way for those musicians to achieve recognition in their homeland was to study abroad, acquire a European reputation and take exotic names. Even such a hallowed name as John Smith had to be distorted into something resoundingly Italian. One of the leading Metropolitan Opera House tenors at the time I joined the company was Edoardo di Giovanni, of La Scala and the Teatro Verdi in Padua. He was none other than Canadian-born Edward Johnson, under which name he subsequently, and with great distinction, guided the Metropolitan as its General Manager. How happy I was that career considerations caused no temptations for me at any time to abandon my name, Ezio Pinza!

Things have improved considerably in this respect

during the past thirty years, with the result that an American artist, possessing a fine voice, dramatic flair and diligence, has as good an opportunity here as does a European endowed with similar gifts. It may be too much to hope that this country might produce in the near future as many good singers as Italy, for there, grand opera is in the very air people breathe, in the wine they drink with their daily bread. Yet much can be achieved through the establishment of small opera groups throughout the U.S.A., in which young people could have their rough edges smoothed down before they drifted to the all-too-few large centers, where competition with European-trained artists is fierce.

While in mid-ocean, en route to the United States, I received a cablegram from Giulio Gatti-Casazza, the General Manager of the Metropolitan, stating that my debut would take place on the opening night of the season, November 1, 1926, in Spontini's *La Vestale*. I was to sing the role of Pontifex Maximus, in support of Rosa Ponselle and Lauri-Volpi. Fate had brought Volpi and myself together several times, but Ponselle was only a name to me, and little did I dream that she would afford me so many unforgettable hours on the stage, during which, instead of thinking of my own role, I would be lost in the dark splendor of her voice.

On board the ship, however, and immediately after my arrival, I gave little thought to Ponselle, for time was short and I knew not a note of my part. With the help of the coach, Maestro Dellera, I managed well during the rehearsals, and through the performance itself. While they did not make an overnight sensation out of me, the reviews were kind and helped me establish myself as "a useful supporting singer," to cite one of the critics. Another, Lawrence Gilman of the *Herald Tribune,* praised my "imposing figure," "excellent voice" and the fact that I used it, he said, "with brains and discretion."

A young singer, with salary to match, I was given a second-class dressing room up two terrifically steep flights of stairs. The small room, which I shared with another singer, was tolerably clean, but, painted a sickly olive green, it was depressing, gloomy. Most of the inadequate space in it was taken up by an old upright piano. There were no private toilets in any of the men's dressing rooms. As for the ladies, only the stars could boast of possessing such a luxury.

If, as a newcomer and a supporting artist, I accepted uncomplainingly the confinement and dinginess of my quarters, the carpenter in me violently protested against the primitiveness of the dressing table placed at my disposal. My first impulse was to build one myself, but I gave up the idea, for fear of offending the carpenters at the Met. The mirror above the dressing table was cracked, which did not exactly facilitate the task of make-up. Yet I would not have it replaced, since a cracked mirror means good luck in my book of superstitions. As a matter of fact, as my star kept rising at the Metropolitan, causing repeated offers of a private dressing room on the floor below, I consistently refused to move, fearing to break the luck my first dressing room had brought me. I was completely satisfied, so long as the dressing room remained mine alone and was tidy, had a mirror for make-up and a table for my paints, greases, beards, mustaches and, last but not least, my luck charm, Licia's little doll. Permanently established in the room, I squeezed a small trunk into it for my belongings.

The most desirable dressing rooms were assigned to the leading prima donnas who, with the help of secretaries and maids, achieved miracles with their larger but equally shabby quarters. The scent of perfume, the colorful screens that hid wash basins and toilets, the precious scarfs thrown as though carelessly on unsightly sofas, the vases always full of flowers—all this plus a star's personality, vitality and charm converted her room into a place of glamour, intimacy and loveliness.

I had formed the habit at the very start of my career of being in my dressing room a full hour before the performance, so I could give the most careful attention to my make-up and costume. When completely ready, I would leave my dressing room, walk up and down the hall and vocalize to myself softly. On one occasion, soon after I had joined the Metropolitan, I ended my little exercise with the sonorous word "Carolina," unconsciously giving it full voice. "Carolina" is an especially good word because it contains many vowels, on which a singer can test his voice. All of the sounds—musical and otherwise—coming from the three floors of men's dressing rooms suddenly came to a halt. Then, as though at the imperious command of an invisible conductor, the artists responded with a "Ca-ro-li-na" that resounded throughout the house. This was followed by laughter on all sides, intermingled with applause, releasing the tension that always precedes a performance. I repeated "Carolina" before my next per-

formance, getting the same response and laughter—and
a custom was established to which I adhered throughout
the years I remained with the company. From that time
on I was always known, backstage, as Carolina.

All in all, my first season was a happy and pleasant
one, easing me into the routine of the Metropolitan and
bringing me in contact with people from all over the
globe, who had been assembled to make a thing of beauty
and perfection out of grand opera in a non-opera-minded
country. Among my roles that year were those of Ramfis
in *Aïda,* Barnaba in *Gioconda,* Sparafucile in *Rigoletto,*
the Abbott in *La Forza del Destino,* Basilio in *The Barber
of Seville,* Raimondo in *Lucia* and Pimenn in *Boris
Godunov,* with Chaliapin in the title role. Dreaming of the
day when I would sing Boris at the Metropolitan, I was
now listening to Chaliapin himself in his greatest role
instead of carrying in my memory Zaleski's copy which,
however distinguished, was pale by comparison.

The modest success of my first performances, the
magnificence of the casts, the gaiety among the members
of the company (it took time for me to discover in the new
surroundings that gossip and intrigue were as rampant
here as in all the other opera houses) and the majestic
presence of Gatti-Casazza, that benign and inscrutable
despot, succeeded in dispelling my first unfavorable impression. I grew to accept the ugly exterior of the building, the drab dressing rooms and even the glittering box
holders, so many of whom come to the Metropolitan to
see and be seen rather than to view and hear opera. But
the standees more than made up for them. Mostly young
people, the standees endeared themselves to us all for

their love and knowledge of opera and for their spontaneous, uncalculated outbursts of gratitude.

The one thing I have not been able to understand, and still less to accept, is the custom of hiring claques. In addition to making regular seasonal payments for the applause, some stars were in the habit of making arrangements for individual shows, the fees varying with the number of extra persons hired to cheer and clap. The claque was so well entrenched, at least in my time, that even those who, like myself, refused to employ them had to contribute something to the gang at the end of each season because of the terrifying realization that, come next fall, its members would be in the audience, geared for boos and catcalls, as well as for hurrahs and bravos. On the advice of my fellow singers, I forked out fifty dollars during my first season, a sum the claque sometimes got for a single performance. This became my annual donation, which I refused to increase, although my earnings were climbing steadily. At the end of each season, the leader of the claque called in my dressing room, his hand outstretched for the blackmail money, which, I am ashamed to say, I gave. Pocketing the fifty dollars, he would thank me profusely, then add with a sudden sharpness in his voice that others paid more, and so should I. This whole business smacked of Mafia, I would say, and threaten to stop paying even my fifty dollars. "Cheapskate!" he would shout at me, but I had made up my mind and would not budge. The deadlock thus established, he would suddenly flash a smile, thank me again and take his leave.

The claque is an interesting institution. The people

in it have a special way of clapping which makes it possible for a trained ear to be aware of it the moment it goes into action. But frequently the claque is moved to join the audience in applauding an aria or a successful bit of acting even by those artists who pay them little or nothing. In fact, the claque's members are probably the greatest opera fans of all. Just imagine attending *every* performance of the season year after year!

The wide range of my voice made it possible for me to appear in a great many operas at the Metropolitan. It is a source of pride and satisfaction to me that my relationships with the company's personnel—my fellow artists, the stagehands, chorus and others—were consistently happy. The success of a performance and the degree of its perfection ultimately rest on the honest efforts of all concerned. I have a feeling that all of these artists are my friends.

The poor country of Italy has very few natural resources, but God made up for that by endowing Italians with a great love of life and laughter. Life is often cruel and everyone has problems and tensions. I thank God for the greatest gift He gave me—a sense of humor. It is a necessity for me to have good-natured people around me. Most artists have similar natures and it was true of those with whom I worked at the Met. We had marvelously gay times backstage, which helped ease the tensions of a performance.

I loved the horseplay, the movement, the gaiety on and off the stage, the wonderful outbursts of laughter in the audience at some special bit of clowning, such as the little dance I did with Lily Pons in *Le Coq d'Or,* where, made up as King Dodon, I carried my huge horsehair stomach with idiotic dignity.

Then there were the practical jokes which, when perpetrated on stage, made one tread the razor's edge, for the slightest deviation from the routine could upset the whole scene. Only seasoned professionals can take practical jokes in their stride. The best trouper of them all was the lovely mezzo-soprano, Thelma Votipka. One night, during a performance of *Faust* in Canada, I, as Mephistopheles, was to present to her, as Martha, the traditional daisy. This I did, except that I replaced the tiny ornament provided by the props department with a sunflower of enormous proportions, such as I have seen only in Canada, its stem the size of a large stick. Thelma Votipka nearly doubled up with laughter, but when she sang, her voice sounded full and beautiful, as though nothing extraordinary were taking place.

Of course, tricks were played on me as well. During a performance of *Rigoletto* one night, I was to pick up a basket in the middle of a melodious exchange with Lucrezia Bori and Richard Crooks, and exit with it. I took hold of the basket, only to discover that my partners had placed a heavy weight in it. But I was young and strong, and managed the scene, with no one noticing the effect of the effort on my voice, except for the conductor, who raised a pained eyebrow. The plot demanded that I re-enter with the basket and hand it to Miss Bori. Assuming that I had removed the weight, she took it from me with a graceful gesture, singing all the while. Naturally, the basket fell to the floor with a bang. It is hard to believe, but it is true: Bori's voice did not falter for a second, and so absorbed was the audience that there was not a stir in the hall.

As you can well imagine, pranks were in order off stage as well. Once my victim was a concert manager in a large provincial city where I gave two concerts, with a few days in between. I stayed on in the city until my second recital, rented a car and took long drives into the country, my favorite source of pleasure and relaxation. It so happened that Elisabeth Rethberg, one of Metropolitan's finest singers, arrived in town for a recital. On the evening of her appearance, I offered to drive her from the hotel to the concert hall. As always when driving, I wore a cap and sport jacket, so that the manager who met her at the stage entrance, and who, incidentally, had been trying to entice me into giving a concert under his management, did not recognize me and, assuming that I was a hired chauffeur, treated me the way small people treat their servants. Standing at attention, my head lowered, I responded to his imperious orders with "Yes, sir," "As you please, sir," "Thank you, sir." I might have earned a tip from that man, but Miss Rethberg, bursting with laughter, gave me away. You should have seen his anguish and heard his apologies!

Giulio Gatti-Casazza, the General Manager, was *Il Gran Signore* of the Metropolitan, whom we all addressed as *Direttore*. Handsome despite his enormous proportions, towering and inscrutable, he was friendly toward everyone, and on intimate terms with not a single soul. Besieged by ambitious, temperamental stars and by high-strung, unpredictable patrons, he was the consummate diplomat who succeeded in keeping his own counsel while offending miraculously few persons.

Gatti's contacts with me, as with everyone else in the company, were cordial, infrequent and brief. As a matter of fact, during my first three years in New York, we had something resembling a conversation on only four occasions.

The first took place toward the end of my initial season with the Metropolitan, when I walked into his office to suggest a raise in my salary. Characteristically, the doors of that office were wide open to all the artists at any time, but one rarely entered the room without some specific matter to discuss.

Gatti received me in a most friendly way and listened without interruption. Then he asked his secretary for my contract, tore it up and wrote out a new one, giving me a modest raise.

I called on him again at the end of the second season, with a similar idea in mind. This time I put it to him in the following fashion: "I have an aspiration, *Direttore*, a dream."

"What is your aspiration?"

"To earn one thousand dollars a week."

The Metropolitan Opera season in New York at that time lasted for twenty-four weeks, followed by a three-week tour of other American cities, which meant that I was asking for the then tremendous sum of twenty-seven thousand dollars a year. In other words, I wanted a very substantial raise.

Gatti looked at me in his inscrutable manner, then said, "Who am I to stand in the way of a man's aspirations?"

Again he sent for my contract, destroyed it and had a new one drawn up. This time it was a three-year contract at one thousand dollars a week.

[Mr. Pinza's request and the unhesitating manner in which the General Manager of the Metropolitan Opera Company granted it were a consequence of the only thing that matters in any branch of show business—success with the audience and with the critics. The young, little-known singer from Ravenna was on his way toward becoming a matinee idol, an achievement of which few bassos can boast. At the same time, the music critics were rapidly becoming convinced that, in Pinza, a star of the first magnitude had risen at the Metropolitan. The reviews of that period laud his "artistry and intelligence," his "voice and style," his "excellent Oroveso," splendid Archibaldo," "expert Don Basilio." As Don Ruy Gomez in Verdi's *Ernani*, Pinza was hailed for what was a truly miraculous feat: he "clearly outsang Ponselle, Martinelli and Ruffo."

In the words of Irving Kolodin, "What he [Pinza] did was what made the Golden Age golden. He was an actor who could sing, a singer who could act."

Years later, Robert Lawrence wrote of Pinza, the opera singer, in these words, "One felt glad to be alive in Pinza's time. . . . Here was opera at its most beguiling. The gods were good to Pinza. They gave him a magnificent throat, fine appearance, dramatic flair, and rare intelligence—qualities which, in combination made for a top operatic artist."

—R.M.]

My new affluence permitted me to invest a considerable sum in Bologna real estate, of which my father took excellent care, and to indulge in a hobby that was hitherto beyond my reach—automobiles. My cars were always of expensive make, and I traded them in as soon as a new model made its appearance in the showrooms.

Then came the crash of the stock market in 1929. People who had been wealthy only yesterday, among them faithful patrons of the Metropolitan, were now blowing their brains out, or hurling themselves to the ground from the upper stories of skyscrapers. The depression followed, forcing cut-downs on everything—on luxuries first, to which category art is undeservedly relegated.

The wave of retrenchment soon reached the Metropolitan, jeopardizing jobs and salaries. With my contract having two more years to run, I was quite safe, yet I called on Gatti-Casazza once more to talk about money. This time, it was I who asked for the contract and who tore it up.

"What about your aspiration?" asked Gatti.

"Time will take care of it, *Direttore*."

"I'm sure it will."

And we signed a new contract for a smaller weekly salary.

Before long, time did take care of my aspirations, and even exceeded them.

In between my last two calls on Gatti-Casazza in connection with money matters, I had visited him in his office at his explicit invitation. After greeting and seating me, he sat down himself and proceeded to scrutinize me in silence, obviously trying to make up his mind on something. Self-conscious and uncomfortable, I decided that the best policy was to stare back, and this I proceeded to do. But the *Direttore* would not be hurried.

At long last he broke the silence. "Have you ever done a baritone role?"

He well knew that I had already appeared as Escamillo in *Carmen* at the Metropolitan, but I patiently reminded him of it.

"No, Ezio, I'm thinking of something more singable, more delicate, something *mezzo-piano*."

"No, but I think I can, if need be."

"Yes, yes," he said absently, and was lost in a new silence.

"What is on your mind, *Direttore*?"

"Nothing in particular just now. . . . We'll come back to it later . . . perhaps."

The interview was over, I understood. Puzzled and intrigued, I left him. Several days passed by, then a week, and nothing further happened. I could not help thinking about the conversation, vainly trying to guess what Gatti had in mind. Finally, I spoke to Tullio Serafin about it, knowing that he was as close to the General Manager as anyone in the company, which is not saying very much. As it happened, I hit it right, however little good it did me.

"This is something I am not free to talk about," Serafin said, "but I can give you a bit of advice. Try to see the *Direttore* once more. He'll tell you, I'm sure."

I refused to call on Gatti with a question he had once refused to answer, and let it go. As chance would have it, I came across him in the hallway two days later. "This is Fate," I said to myself. To Gatti-Casazza I said, "I am the type of a person who, once you put a bug in his head, cannot rest. What was it about my baritone roles?"

"It's still a secret. There will be hell to pay when it gets out, especially before I am ready."

"I can keep a secret."

As if that were all he was waiting to hear, Gatti went straight to the heart of the matter. "How well do you know *Don Giovanni*?"

"I don't know it at all."

Gatti was somewhat taken aback by the reply, but it was too late now. "Tullio Serafin thinks you would make a good Don Giovanni. Talk to him about it. And also learn the Serenade and the duet with Zerlina, '*La Ci Darem la Mano.*'"

This time Serafin talked freely. He and Gatti were planning a revival of the Mozart opera for the 1929–30 season, the Metropolitan's first *Don Giovanni* since 1908, when Scotti, Chaliapin, Eames, Gadski and Sembrich had combined with the great conductor-composer Gustav Mahler to give an unforgettable performance. There were always requests for the opera, but Gatti had felt he did not have the singers to fill the roles. Now, at last, he decided he had them all—except for a baritone with the voice, physique and style of singing suitable for Don Giovanni. To be sure, each of the leading baritones at the Metropolitan was convinced that he was made for the title role, and was jealously awaiting the news of a revival of the opera. Gatti knew this, and he also knew that all baritones would join forces the moment they learned a lowly bass had been assigned to do Don Giovanni.

"They'll find out sooner or later," Serafin told me, "but the *Direttore* does not want to face the uproar unless he is certain that you are right for the role."

I took the score and the libretto with me, studied them—and my heart sank. The music was absolutely enchanting, but the libretto was a real calamity. I had never questioned a composer or librettist, and knew of no singer who did. Everything in opera is so hallowed by tradition that it rarely, if ever, occurs to anyone to question the unfolding of a plot or the conception of a character. With the one exception of *Boris Godunov*, I had never spent any time on studying the background of a libretto, its sources and the transformations the story goes through in the hands of the librettist. What I usually did was to study the character for interpretation and make-up, memorize the music and the lines and try to sing my best. But in *Don Giovanni* there is a truly monumental discrepancy between the build-up of the hero as a great romantic figure, an irresistible, heartless, dashing seducer—and the failures of his attempted conquests on the stage. All of Don Giovanni's successes are in the past; in the present, there is nothing but boasts and rebuffs. How could I have effectively portrayed such a man when, at every turn, I had the impulse to say to him in good American slang, "Put up or shut up!" The opera, I felt, ought to have been called "The End of Don Giovanni."

My dissatisfaction with the depiction of the hero

provoked me into reading up on the history of the opera, and when I did, I stopped being surprised at the libretto's weakness. The real surprise actually lay in Mozart's ability to fill such a hollow frame with such noble music. The composer's collaborator, da Ponte, was working on two other librettos at the time he wrote the book for *Don Giovanni,* completing all three in the space of two months, thus proving conclusively that speed, wonderful in bicycle and auto races, is not for the opera. Da Ponte, it seems, did not see it this way, for he actually boasted of his speed. His attitude toward the three librettos he was working on throws additional light on the man. His mornings were devoted to *L'Arbore di Diana* for Martin y Solar, which he considered as pleasant a task as reading Petrarch; his evenings, to *Tarare* for Salieri, every bit as enjoyable, said da Ponte, as reading Tasso; and, finally, in the depth of night, he would turn to *Don Giovanni,* the equivalent to him of plunging into Dante's *Inferno.* Alas, even Dante could not add glow to mediocrity.

Despite my misgivings, I worked hard on the Serenade and the duet, as Gatti had suggested, with the expert help of Tullio Serafin and the coach, Dell' Orefice. In due time, I sang before a very small group headed by the *Direttore,* who listened impassively, thanked me politely and left the hall without adding another word. I waited for the verdict, but no one said anything, and I was too proud to ask even my good friend Serafin. The decision must be against me, I thought, and made no further attempt to study the role. As an artist, truth to tell, I was not disappointed, but as a man of ambition I was. The public kept clamoring for *Don Giovanni,* and Gatti's

failure to revive it was criticized in the press and in letters
from numerous music lovers.

Once again I happened to come across Gatti in the
corridor (just how "accidental" those meetings were is
something I have often wondered about), and he stopped
me to ask in a conspiratorial whisper, "How much progress have you made with *Don Giovanni?*"

"None at all, *Direttore*. I never study a role unless
it has been assigned to me."

"Well, it is, as of now. But I want no one to know
about it just yet."

The assignment of the role of Don Giovanni to me
must have been the Metropolitan's best-kept secret in
years. When, according to tradition, the next season's
program was published in the late spring, 1928, the news
that I, a basso, would sing *Don Giovanni*, thus probably
setting a trend, caused a furore, especially among the
baritones. Two or three of them threatened to resign.
Particularly indignant were the Don Giovannis of bygone
years—Pavel Ludikar, Giuseppe de Luca and even Antonio Scotti, who clung to the memories of his triumph as
Don Giovanni in 1908.

There were protests, outbursts and angry shouts, but
Gatti miraculously quieted the storm, and soon most of
my colleagues were wishing me success and loading
me with advice. All that remained for Gatti and me to
contend with were anonymous letters abusing us, threatening that disaster would overtake the rehearsals and the
performances themselves. Gatti-Casazza dismissed those
letters with a shrug of his massive shoulders, but I dreaded

them, fearing what they might do to our *Don Giovanni*.

The Metropolitan sent Serafin and me to Salzburg to study the production of the opera at the Festival. When we returned to New York, we began rehearsals. Rosa Ponselle was to be the Donna Anna and Editha Fleischer was Zerlina, which provided great excitement for all of us.

For unknown reasons, everything went wrong from the very start. As we worked together, we felt, unaccountably, that something was missing. We, as a group, had failed in our combined search for the key to Mozart's music. The opera, long acknowledged as a musical masterpiece, managed to elude us. The stage director, a man of unquestionable gifts and knowledge, was unable to overcome the frustrations and tensions among us. I must have been the worst of the lot. Normally calm, businesslike and hard-working, I became prey to frayed nerves and gave a poor account of myself.

The fault was not altogether mine. True, I suffered from a lack of sympathy with the role, and I allowed the continuing flow of anonymous letters to upset me. But there was something else: for the first time in my life as an opera artist I was up against sabotage aimed at me brazenly, almost openly, by a colleague in the cast. Whenever we did a bit of business together, Pavel Ludikar, as Leporello, did all he could to wreck my part. I tried to ignore him, but how can you ignore someone with whom the plot of the opera brings you together constantly?

The breaking point was bound to come sooner or later, and when it did, I stopped in the middle of a note, reached for my coat and shouted, "This is ridiculous! I'm going home!"

As luck would have it, Gatti-Casazza had walked in a few minutes earlier and taken a seat on the stage. He had no inkling of what had been going on, I am sure, for he rose to his mountainous height and said in a clear, loud voice, "You stay right here and go on with the rehearsal!"

That did it. I, who had always considered tantrums the doubtful privilege of tenors and prima donnas, turned to face the awe-inspiring *Direttore* and bellowed at him, "What are *you* doing on the stage? Go back to the office where you belong!"

Without saying a word, Gatti-Casazza left.

And I? I stayed on, spiritless and ashamed of what was the first and last tantrum of my entire career. Our gentle stage director took the coat out of my hands, gave the sign, and the rehearsal was resumed.

That night I found it hard to fall asleep. There was the remorse at having offended the man who had done so much for me, and who was essentially right: the show must go on. There was also the realization that I had been working too hard and worrying too much. Every suggestion by Serafin or the stage manager, every little thing that went wrong, began to seem part of a plot against my singing Don Giovanni; whereas, with the exception of Ludikar, everyone was straining for a beautiful production. I decided to take myself in hand and make a new start.

I called on Gatti-Casazza the next morning and

apologized for my outburst. I must have looked the picture of contrition, for Gatti suddenly laughed, placed his hand on my shoulder and said, "Don't worry about it. Don't worry about anything except your Don Giovanni, and all will be fine."

I agreed with him and started for the door, when he unexpectedly drew me into the only long, informal chat I was ever to have with him. Normally, Gatti was aloof with all of us as a way of keeping above the battles of ambition and clashes of temperament that rage forever in the opera world.

Things began to go better after that. I was my co-operative and businesslike self again, and so was everyone else, including Ludikar. Then, on the eve of the first performance, Ponselle fell ill and was hastily replaced by Corona, who had had too little rehearsal time to do justice to her role.

The audience, however, was enchanted with the performance and made it a great success, especially for me. The demand for *Don Giovanni* became so great that we presented it several times each season thereafter. On tour it was the most successful Metropolitan Opera production in which I participated. The insatiable demand for *Don Giovanni* and the Metropolitan's financial difficulties compelled the management to hire ever-larger theaters for the opera that cries for an intimate hall. In Cleveland, for instance, a great big auditorium seating nine thousand persons was sold out every year, with results that were beneficial to the company's treasury, but harmful to the performance.

I was Don Giovanni so often and in so many places

(Italy, France, Austria, England, Sweden, Czechoslo-
vakia—over one hundred and fifty performances in all)
that the name had become a kind of a trademark for me,
the source of the legend of Ezio Pinza, the romantic lover,
a legend that kept growing until it burst into full bloom
some twenty years later with my first role on the popular
stage, that of Emile de Becque in *South Pacific*.

With *Don Giovanni*, I was, at last, beginning to taste
sweet revenge over my eternal "enemy," the tenor, who
always gets the girl, the best arias, the loudest applause,
the highest salaries and the privilege of tantrums! True,
I was not getting the girl in *Don Giovanni*—an oversight I
shall never forgive the librettist—but I was beginning to
get pretty nearly everything else!

Unlike the audiences, the critics reacted to our *Don
Giovanni* with very little enthusiasm. I do not read reviews as a rule, and would have missed them that time,
too, were it not for some anonymous "friend" who took the
trouble to mail them to me. The notices did not blast *Don
Giovanni;* they killed it with faint praise—the production
and everyone in it. That is, everyone except for Editha
Fleischer, our exquisite Zerlina. As for myself, Lawrence
Gilman of the *Herald Tribune* found me wanting "in the
elegance, the grace, the adroitness, the magnetic charm"
that a successful Don Giovanni should possess. Still, the
critic charitably credited me with "surviving the ordeal
more happily than one had supposed Pinza would."

To be perfectly frank, I hate to agree with reviewers
because they are often so all-knowing and didactic, so
determined to force their own conceptions and misconceptions on artists and audiences alike. But this time,

despite my wonderful popular success in *Don Giovanni*, I agreed with the critics, and I would not have been too disappointed had Gatti taken the opera out of the Met's repertoire. Fortunately, he was too good a businessman to do it, and had sufficient faith in the cast to sense that, given time and opportunity, we would improve. This we all did, I probably more slowly than anyone else because I lacked sympathy with the character I portrayed.

Gatti's persistence and *Don Giovanni's* continuing success with the public kept me in the title role until, in 1934, I met Bruno Walter, the best exponent of Mozart among the world's great conductors, whose wisdom and imagination subsequently converted that opera into an enchanting experience for me. Fate decreed that Walter also play a vital part in my personal life.

CHAPTER SEVEN

Salzburg: Enchantment and Tragedy

🎵

*T*HE TIME has come to reveal the most important reason for my temper and churlishness during the rehearsals of *Don Giovanni.*

Everything I have said about the anonymous letters and Pavel Ludikar was true enough, God knows, but I had become too much of a professional by then to allow such things to distract me completely from my work. Something else was in the picture, something so deeply personal and passionately felt that I was losing my sleep, my appetite and with them that sense of well-being so essential to the communicative powers of a performing artist. As you may have guessed, this something was the immense and ever-mounting unhappiness between Augusta and me. We had become such strangers that even our joy in little Claudia was a thing we experienced apart from each other.

Augusta's obsessive jealousy had grown to such incongruous proportions that violent scenes were a daily occurrence, irrespective of time, place, cause—or lack of it. She had made up her mind that I was being unfaithful to her, and was determined to frustrate my infidelities or, at least, make me pay for them by subjecting me to the indignity of public scenes. However hard I sought to avoid them, however little cause I gave her, those scenes, in whose violence Augusta seemed to take a perverse joy, became daily occurrences.

As though this were not enough, she treated any willing ear to fabricated stories about me and my lady loves, stories so fantastic that, by comparison, they reduced Don Giovanni, with his score of 2,065 conquests, to the rank of mere amateur.

A strict Metropolitan Opera House rule allowed no one backstage except those who had business there, but this did not prevent Augusta from attending all my rehearsals. During performances she sat in a box as close to the stage as possible, watching my curtain bows with the same alertness she had displayed at La Scala. And later, of course, she would nag me with the familiar questions: "Why did you bow to the right? . . . The left? . . . Who is she?" Even had I bowed to the ceiling, I suspect, she would have imagined an invisible woman there, lounging voluptuously in an invisible net.

We had no social life whatsoever. When we first came to New York, we were showered with invitations to the parties that go with a place of glamour such as the Metropolitan Opera House. My English was poor enough, but Augusta's was nonexistent, so she simply clung to me at these parties, inattentive when I talked to men, but fiercely alert the moment a lady, any lady, stopped to talk to me. "What did she say? What did you say?" she kept interrupting with no regard for amenities. As a result, people gave up inviting us to their parties.

The walks I liked to take were another source of irritation. They were a necessity, too, for I had been used to physical activity since childhood. My body ached for it, and because walking was the most available form of exercise, I tried to walk a mile or so every day. Suspecting the worst, Augusta insisted on accompanying me, although this was much too great an effort for her. If I had to slow down to her pace, I was frustrated and irritated. If I did not, there were scenes. On the days she was unable to join me, Augusta would try to get me to give up my walk. Failing, she would send little Claudia as chaperone, first going through my pockets to count the money in my possession. There was another count upon my return, and the inevitable belligerent questions should any coin or bill be missing: "What did you buy? . . . For whom? . . . Where is it? . . . Who was the lady you called on?" And all this in front of our child.

Like all the Casinellis, Augusta had the makings of a gracious hostess. She often invited our Italian friends to the apartment we had rented soon after our arrival in New York, and later to our large suite at the Hotel Ansonia. I, too, liked to entertain friends, and share with them the excellent Italian dishes Augusta knew how to prepare, but I resented the reason for her hospitality. She invited guests not for the pleasure of their company but because their presence would keep me at home, under her surveillance.

For years our meals were the only oasis in the stormy, barren desert of our life together, for the enjoyment of food was the one thing we could still share. But finally her obsession began to invade even that last refuge, her nagging affecting my appetite and my digestive system. I lost weight and grew increasingly irritable. It was at this point that *Don Giovanni* entered my life, the nerve-wracking rehearsals adding to my burden. Fortunately, relief and help also came to me at about the same time, in the shape of my good old friend, Otello Ceroni.

Ceroni had written from Rome, saying that he would like a job at the Metropolitan as prompter. I immediately spoke to Gatti about him, and so glowingly that Ceroni was hired simply on my recommendation. Wonderful prompter and musician that he is, my friend became the pet of all the singers, who often spoke of him as the Toscanini of the prompters. Some soloists became so dependent on his intuition, his miraculous ability to forestall mistakes, that they refused to set foot on the stage unless Ceroni sat in the prompter's box. His presence alone gave them such reassurance that they seldom needed his prompting. Though I was never that dependent on his presence, it did me good just to see his round head in the box.

Ceroni's arrival in New York brought a welcome change in some aspects of my personal life. We were living at the Ansonia then, and he settled down at the same hotel—a good friend within easy reach. Augusta, too, liked and trusted him, and was tremendously relieved when he took her place as a companion on my long walks. She no longer raised objections to my spending an evening away from home, playing poker or other card games, provided Ceroni was with me, and also provided that the other players were all men. As though anyone would care to play poker with women! Most wonderful of all, I could now go away on long drives, exploring the many beautiful spots around New York, upstate and in New Jersey. Ceroni, of course, had to be with me, but I wanted his company anyway.

One of the most ridiculous incidents of my entire life happened on such a trip. Ceroni and I had a great longing to see Niagara Falls, of which we had heard a great deal as schoolboys in Italy. We set out one hot morning, with the four-year-old Claudia in the back seat. We should have been forewarned when, after only a few miles, we had a flat tire; but we changed it and plowed on. That afternoon I passed a car in a no-passing zone and soon heard a police siren. The policeman who talked with us kept staring, dumbstruck, into the back of our car. I turned around to see that Claudia had removed every stitch of her clothing in an effort to find release from the heat. Apparently he regarded us as suspicious characters, for he was not content with giving us a ticket, but ordered us to the police station, where telephone calls were made to New York to clear us. Finally, on our way again without even a map, we asked many people the direction of "Nee-a-*gaa*-ra." Not one soul could tell us where this wonder of the world was located. We found ourselves in the city of Buffalo—and asked once again, this time of the right person. After correcting our pronunciation, he told us we were practically at the Falls, and to be sure to see them at night, when they were lit. As it was indeed night by then, we two hot-headed Italians hastened to the bridge and proceeded to gaze upward, expecting to see the water falling from heaven, at least. How completely disillusioned we were to see it all beneath us!

We continued to the Canadian side of the bridge, where the officials asked our nationality. When we said Italian, we were asked for passports! Ridiculous, we said, whoever traveled in America with passports? Then you had better go back to the American side, the authorities said, we cannot permit you to enter Canada. We were dirty, tired and hungry, so we returned. What nationality? the American immigration officials asked. Italian, we replied. Passports, please. Now what? Would we have to spend the rest of our lives in the middle of a bridge? Like men without a country? Our English was terrible and it worsened as we got more excited. We sputtered and pleaded for what seemed hours. Finally, a higher official was called, a former waiter on the Italian Line. He not only spoke Italian, but remembered having served me, so we were saved.

We rarely talked, Ceroni and I, understanding each other without words, finding a quiet, restful comfort in each other's presence—a refueling, if you will. Too many people talk all too much because of a nervous urge, giving neither themselves nor others the needed breathing spell to absorb and reflect.

Augusta provoked fewer scenes now, but we had them just the same. After one particularly stormy session at dinnertime, I invited Ceroni, who was a bachelor, to have his afternoon and evening meals with us, hoping that the presence of a stranger would keep Augusta within bounds. For a while the scheme worked. Soon, however, she started taking Ceroni for granted and things returned to "normalcy." Poor Ceroni! Dear friend! Time and again he would flee in misery and disgust, determined not to eat with us any more, only to come back in response to my desperate pleas.

One day it was I who fled. Though I soon returned, the thought of separation stayed with me day and night from then on, despite my vow of "for better or for worse."

In reciting my case against Augusta, I am not unaware of her side of the story. I am not the easiest person to live with, having inherited my father's tendency to dominate the household, and also his impatience with the little things that so often go wrong in one's daily life. I insist on neatness, for instance. I must have solitude from time to time, feeling a sharp physical need of it when exhaustion and emptiness set in after I have given all to a performance. Augusta, however, never left me alone. I need to feel that I am master of my own life, free to go wherever I choose, whenever I choose.

Yes, Augusta was right; I do thrill at the sight of a beautiful woman, and shall think myself ready for the grave the moment I lose that feeling. In trying to keep me away from women—and women away from me—in so melodramatic a manner, Augusta actually endowed other women with all the glamour and desirability of the forbidden fruit. Hers was the fatal failure to understand that her efforts to keep me lashed to her with the bonds of jealousy were self-defeating. True, she succeeded to the extent that I rarely dared to speak to another woman, but at the price of mutual alienation, until neither the marriage vows nor our devotion to Claudia was able to keep us together.

It was during my last months with Augusta that *Don Giovanni* brought me in contact with Bruno Walter, the world-famous conductor who was destined to play a vital role in my life. He was at the time—1934—planning opera productions for the Salzburg Festival that summer. From here on, I shall let Walter himself tell the story of our meeting:

> The major part of my endeavors was naturally centered upon Mozart, whose *Le Nozze di Figaro* and *Don Giovanni* performed in Salzburg for the first time in my life in the original language. I had always been troubled by the fact that many details of the German translation were incompatible with Mozart's music. At last I was able to enjoy the longed-for harmony between words and music. Some of my previous productions of *Figaro*, which presented no difficult problems, had turned out quite well. I had been less fortunate in my endeavors to cope with the problems of *Don Giovanni*. At any rate, my repeated experiences and disappointments had made me thoroughly acquainted with them, and now, in Salzburg, with the assistance of Strnad and Karlheinz Martin, I was ready to risk a well-planned attack upon the seemingly impregnable fortress. I had succeeded in coming to an understanding with my collaborators about the dramatic and scenic difficulties, and our plans for the performance held out the promise that this time we would overcome them. But of what avail was the best solution of all these

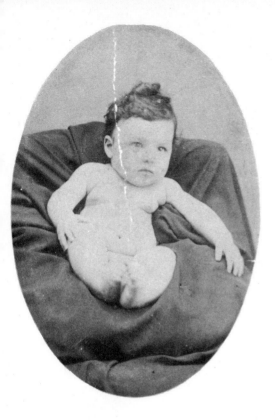

Ezio, the bambino.

With the Burgarellis. Gino is at the far left (next to myself) and in front of him Adele holds their baby.

With my father and mother, in Italy.

This is how I looked during World War I.

On board ship with Claudia.

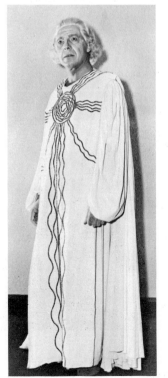

(*Above*) Bruno Walter rehearsing Jarmila Novotna and me for our roles in *The Bartered Bride*. (*Left*) Sarastro in Mozart's *The Magic Flute*. (*Below*) During a Met performance of *Figaro*, with Bidù Sayão as Susanna.

Lothario in Thomas's *Mignon*.

Russell Birdwell & Associates,

Kezal in Smetana's *The Bartered Bride*.

Opera News

Dodon in Rimsky-Korsakov's
Le Coq D'Or.

Guaranteed to scare both children an
adults—Mefistofele in Boito's opera.

iesco in Verdi's *Simon Boccanegra*.

As the father in *Louise* by Charpentier.

ounod's Mephistopheles.

Archibaldo in Montemezzi's
The Love of Three Kings.

Padre Guardiano in Verdi's
La Forza del Destino.

Russell Birdwell & Associates,

Don Basilio in *The Barber of Seville*.

The New York Times

The Hebrew Priest—*Samson et Dalila*
by Saint-Saëns.

My early—and perhaps wrong—conception
of Don Giovanni.

Here is how the Don eventually turned out.

Boris Godunov.

In 1946 I celebrated my 20th anniversary with the Met. Here is Edward Johnson presenting me with a silver bowl in commemoration.

At a broadcast, with Salvatore Baccaloni.

This picture of Doris and me was taken the summer of 1940, just before we were married.

The Pinzas — Doris, Pietro, Clelia, Ezio and Gloria.

Jane Froman, Danny Kaye and I, after entertaining President Eisenhower.

When President De Gasperi of Italy visited Washington, I was invited to sing for him, with President Truman in the audience.

With my good friends, Wal
lace Magill, producer, and
Don Voorhees, conductor, of
The Telephone Hour.

With Gibner King, my accompanist, coach and friend.

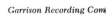

1953, in Baltimore,
with Rosa Ponselle.

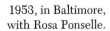

circle. Here, in Beverly Hills, Pietro and Clelia and I go bicycling.

th Pacific . . . and Mary Martin.

Broadway again:
onstage in *Fanny*.

Backstage at *South Pacific*,
with my good luck doll
and other treasured mementoes.

and my *Bonino* series; I was surrounded
children and I loved it.

Pietro and I
striding along a hilltop.

With Clelia and Satan.

Ronny Jaques, Oneida,

Spoon feeding—this time with Gloria.

problems as long as the most important question remained unanswered: where to find an artist for the
title part? I knew of none. The best of those who had
sung the part for me were lacking in some particular.
Even the excellent D'Andrade of my recollections
failed to measure up to the standard that a life-long
study of Mozart's figure had made to rise up before
my vision. We made every preparation, but I warned
Kerber that I would abandon the project unless a
kind fate helped me to find a suitable Don.

Among the singers of romance languages—for
only they could be considered—I knew a number
whose vocal accomplishments, diction, style and even
appearance called for serious consideration, but they
were all lacking in that immediately convincing
personal fascination which is an essential of the part.
Then I heard that Ezio Pinza, of whose voice, talent
and appearance Artur Bodanzky had spoken to me
enthusiastically several times, had scored a striking
success as Don Giovanni at the New York Metropolitan Opera.

An amusing incident inspired the hope that, in
addition to his general artistic suitability of which
all reports had made me convinced, he would also
be endowed with the ability to produce that immediate personal effect. We had taken with us to
New York our Bohemian cook, an efficient but quite
unimaginative middle-aged person. I called up Pinza
and told him I should like to make his acquaintance.
He kindly offered to call on me. There was a ring,
and Anita went to answer it. She came rushing back,
flushed, confused and excited, and whispered to my
wife: "Ma'am, there's such a beautiful man outside."

I said to my wife: "I think I've found my Don Giovanni for Salzburg." I had.

I, for my part, felt deep respect and affection toward Bruno Walter from the day we met, and I was eager to work with him on whatever terms he might suggest. The terms proved to be as generous as the man himself. We signed a contract and in due time I left for Salzburg, accompanied by Augusta and Claudia—the last trip we were to take together before our little family broke up.

So much has been written about this noblest of all music festivals that I can add little beyond affirming that it takes place in one of the most exquisite spots on earth, amid lakes and wooded mountains, against the majestic background of Alpine glaciers and snow-capped peaks. The medieval town where Mozart was born has retained its historic identity through its towers, churches and monuments, which give the town a solemn religious aspect, without at the same time depriving it of a sunny enchantment, grace and joy.

Nowhere else have I seen as many happy faces as in Salzburg, and nowhere else have I found the magic which music works there. People were drunk with music, and I along with them. Never a concertgoer before or since, I attended concerts in Salzburg whenever time permitted, and found the rewards great, for Toscanini and Walter shared the leadership of symphonic and operatic works that season.

The most moving event of the entire Festival, for me, was a performance of Max Reinhardt's *Everyman*, the majestic, simple story of man's life and death, staged on the Cathedral Square. The opening fanfares were sounded from the portals of Salzburg's splendid cathedral; the warning voices were heard from the spires of the town's churches, whose evening bells mourned the passing away of Everyman. The grandeur and truth of the production drew me to it each time I returned to Salzburg, never failing to move me anew.

Bruno Walter's impact on me was, in its own way, no less profound and lasting. Once more I found myself working with a person of Toscanini's caliber, but one who was neither distant nor harsh. Like Toscanini, Walter was able to raise the singers and orchestra musicians to the greatest heights of which they were capable. But there was this difference: whereas the former achieved his goal through a will of iron, the latter made us partners in his search for the right interpretation of the work.

Possessed by his own vision of the composer's intentions, Toscanini tolerated no other visions and crushed all opposition with sheer force of personality and authority. Walter welcomed challenge, meeting it in the spirit of intellectual and artistic give-and-take, making of it an enriching experience. Where Toscanini subdued wills, Walter molded taste and intelligence. Both men have achieved greatness, and the achievements of each are valid in their own way. I prefer Bruno Walter's method because we all were welcomed to participate as colleagues; in Toscanini's, we were permitted to take part only as awe-stricken and obedient followers.

The Salzburg rehearsals were a joy from beginning to end—all fourteen of them, including three dress rehearsals, an unheard-of luxury at the Metropolitan. The intimate theater, the stage, the scenery and the costumes were ideally suited to Mozart's work, and so were the people working with us. I particularly remember my good friend Virgilio Lazzari, who played Leporello; Dusolina Giannini, who was our Donna Anna; and Karlheinz Martin, the stage director. Martin possessed a most unusual quality: himself nervous, excitable, erupting with new creative ideas every few moments, he somehow had a most reassuring, even calming effect on all of us. Any other stage director, who, instead of walking, would slide up to you, like a baseball player stealing base, would make you jump. But not Martin. One smiled at his eccentricity, but listened to him carefully, for the man was a master of stagecraft.

The guiding genius, of course, was Bruno Walter—patient, kind and persuasive.

Mozart's spirit may have pervaded every aspect of the Festival, but do not think for a moment that it is easy to play and sing Mozart even in Salzburg. His music is too pure, too perfect. Perfection of course, is easy to unbalance. No wonder I have heard performers say that Mozart is the most inaccessible of the great masters. In discussing him, Bruno Walter once remarked to me, "It is not enough to feel Mozart; one must also understand him."

Understanding Mozart was precisely what presented the greatest difficulty for a person like myself who absorbed music instinctively—and with good results when it came to composers like Rossini, Bellini, Donizetti and the incomparable Verdi. What I was now trying to do was to attain an understanding of Mozart, and particularly his *Don Giovanni*, without at the same time ignoring the promptings of my instinct.

Guided by Walter, I concentrated on the composer's score, rather than on da Ponte's plot and words, finding in the music the psychological insights that helped me correct my original, somewhat literal, approach to the opera. I now perceived its majesty as well as its elegance, sensuousness and mockery. The main character, in whom I had seen merely a conquering male, hopping from bedroom to bedroom, gradually emerged in my imagination as the magnetic rogue he was, yes; but one doomed by his quest for the perfect woman, by his mad courage and irreverent sense of humor.

Don Giovanni, I grew to believe, is the most tragic of all the Mozart operas. The last scene, which had once contained for me nothing more catastrophic that the destruction of a scoundrel's body, now symbolized the punishment of a man's soul. The very heaviness of my voice (I am, after all, a bass), to which some New York critics had objected, became an asset in my eyes—and in those of Bruno Walter, I have reason to believe—for it helped me to communicate to the audience the tragic element of the opera.

As for the excitement, the action, the sex, I tried to stress Don Giovanni's virility and elegance rather than to portray a man moved by sensuality alone.

Most important, the opera and my own part in it grew on me in the course of the rehearsals, enabling me to give

Don Giovanni my all. I had appeared in other roles which I cherished much more—Figaro and Boris Godunov, for instance—and I had worked as hard on mastering them, but no part ever gave me as complete a sense of having met a challenge. With *Don Giovanni*, I overcame the taboo on bassos invading baritone territory. More significantly, I overcame my own misconceptions regarding the opera, and achieved a victory over da Ponte's uninspiring libretto.

The reception given our *Don Giovanni* by the Salzburg audiences remains an unforgettable experience for me, one of the high lights of my entire life, a veritable triumph that carried me in the title role to all the corners of the world, and, not the least, back to New York, where the critics happily joined the audience in accepting my more mature interpretation.

The happiest result of my success as Don Giovanni was an invitation to come back to Salzburg again and again and again. I did so because I wanted to breathe its air, to see *Everyman,* to work with Bruno Walter. And also because wherever Walter was, I could see his younger daughter Gretel, or Greta, as I called her.

She was an exceedingly attractive young woman, full of vitality and charm. Like her father, mother and her elder sister, Lotte, she was a most gifted pianist and possessed a mind of great sophistication and many-sidedness. "Gretel is the best and severest critic of my work as conductor," Walter used to say. Yet she usually spoke little, concealing her knowledge and insights behind the sweetness and simplicity of a country girl's looks.

Greta and I hardly got to know each other during my first Salzburg season, which, you will recall, was in 1934. To be honest about it, I was attracted to her from the moment we met, but Augusta was still with me and, although our life together was nearing its end, I did not dare as much as look at Greta, for fear of spoiling the sunny happiness of our stay in Salzburg, and of involving the deeply respected Bruno Walter family in one of Augusta's terrible scenes.

Even had I not forced myself to be reserved with Greta that summer, her attitude toward me precluded any possibility of friendship. I saw her often, for she accompanied her father to all rehearsals and performances; but, for no reason that I could see, she took a strong dislike to me from the very start, treating me with that special brand of cordiality which civilized people use to place the objects of their dislike in a very very deep deep-freeze.

Greta was married to a German architect who lived in Zurich, a man she had stopped loving long before she met me, and from whom she had been separated for many months. Still desperately in love with her, he refused to give Greta a divorce, in the hope that she might come back to him. This she was determined not to do.

Upon leaving Salzburg I had no contact whatsoever with Greta, and did not see her until the following summer. In the meantime, Augusta and I had reached an agreement. In exchange for her promise of a legal separation and her return to Italy for permanent residence, I agreed to give her my automobile, residence in our beautiful villa and the entire income from my investments in Bologna. This settled, I already felt myself a free man, with all the excitement and the wonder that freedom meant after those sixteen years.

In saying this, I do not have Greta in mind, for the memory of her chilly cordiality was not conducive to any flights of fancy. Furthermore, she greeted me rather distantly when we met again in Salzburg in 1935. I have in mind something general, a sense of happiness and well-being that embraced everything and everyone. All of Salzburg looked lovelier and more enchanting than the year before, although I would hardly have thought it possible. The air was clearer, the sun shone brighter, men and women showed more beauty in their faces and there was more grace in the way they moved.

I was seeing much of Greta, as I did the year before. I soon knew that I could love her, but I said nothing, demanded nothing, and still was happy, so long as I could see her at rehearsals, at her parents' home, and have an occasional meal with her and her family in a restaurant.

Then came an evening which changed everything. A gala reception was held at the Residential Palace of the bishop, in celebration of the Festival's fifteenth anniversary. The party was dignified by the presence of a cardinal wearing a red beret which, along with the period costumes many people wore, enhanced the sixteenth-century atmosphere of the festivity. Some of my friends urged me to wear my *Don Giovanni* costume, but I came, instead, in the brand-new tails I had brought with me from London, where I had sung prior to the opening of the Salzburg Festival. Those were the first tails I had ever owned, and I was very proud of them, the more so after Lotte and even Greta herself, the always critical Greta, complimented me on their elegance. Emboldened by the compliment—or was it by the beer that had been served in abundance?—I invited the sisters to wind up the festivities in a night club with me. As it happened, they had been planning such an excursion in the company of a music critic from Vienna. I was invited to complete the party.

What followed was a never-to-be-forgotten mixture of the heavenly and the ludicrous.

The Viennese critic ordered a bottle of champagne. Considering the number of toasts our exuberance prompted, the bottle did not go far, and he was expansively ordering a second when I intervened, insisting that it be on me. The music expert objected, then hesitated, then yielded with such totality that I paid for both bottles and for the after-midnight supper as well. This, naturally, did not improve my opinion of music critics, but failed to dampen my spirits, which kept soaring even after my tails and the chair I was sitting on caught fire. Someone, it seems, had left a lighted cigarette on the seat of my chair. This meant that, in addition to paying the bill for the champagne and food, I also had to pay for the damaged chair and to order a new evening outfit from London. On top of all that, I had a flat tire near my hotel after I had chauffeured my companions home, and had to change the tire without anyone helping me. But this did not matter. Nothing mattered after the sudden realization which had come over me while I was dancing with

Greta that she liked me the way I liked her, and found a happiness and a fulfilment in my presence just as I did in hers. She who had been distant, superior and sarcastic was now confiding and tender.

From that night on, I saw as much of Greta as my busy schedule permitted. We took automobile rides to the many beautiful spots around Salzburg, climbed mountains and hiked in the valleys, discovering each other and learning about each other's life. She told me about her husband and the separation from him, and I told her about Augusta. Greta was possessed by a sense of loyalty I found difficult to share, but this did not diminish my joy in her presence.

Soon, all too soon, the holiday came to an end. I had to return to New York, leaving Greta in Europe. The season at the Metropolitan allowed me to arrange appearances on the continent for the following spring, where it was easier for us to meet. I was the more anxious to do so because I had committed myself to an Australian concert tour and was unable to take part in the Salzburg Festival in 1936. The commitment, incidentally, was made following my first and only difference of opinion with Bruno Walter regarding an operatic role for me, a difference which I shall recount in the next chapter.

Prior to my departure for Australia, I took part in two performances of *Don Giovanni* at the Grand Opera of Paris, with the entire Salzburg cast, headed, of course, by Bruno Walter. This meant also a brief reunion with Greta.

The trip to Australia from Marseille via the Suez

Canal was memorable, full of exotic sights such as a camel caravan in the distance, or the stars at night so large and seemingly near that you got the feeling you could touch them if you only reached out eagerly enough.

Australia was huge and tiring, a succession of one- or two-night stands, so that my impressions of that continent are hazy and superficial. We sailed from Sydney to San Francisco—it was a round-the-world trip—stopping off at the Fiji Islands, where I saw an authentic war dance and witnessed an impressive, song-filled religious ceremony. There was also a stop at Pago Pago, where the natives sold finely fashioned baskets, boxes, rings and other trinkets, all adorned with an inverted Swastika, which is one of the most ancient and widespread ornamental forms and the sun symbol of many primitive tribes. I bought a turtle-shell ring, the exquisiteness of which delighted my colleagues at the Met when I showed it to them upon my return. The shell proved brittle, though, and the ring disintegrated within a year's time. I threw away the pieces and forgot all about them until, years later, a blow struck like sudden lightning to remind me of them.

Time was passing, and with it came further bittersweet reunions and partings with Greta. One day, looking preoccupied and worried, she told me that she was about to leave for Zurich. Her husband wanted to see her urgently. I took her to the train. At the last minute, Greta embraced me, exclaiming, "I don't know if we'll see each other again, but if we do, I'll go mad with happiness!"

I became alarmed. "Why the 'if'?"

"Just a figure of speech—a woman's whim . . ." She laughed it off, then repeated, "I'll go mad with happiness!"

Although my time was filled with the never-fading excitement of the Salzburg Festival, the next three days were days of waiting, suspense and silence. As I entered my hotel after the performance at the end of the third day, I received a telephone call from Zurich. It was Toscanini's daughter, Wally.

"Gretel's husband shot her and killed himself," she said.

"How is she? How is Greta?"

"She died at the hospital. Mr. and Mrs. Walter are already here."

That night I got in my car and drove alone from Salzburg to Zurich. When I arrived in Zurich, Lotte took me to the cold, white hospital room where Greta lay. The strain of the long journey and my own emotion at the thought of this terrible tragedy caused me to break down. The understanding and sympathetic Lotte and a doctor led me from the room and out of the hospital. With Lotte I went to the hotel where Mr. and Mrs. Walter were staying, to pay my respects to my "second parents." As I entered their suite, Bruno Walter came up to me and placed his arm around my shoulder.

I remained with them for the rest of the day, then drove to Salzburg where another performance awaited me the following evening. Taking just enough time to change, I started on the lonely all-night drive back to Zurich once more.

The cremation of Greta's body was followed by a solemn farewell ceremony in which her family, Toscanini, his daughter and I took part. The next day I drove the Walters to their home in Lugano, the urn with Greta's ashes in my car, the man I had grown to love like a father sitting beside me, silent with grief.

CHAPTER EIGHT

Figaro and Boris Godunov

*T*HE DIFFERENCE of opinion between Bruno Walter and myself, mentioned in the preceding chapter, had to do with the title role in Mozart's *The Marriage of Figaro,* one of my favorite operas ever since I first heard it many years ago. I had always wanted to sing Figaro, but the part had been consistently denied me, as was that of Boris Godunov, at both La Scala and the Metropolitan Opera House.

I was particularly unhappy at not having had the opportunity to sing in *The Marriage of Figaro* after having first seen it at Salzburg. My chances to sing Figaro at the Metropolitan were altogether nonexistent. Gatti-Casazza had burned his fingers on a revival of *Figaro* as far back as 1917, and was steering clear of it. At the same time, Rossini's *The Barber of Seville,* where the same Figaro is the leading character, enjoyed great popularity and was indeed one of the mainstays of the Met's repertoire.

There were two reasons for that peculiar state of

affairs. First, Mozart's perfect creation required a near-perfect ensemble, and this was not always available, even in the world's best opera house. Discussing the casting problems connected with *The Marriage of Figaro*, Gatti-Casazza writes in his autobiography:

> Of the Mozart operas, I believe that *Figaro* is the best. . . . Mozart is a composer who does not permit of mediocrity in his operas. Compare his treatment of Beaumarchais' comedy with the livelier manner of Rossini. Four or five mediocre artists are all that is necessary for Rossini's *Barber*. Figaro is a role for a great artist, and Almaviva must be sung well. To spoil the Rossinian parts of Rosina, Basilio or Bartolo, the singer needs to be pretty bad. . . . But what has been said for Rossini does not hold for Mozart. Every role requires a fine interpretation, or the performance will fail.

Secondly, there was the ridiculous convention which goes all the way back to the eighteen eighties, that an opera is not worthy of its *genre* unless the hero is a tenor, and the heroine a true soprano. The battle cry seemed to be, "Down with the bass and the baritone! Down with the contralto and the mezzo-soprano!" How else can you account for the almost total disappearance from the Metropolitan's repertoire for years on end, of such operas as *Don Giovanni, The Marriage of Figaro, La Favorita* and *Hamlet?*

One might have thought that the success of *Don Giovanni* would encourage Gatti-Casazza, at least in respect to *Figaro,* but it did not. After Gatti left the Met in 1935, his successor, Edward Johnson, also kept avoiding the opera.

You can imagine my joy, therefore, at Bruno Walter's suggestion in 1935 that I return to Salzburg the following year for performances in *Don Giovanni*—and also in *Figaro*.

"How wonderful!" I cried. "I've always wanted to sing Figaro!"

The gentle Bruno Walter looked terribly embarrassed, "I'm afraid I haven't made myself clear," he said. "I had you in mind for the part of Count Almaviva."

Still, I refused to give up. Counting on Walter's kindness and understanding, and on his appreciation of what I had done with *Don Giovanni,* I pleaded for a chance, I argued, only to learn that gentleness is not always synonymous with weakness.

"Sorry, Ezio," was Walter's ultimate answer. "I simply do not see you as Figaro. He is too light, too mercurial for your style."

I had no answer for that. It was, after all, a matter of opinion, and Walter had as much right to his as I to mine. We took leave of each other in a most friendly fashion, but made no arrangements for my return to Salzburg in 1936. As though to rub salt on the wound, I chanced upon Sena Jurinac of the Vienna Opera soon after my conversation with Bruno Walter, and she proudly mentioned to me that she would be making her one-hundredth appearance in *Figaro* at the forthcoming Edinburgh Festival. A very young woman, Jurinac had the enchanting role of Cherubino.

You have been wondering, I am sure, precisely what

it was that attracted me to Mozart's opera so strongly that I—who hated the very thought of forcing myself on a conductor and who feared to jinx a role by asking for it —should stubbornly seek a chance to sing Figaro.

The answer is very simple: I loved that opera and everything about it. Even the libretto. For once, Lorenzo da Ponte came through with a text that does no damage to Mozart's music. And why should it? The libretto is, after all, based on a play by Beaumarchais, a man who knew the stage and could write excellently. It was he who infused *Figaro* with the action, spontaneity and laughter that helped the composer to break away from the remote grandeur of pre-Mozartian opera. As for Figaro himself, he is the only character of the one hundred I portrayed on the opera stage with whom I found perfect self-identification. I believed myself a natural for Figaro. Largely because I had been typed as Don Giovanni, no one agreed with me. People insisted that I was deluding myself in thinking that I could re-create Figaro as convincingly.

Everything in me protested against such a judgment, for I *knew* I could do Figaro more convincingly. While it was true that I had modified my first negative reaction to Don Giovanni, I still continued to resent the violence of his courage and his irresponsibilty. There is a certain inhuman quality about Don Giovanni that makes him more a symbol than a man, whereas Figaro is all man. I grew to appreciate the philosophical-religious overtones in *Don Giovanni*, but to Figaro I responded spontaneously and completely. There was a personal involvement on my part, as well as deep sympathy with the dignity and earthiness of *Figaro's* challenge to the feudal times. Myself an itinerant carpenter's son, I could not but rejoice in the superiority of the barber-valet and his friends over an arrogant aristocrat. Theirs is a moral superiority, as well as the advantage of greater wit and resourcefulness.

In this they were not unlike Mozart and da Ponte themselves, who were up against the thick-headed censorship of their patron, Emperor Joseph II of Austria. He had banned the Beaumarchais play for its dangerous ideas, but allowed the sparkle of the music to lull him into giving his approval to the opera, which actually retained the rebellious spirit of the original.

Bruno Walter never told me what had led him to change his mind, but that change took place some months after our conversation in the summer of 1935, with the result that he invited me to sing Figaro at Salzburg in 1937. And once more came the joy of rehearsals with a perfect ensemble under the guidance of the man whose knowledge of Mozart was peerless, taste immaculate and tempi faultless!

The success of our *Figaro* rivaled that of *Don Giovanni*, completely vindicating my feeling about the title role. The ultimate praise came from Bruno Walter, when he entered my dressing room after the first performance, embraced me and said, "You were right, Ezio!"

The success of our Salzburg performance also revived the interest in *The Marriage of Figaro* among the leading spirits at the Metropolitan, most importantly the Met's General Manager, Edward Johnson. With a Figaro already in his company, he started a search for suitable singers to fill the other roles—and unearthed them. The next problem was to find a director with sufficient experience and imagination to adapt the Met's colossal stage to the requirements of what one might call an intimate grand opera. Herbert Graf took on the difficult task, which he discharged with miraculous inventiveness, aided by Jonel Jorgulesco's splendid settings.

The cast, headed by the great, fiery conductor Ettore Panizza, was as follows:

John Brownlee and Elisabeth Rethberg enacted Count and Countess Almaviva; Bidù Sayão was our Susanna; Risë Stevens, Cherubino; Irra Petina, Marcellina; Alessio De Paolis, Basilio; and Giordano Paltrinieri, Virgilio Lazzari, Louis D'Angelo and Marita Farell, respectively, sang the roles of Don Curzio, Bartolo, Antonio and Barbarina. Each and every one of the participants loved the opera and cherished the gaiety and inspiration of the rehearsals.

The Marriage of Figaro was revived at the Metropolitan on February 20, 1940, twenty-three years almost to a day after its last performance there. The revival happened to coincide with the one hundred and fiftieth anniversary of the death of Emperor Joseph II, whom we did not begrudge the accidental tribute.

The reception given *Figaro* was of the stuff that all producers and artists dream on. It was a veritable feast of gratitude and recognition. Exhilarated, I stayed up all night, along with the rest of the cast, to wait for the reviews.

Oh, those reviews . . .!

Fair and objective to the bitter end, the critics dutifully reported that the audience had had a terrific time, and stated just as dutifully that it had been treated to a vaudeville act, not Art. All fire, comedy, sensuousness and beauty which we had thought we had communicated to the audience had somehow missed the critics, without a single exception. Their unanimity threw the management into confusion, and the cast into despair. *Figaro* seemed doomed to oblivion once more.

What followed was nothing short of a miracle.

Undaunted by the accusation of having rejoiced in a bit of vaudeville, the public rallied to the defense of our *Figaro*. Letters, telegrams, phone calls came pouring in to the management, blasting the reviewers and demanding repeat performances. The situation created was described in an article by Samuel Chotzinoff (in the New York *Post*), aptly headlined: "Marriage of Figaro is Tough on the Critics." This same Chotzinoff, by the way, had spoken to Bruno Walter a day or two after the performance, blasting the production with anger and indignation.

"Just imagine!" he said. "Pinza is about to sing that great last-act aria, and what does he do? He walks up to the prompter's box, plants one foot on top of it and starts singing."

"I can well imagine it," replied Walter. "This is how I taught him to do it in Salzburg."

Encouraged by the public reaction, the Metropolitan decided to risk another performance. The rousing ovation given it by the audience confirmed the public's original verdict. The critics honored our *Figaro* with an unprecedented second review, and were more indulgent this time. The opera soon became firmly entrenched in the Metropolitan repertoire, its popularity rivaling that of *Don Giovanni* and *Barber of Seville*. More performances of *Figaro* were given in the next decade than in the preceding fifty-seven years of the Metropolitan Opera's history, and always to packed houses.

How right Verdi was in advising managers and impresarios to read box-office reports with greater care than newspaper reviews!

If Figaro was my favorite role, Boris Godunov was a close second. Having heard me say this, some of my friends were surprised, for they knew that I have always preferred operas that are gay and full of movement and laughter. Yes, provided the gaiety and the fun are part of the truth of life. That is the supreme consideration. I have never been able effectively to portray people who are not real, or to enact situations that are phony. Thanks to Bruno Walter, I arrived at the truth and the greatness of *Don Giovanni*, but the hero of that work, unlike Figaro, has remained to me a brain child, not a man. In a different way, of course, Wagner's characters, too, are no more than brain children and symbols to me, which is why I gave up Wagnerian roles a long time ago. Perhaps it is just as well that when I arrived in America and found these operas performed in their original language rather than in my native tongue, as in Italy, I gave up singing them. I did not know German then and could never do justice to a part sung in a language I could not speak.

Boris, on the other hand, is real to me, and always was. As with Figaro, I was able to place myself inside the man who was Russia's tragic tsar, and to emerge with a portrayal that held conviction for audiences. If, as I have been led to believe, it was in my power to convey the tsar's majesty, drama and deterioration, that was only because there is deep truth in Mussorgsky's music and in Pushkin's play on which the libretto is based. It was this quality that attracted me to another opera—Italo Montemezzi's *The Love of Three Kings*—for it, too, is distinguished by a similar depth of truth, and Archibaldo is a great dramatic role.

I was aware of the dramatic opportunities inherent in *Boris Godunov* when I first became acquainted with it, all the way back in 1920. Look at the gamut of mood and emotion for the singing actor to run: Boris' tender love of his children; his pride in the power and majesty of being tsar; torture by guilt and remorse; lastly, fear, insanity and self-destruction. To me, *Boris Godunov* is the greatest dramatic opera ever written. Far from luring the artist into a contemplation of the beauty of his own voice, Mussorgsky's music demands of him as much acting as it does singing. The pauses in the score are as pregnant with meaning as those in a Beethoven symphony, testing the artist's intelligence and histrionic gifts with an implacability I have found in no other opera. A performance of *Boris* used to take more out of me than any other opera in which I sang. Ordinarily, I switched to my normal routine and pursuits almost as soon as a performance was over, irrespective of the role I played, but *Boris* always haunted me for some time afterward.

This part differed from others in still another way. As you have surely gathered by now, I am not a scholar given to contemplation and analysis, nor an aesthete in

search of fulfilment, but a man of action whose natural
endowments destined him for the stage. I cherished my
work at the opera because I was happiest in it, and because its rewards were magnificent in every way. In
return, I gave the maximum of what was mine to give:
voice, instinct for music and acting, the time and effort
needed to master a role. *Don Giovanni,* you will recall,
was a challenge. *Boris Godunov* represented an even
greater one, for the world it contained was completely
alien to me—alien and irresistibly fascinating. But let me
start from the beginning.

I first became acquainted with *Boris Godunov* at the
time I sang at the Teatro Constanzi in Rome, in 1920,
when I was assigned the role of Pimenn, the monk and
chronicler, to Sigizmund Zaleski's Boris. I conscien-
tiously studied my part, of course, but it was the tsar who
captured my imagination. The transition within Boris
from majesty to madness was depicted by the composer
with an intensity and truthfulness I had not imagined
possible on the opera stage. Baffled and captivated, I
decided to make the role my own, and to learn all I could
about the work, the composer and the historical background.

Zaleski, always the loyal colleague, answered my
questions willingly, but he could not be as helpful with
Boris as he was with other roles or the art of make-up.
Frankly admitting that he based his Boris on the portrayal
by Chaliapin, who had created the role, Zaleski showed
little interest in the tsar as man or ruler, or in the morbid
chapter of Russian history that was his setting.

I began to read everything available on the subject.

I also hired the services of a coach to go through the role of Boris with me. That happened after I had joined La Scala, where I met a man ideally suited for the task. He was Victor Andoga, baritone of Italian parentage, born and raised in Russia where he had sung in *Boris Godunov* and even directed it. Andoga was also responsible for La Scala's production of the opera.

You will recall the plot: The tsar's brother-in-law, Boris Godunov, gains the Russian throne following the murder of the lawful heir, a murder Godunov has arranged. He rules peacefully for some years, rejoicing in his power and in his children, but is ultimately punished for his crime, first by a series of calamities that befall his realm—natural disasters such as flood, fires and famine—and then by the emergence of a man who claims to be the rightful heir. The ultimate executioner of Tsar Boris is his own conscience, which tortures him into insanity and suicide.

The situation, as you see, is not strikingly different from that in many another tragic opera, and indeed Boris is often spoken of as the Russian Macbeth. What is different is the treatment, the emphasis, the psychological twists. And, of course, the music.

For all my immersion in the title role, I could not but realize in studying the work as a whole that the central character in the opera is the Russian people, not Boris; and that the main conflict lies not so much in his remorse at having murdered a child as in his guilty realization that he has failed the Russian people. Their spirit, their speech and song pervade the lines sung by their autocratic ruler and the liturgical choruses that are so vital a part of the opera. Not until I began to read about Mussorgsky, and to discuss *Boris Godunov* with Victor Andoga, did I learn something which I had sensed intuitively: namely, that the composer consciously treated people *en masse* as though the mass were one human being. More than that, Mussorgsky's search for the most effective way of accomplishing this treatment enabled him to make his major contribution as a composer. The Metropolitan Opera bulletin dedicated to the revival of *Boris Godunov* in 1938, in which I sang the title role, quoted from a letter by the composer:

> To search for the peculiarities of human nature, not only in the individual, but in the masses, to explore them and bring their beauties to the light of day—*that* is the mission of the artist. In the masses there are treasures which no one has yet touched; to seek until I find them, to offer them to the world as fresh, invigorating fare, that is my task, and I know of no greater joy!

In still another letter, Mussorgsky wrote:

> Sleeping or waking, I have the masses in my thoughts. They rise before me incessantly, in all their reality, colossal, unvarnished, with no tinsel trappings.

As a result of these visions, Mussorgsky revolutionized the presentation of mass scenes on the opera stage, a presentation that hitherto had been as formalized as a minuet.

I have never ceased to marvel at the Russian musical giant who, with little knowledge and still less training in his chosen field, created a major work of art. Violating all rules of composition and ignoring all conventions, he preferred to be a first-class barbarian rather than a second-class Mozart, and succeeded, insofar as he made lasting innovations in opera and in music in general.

Mussorgsky, the man and the musician, fascinated me in a strange, incomprehensible way. I say that because everything about him was alien to me both as a person and as a singer: the despair and drunkenness that carried him to the grave on his forty-sixth birthday; his aversion to women and to marriage (" . . . when you read in the morning papers that I've put a bullet through my head or hanged myself, you may be certain that I was married the day before"); his lack of discipline in work; and his refusal to recognize the authority of tradition and of the great masters. Yet Mussorgsky's music gave me a sense of direct contact with the throbbing heart of a genius, such as no other composer's ever had.

Possibly there is an explanation somewhere, but a search for it would require a voyage through time, history, geography and psychology. Had not Rieseman, Mussorgsky's biographer, written in connection with *Boris Godunov:* "The mystic twilight chants pierce through; the brazen trumpet calls . . . the mosaics of Ravenna, the black and gold ikons of Russian saints, the aureoled saints . . ."

I have never undertaken that voyage. Still, year after year, I kept gathering knowledge and understanding of *Boris Godunov* until a conception of the tsar evolved within me, dominated by a compassion people usually reserve for tragic victims of circumstances rather than for ambitious autocrats whose villainy creates those circumstances. This approach was further strengthened when Andoga told me that historical research has failed to prove Boris' guilt in the murder of the child-heir.

I sang my first Boris in 1925, in Mantua, a city distinguished even in Italy for its devotion to opera, where anyone you meet is a music expert, severe in judgment and liberal with advice. It was impossible for me to step out of my hotel room without being cornered by one or more persons questioning me about the opera and giving opinions on how to approach my role. To hear them talk, you would have thought that nothing in the world interested them more than old Muscovy and the brooding tsar. Incomplete as my ideas on the subject were at the time, I could not help noticing the striking similarity between the Italy of the Borgias and these people's conception of ancient Muscovy. In my mind, I could hear the groans of disappointment and the catcalls of indignation filling the opera house.

To my surprise, the first-night audience received *Boris Godunov* with a most uncharacteristic perplexity. Italian audiences know exactly what they want in opera and, depending on what they get, lift you to the skies with their rapture or crush you to the ground with derision. But, as we stood behind the drawn curtain, we heard only scattered applause; our bewildered audience was giving us a little credit for our effort. But then, a very strange thing happened: all tickets for the second and third performances were sold out the very next day. Many of the buyers, the management told me, were people who had been at the theater the night before. They were giving us, *Boris* and themselves another chance.

The situation was repeated in the other Italian cities where I sang *Boris* during my "free-lance" year between La Scala and Buenos Aires' Colón. In the end, Mussorgsky always triumphed, and his opera was accorded an ovation usually reserved for the works of Verdi or Rossini.

When I joined the Metropolitan Opera Company in 1926, I brought with me an ambition to do *Boris*. The opera had had a glorious history there ever since 1913, when Toscanini conducted and Adamo Didur sang the title role. So gratified was Gatti-Casazza with the production that he wrote, "I consider *Boris* the most important performance artistically I have given at the Metropolitan."

The interest in the opera mounted after Chaliapin joined the company in December, 1921, continuing the tradition of annual performances of *Boris*. For so long as the great Russian bass was available, there was no question in anybody's mind, and least of all in mine, that the title role was his. I was happy to sing Pimenn and watch Chaliapin as Boris. The singer was rapidly aging, but, tall and straight, he was magnificent to behold. As he walked about the streets of New York in his enormous fur coat, he looked not so much like a man as a monument come to life. And he was a superlative actor, so compelling that only my professional experience and a perfect knowledge of my role saved me time and again from missing my cues, so absorbed was I in watching him act. What impressed me most was the intelligence with which he limited his movements and gestures to psychological necessity. They were very sparing, but when Chaliapin moved, the whole stage shifted with him.

The Metropolitan's custom was to have all Russian operas sung in French. With *Boris* it was different: Chaliapin sang in the original, while the rest of us and the chorus sang in Italian. The clash of the harsh, powerful Russian with the liquid, melodic sounds of Italian was so disturbing to me that I decided to learn the part of Boris in the original, if and when I should have the opportunity to do it. I hoped I would be able to insist that the others, too, learn to sing their lines in Russian.

Chaliapin's notorious temper seemed to grow with time. Every rehearsal provided a repetition of terrible scenes, which are remembered even today by old-timers at the Met.

Chaliapan was late for a rehearsal one day, while the entire cast waited, including Gatti-Casazza, who sat in the front row biting his fingernails, obviously not knowing what to do. All means of finding Chaliapin had been exhausted. Just as the *Direttore* seemed to have made up his mind to start without him, Chaliapin appeared on the stage, muttering something to himself, then saying loudly in French, a language nearly everyone understood, "Do you call this a temple of music? This a stable, not a temple!"

There was a moment of shocked silence. Then Gatti-Casazza calmly gave the signal and the rehearsal started.

Chaliapin could be equally rude toward conductors and fellow singers, although I must say that for some reason he was invariably gracious toward me. One time after a performance, he put his hands on my shoulders and said, "I like your Pimenn, Ezio. Let me take you home in my taxi!"

As we were parting, he pulled a watch out of his pocket and presented it to me with a flourish. It was a one-dollar Ingersoll which I treasured and always carried with me. One day, alas, someone stole it.

Chaliapin's farewell performance at the Metropolitan took place in March, 1929, and it was a sad evening. With his leaving, *Boris Godunov* disappeared from the company's repertoire. Year after year, I waited for the summons by Gatti, but the *Direttore*—who, as I later learned from his memoirs, had thought of me as Chaliapin's natural successor to the role of Boris—did nothing. Then, in 1935, he, too, left the Metropolitan Opera House. More time went by. Still I waited in silence. Then, one day, Edward Johnson announced a revival of the opera with me in the title role. *Boris Godunov* was to close the opera season with two performances in March, 1938.

I was ready. I had been studying my part with Victor Andoga, who had emigrated to the United States, and I was eager to learn it in Russian, but on the condition that the other artists and the chorus sing their lines in the same language. I was told that the effort would involve too much time and too much money; indeed, a small fortune. We ended up by giving the opera in Italian, much to my regret. I never did get to sing *Boris* in the original, except for two scenes which, years later, I performed in a film called "Tonight We Sing."

The magnificent sets and costumes, originally made in 1908 for Chaliapin's three performances of *Boris* at the Paris Opéra, and later bought by the Metropolitan for a fraction of their cost, were now being restored in all their authenticity by Joseph Novak.

The rehearsals, guided by one of the Met's finest conductors, Ettore Panizza, and Leopold Sachse, the stage director, went smoothly, involving much work and patience but no real problems, for the cast was excellent.

I did have problems, however, but they came from an unexpected quarter—the press. The cumulative effect of the good notices I had been receiving, the sensational success of *Don Giovanni*, and now the announcement of my forthcoming debut as Boris, attracted the attention of reporters and columnists. I was besieged with requests for interviews and for opinions on subjects ranging from *Boris Godunov*, Chaliapin and Toscanini down to the fair sex, food and poison rings. I did not mind talking about food, which is one of life's greatest delights; or about the fair sex, which deserves the adoration bestowed upon it by the male half of mankind; or even about poison rings, of which I knew absolutely nothing; but the newsmen made things awkward for me by pressing for opinions about conductors and my fellow singers, or for a comparison of my Boris with Chaliapin's classical portrayal. I was accused of being too diplomatic in my response to the last question, but what else could I say except state as I did, "There are only three kinds of opera singers: those who cannot act at all; those who imitate and copy; and those who try to create according to their own conceptions. Only the latter deserve to be called artists."

I was happy, indeed, when my conception of Boris was received kindly by audiences and critics alike. Irving Kolodin summarized the reaction by saying that "Pinza survived a flood of comparisons [with Chaliapin] to establish a conception wholly his own, more lyric and less pathological than his predecessor's."

One of the most pleasant aspects of singing Boris centered around my old friend Alessio de Paolis, who sang the role of Shuisky. Seldom have I felt such rapport with another singer. We complemented one another beautifully and I learned to value his presence on the stage with me. I remember to this day my shock during a performance of *Boris* when, instead of finding de Paolis as Shuisky, I discovered that another singer was substituting for him at the last minute.

The final performance of *Boris* coincided with the announcement that a revival of *Figaro* was scheduled for the next season, with me in the title role.

I had now reached the high point of my career. I had also reached its turning point, with a prospect of new fields to conquer. Although the wheel of Fate was to move slowly in that direction, it moved rapidly in another—in my personal life, ultimately leading me toward the altar for the second time.

PART THREE

"They Dreamt Not of a Perishable Home"

Nerved to either event, whether to spin his toils, or to fall under death inevitable.

VIRGIL

CHAPTER NINE

My Wife Doris

THE PATTERN of my life had undergone a radical change by the time the 1938–39 Metropolitan Opera season got under way. The separation from Augusta gave me the feeling of being a free man once more. I came and went as I pleased, attended parties, absorbed the sights of America. I was speaking English with increasing facility and, in general, was beginning to reach out beyond the cherished yet confining opera world, where most of my friends were Italians, constantly speaking our language, observing the customs and adhering to the cuisine of our native land.

Whereas hitherto I had regarded myself a visitor in the United States, as I was in many countries, I now began to think of myself as an American, and applied for my first papers in March, 1940. This country was, at last, becoming home in my own consciousness and in my acceptance as an artist by an ever-growing number of Americans from coast to coast. The word for it is "popularity." While the starting point was, of course, my success on the opera stage, the rest was being achieved with the help of two typically American institutions—concert tours and the services of a publicity agent.

My concerts repeatedly brought me to every nook and corner of the United States, while the country's major musical centers kept inviting me year in, year out, to sing before huge, sold-out houses. To their credit, the audiences and local managers rarely, if ever, requested that I lower the standards I had set for myself in working out my repertoire.

In addition to managing my concert career with an experienced and friendly hand, Marks Levine of NBC and, later, of NCAC (The National Concert and Artist Corporation) was responsible also for my retaining the services of a publicity agent. True, at first I strenuously objected to the idea.

"To pay for publicity out of my hard-earned money!" I remember myself exclaiming when he first brought up the subject. "I'm not that vain!"

"Vanity has nothing to do with it," Levine replied. "It's an investment, like advertising, display windows or painted signs. If you want more concerts and sold-out houses, if you want Hollywood offers, you must become a celebrity. I don't mean a celebrated artist—this you already are. I mean a celebrity in the American sense, a person everybody's talking about; discussing his comings and goings, his opinions, hobbies, friends, clothes and, of course, his performances. Reviews of your concert and opera appearances are not enough. There must be a steady flow of articles and notices about you in the newspapers, repeated mention of your name in gossip columns, interviews with you in the press and over the radio. Only a professional publicity agent can achieve this for you."

Having thus weakened my opposition, Levine suggested that I retain the firm of Constance Hope Associates, at least on an experimental basis. This I did, although I must admit that Miss Hope impressed me as too feminine and attractive to be capable of putting in the long hours and the sustained hard work that her publicity job demanded. I was therefore quite surprised at her industry and efficiency. She started out by patiently extracting from me half-forgotten incidents and anecdotes from my earlier life. These she wrote up entertainingly and distributed to anyone willing to read and print them. Any and all of my activities considered newsworthy were reported to the press. If I went on tour with the Metropolitan, Miss Hope would, in competition with the publicity agents of other stars (most of whom, I discovered, had the services of such agents), try to get the maximum possible newspaper space devoted to me. Wherever my concert tours led me, Miss Hope supplied the local newspapers and radio stations with my biography, achievements, quotes from the New York press and sundry episodes and side lights of my life. Very often, of course, editors, reporters and columnists asked for materials and interviews of their own accord. Not being bound, as was Miss Hope, by my natural reticence, they at times let loose their imaginations and cloaked their prose in the purple of sensationalism.

My collaborator on this book amused me one day by showing me a list of descriptions of a man named Ezio Pinza, culled from my clipping books: "A bronze Roman god come to life," "Ezio the Magnificent," "Don Juan of the Metropolitan," "One of the fourteen most glamorous men in the world," and "The only living example of the great vocal tradition created by Pol Plançon, Édouard de Reszke and Chaliapin."

It would have been easy to be cynical about the whole matter of build-up, were it not for Mr. Levine's words of warning: "A celebrated name will open all doors for you, but after that you're on your own. If you have no talent, or should you lose your voice or lower your standards, a well-publicized name will be of no use whatever. Unless you can deliver the goods, there would be nothing in it but tragic mockery."

I continued with my concerts, in every corner of the United States. The audiences were always very musical. Some artists reserve the obscure and the more "musical" selections for their New York and other large-city recitals, and sing only the most hackneyed programs when they tour. But audiences in Wichita heard the same songs I sang to supposedly more sophisticated audiences in New York or Boston. My favorites—and evidently the favorites of the people who attended my recitals, for they were requested everywhere I went—were the wonderful Mozart aria, *"Non Piu Andrai,"* from *The Marriage of Figaro; "Il Lacerato Spirito,"* from Verdi's *Simon Boccanegra;* and *"La Calunnia,"* Don Basilio's aria from the Rossini *Barber of Seville.* Then there were the "art songs": Flegier's *"Le Cor," "Caro Mio Ben"* by Giordani, Beethoven's *"In Questa Tomba Oscura,"* Cimara's *"Fiocca la Neve"* and that brilliant short song, *"La Girommetta,"* by Sibella.

I would like to pay tribute here to the ten happy years
that I appeared on The Telephone Hour. While I sang for
them, no other basso was engaged, a compliment I treas-
ure highly. Conductor Don Voorhees was a joy to work
with, as was Wallace Magill, producer of the radio broadcast. And always on hand to help me was the invaluable
Gibner King.

The greater the commotion around me and the more
recitals I gave across the country, the less opportunity I
had of seeing old friends, even Ceroni, and of making new
ones. Worse still, the people who were seeking me out
did so mostly for the prestige of exhibiting a social lion
at their parties. One hardly invites a social lion for a
quiet home dinner with the family, although this particular lion would have enjoyed nothing more. My reputation as a Don Juan did not help matters any. The gossip
Augusta had spread about me, and her scenes of jealousy,
the memory of which was not allowed to die, had started
rumors about my private life. wherein truth was mixed
with most fantastic fabrications. As a result, men regarded me with envy and suspicion, and the women with
amusement and interest.

The plain truth is that, to me, there is no greater
bliss on earth than the quiet peace of a happy family, a
contented home to come to, filled with the laughter of
children. I revel in the sight of a beautiful woman, but
the sight of a laughing child makes me happier still. I
would do anything to make a child smile. Many a time
I have stopped in front of a baby carriage in the street to
look at a child, smile at it and sometimes sing a few bars

or make clucking sounds which people would be surprised to hear an opera singer produce. Occasionally, to the mother's astonishment and horror, I would bend down and kiss the baby, then quickly walk away for fear of a scene, thinking of my own child in Italy with Augusta, and dreaming of the half-dozen children I should like to have in my home, all calling me *Babbo* (Daddy).

If this sounds oversentimental to you, just you try years of incessant travel, with no cherished face to gaze at, with only a train compartment or a hotel room as your home. Yes, I longed for a real home of my own, a wife to love and children for us to raise together. I am not ashamed to confess that I kept searching for her wherever I went, incessantly, until at last I found her in the most improbable of all places—on the stage of the Metropolitan Opera House.

It was winter, 1938. The opera was Delibes' *Lakmé*, a beautiful, tragic work, the thought of which, nevertheless, always makes me smile, because a program note I once read describes Lakmé's lamentable end in the following words: "She makes the best of the situation by committing suicide." My role was that of her father, the fanatical Brahmin priest Nilakantha, whose intolerance drove the girl to her act of desperation.

A new ballet was being introduced that night in the second act. I stood in the wings to watch the Metropolitan's recently revamped ballet company in a number of wonderful Hindu dances. A tall young girl attracted my attention, first by the grace of her movements, then by her face, whose pure loveliness shone through the make-up. A thought came in a flash, so distinctly that I involuntarily looked around to see whether anyone had overheard me say in my mind, "This is the girl I would like to marry."

I made inquiries during the intermission and learned that she was Miss Doris Leak, daughter of Dr. William Leak, a dentist with an office in New York and a home in the suburban village of Larchmont. Everyone in the ballet group seemed to know about Dr. Leak, because he called for his daughter, after each performance in which she participated, to escort her home. Miss Leak, I learned, was never available for after-the-show suppers and parties, as she was always whisked off home to Larchmont by her father.

I sought her out after the performance and introduced myself. Miss Leak was already in her street clothes, looking exceedingly young and beautiful. She had a clear white skin and clear, virtually translucent light-green eyes that looked at me with an almost childlike directness.

Why does she have to be that young? I thought. Then I said, "Will you lunch with me tomorrow?"

The look she gave me left no doubt that she knew all the backstage gossip about Pinza. She looked pleased, scared, confused, utterly enchanting—and obviously wishing she were a thousand miles away. She mumbled a polite refusal and hurried off, graceful, lovely and unattainable.

I did not follow her. For all my indulgence in romantic dreams, I could not make myself forget that I was in my middle forties, whereas she must have hardly turned twenty. Yet, working in the same place, we could not help bumping into each other from time to time, coming or going, or at rehearsals. On each such occasion my will weakened and I would ask her to have a meal with me, or take a ride in my car, or simply join me for a walk. "I would like to know you, see you, just to talk to you," I would say.

But the last thing Doris appeared to want was to be seen talking to Ezio Pinza. The wave of pleasure and excitement which broke over her expressive face at the sight of me would recede. She would just return my greeting politely. What could I do in the face of such determination? Discouraged and dismayed, I would resolve to ignore her in the future—only to fail and have the scene repeat itself.

You may not believe it, and I hardly believe it myself, but fully two seasons passed in that strange, practically wordless courtship, my pride pitted against her loveliness, my adoration against her fears. I loved her, I knew. I wanted to marry her, call her my own and remain at her side for the rest of my life, although I still knew no more about her than at the beginning: she was Miss Doris Leak of Larchmont, who went her way alone, or with her father, her only escort. I also knew that she was a beautiful dancer, but, somehow, she did not seem to belong to the gay, ambitious, Bohemian world of the stage. What world *did* she belong to?

Then spring came, the spring of 1940. The New York season over, the company went on tour aboard the special Metropolitan Opera Train. I caught sight of Doris getting on it, looked the length of the train for her, but found her

nowhere. In city after city she eluded me, until we came
to New Orleans. There, one of the dancers, a native of the
city, whom I occasionally saw in Doris' company, invited
me to a party. I accepted eagerly—and spent my time
wandering from room to room in search of Doris, cursing
the spaciousness of old Southern mansions. She was nowhere to be seen. Finally I gave up and decided to leave,
only to come face to face with Doris in the hall; she, too,
was leaving. One of the ballet girls was with her. I jumped
at the heaven-sent chance.

"May I take you to the hotel in my taxi?"

"I was leaving with Ruth Harris. May she come
along?"

"The pleasure is all mine," I said none too convincingly.

Inside the taxi, I took Doris' hand and pressed it.
After the briefest second she pulled it away and, with
seeming unconcern, turned to chat with Ruth about the
party. I had to act quickly, for we were going to Atlanta
the next day, our last stop, where I had to leave the company to give a few recitals in other parts of the South.

Risking a rebuff in a stranger's presence, I said, "May
I see you when we are all in New York again?"

"I'm not sure," she hedged.

"May I have your telephone number, so I can call
you and find out?"

"I'll leave it in your mailbox."

My mailbox remained empty up to the last second
before my departure. It's no use, I thought; forget her.
This time I made no effort to find her on the train bound
for Atlanta; then, on the morning after our arrival, I saw

her in the hotel lobby, alone, waiting for the elevator. Forgetting my brave resolutions, I suggested that she make up for her oversight by having lunch with me that day.

"Sorry, I'm engaged for lunch," she stammered, obviously lying and looking terribly uneasy about it. But I asked again for her telephone number.

"Very well. I'll leave it in your mailbox. This time I promise."

She looked me straight in the eyes as she said it, and the ring of determination in her voice was completely out of proportion to the trivial business of giving an acquaintance your telephone number. I knew then that she would keep her promise, and she did. There it was, at last, written in a bold, handsome style.

Only after I had boarded my train did I realize that I had failed to mention my brief concert tour to Doris, which meant that I would not be able to contact her for two weeks. I could have telephoned, of course—I was dying to do it—but I felt that she and her family would resent a long-distance call from a stranger.

On my return to New York, I telephoned her. It was May eighteenth, my birthday. But before making the call I paid an urgent visit to my lawyer in an attempt to settle once and for all the question of my divorce from Augusta. She and I had agreed on a settlement all the way back in 1935, but each time I pressed for the divorce, her demands would go up. No sooner would I agree to the new conditions than Augusta's price would rise again. Knowing full well that I had all my savings tied up in Bologna, for I had intended to settle there after my retirement, she seemed to aim at cleaning me out of everything I owned. So far I had been putting up a strong resistance, but that day I said to my lawyer, "Give it all to her! The three apartment houses, the villa, the insurance, the bonds and the savings on my bank account—everything I have. My one condition is an immediate divorce. If she refuses or insists on a part of my future earnings, tell her that I withdraw all offers and that she will get absolutely nothing from this day on. And do it all by cable!"

Augusta knew me well enough to realize that, once it came to the point of an ultimatum from me, she would either have to accept it or admit that she was really determined to hold on to me "until death do us part" and spend the rest of her days alone and on an allowance, whereas this arrangement would make her a wealthy woman in Italy. My guess was that she would accept.

Having finished with the lawyer, I telephoned Doris. "May I see you today?" I asked urgently, having first explained that I had just returned from my tour.

"Well, I am busy today in New York. I'm not sure . . ."

But I would not be stalled off this time. I had missed her too intensely. I had been rebuffed too obviously for too long. And I had just gambled on my future, perhaps too riskily. I was like a man possessed, feeling that I had not a day to lose. Our first real meeting, the first conversation, had to take place on that birthday of mine—or never. Let Fate decide. Trying not to scare her by betraying my win-all or lose-all mood, I made what I knew was to be my final attempt.

"I shall be in my room at the Mayflower Hotel until

three o'clock this afternoon, waiting for your call. Please call, if you can see me today, at any time."

At just a few minutes before three, Doris telephoned, asking me to meet her in an hour at her father's office on Park Avenue. She was there when I came and introduced me to Dr. Leak, a trim, graying man who had the same way of looking you directly in the eyes as Doris had.

There was an easy friendliness in his manner, yet I felt it necessary to ask his permission to take his daughter out for tea, which he gave graciously, though with the air of one conscious of his right to withhold it. Doris and I took the short walk to the Hotel Commodore, where I ordered two teas, although I would have preferred coffee —and so would she, as she laughingly confessed to me later. I had a million things to tell her, but all words suddenly fled from me, and we sipped our tea in an almost total silence. But somehow there was nothing constrained or embarrassing about it, as though we both understood that there was a lifetime ahead of us to talk to each other. It was this very understanding, perhaps, that made us too tense for conversation.

Still hardly saying anything, I drove Doris home to Larchmont in my new Lincoln Zephyr convertible, stopping in front of a rambling three-story house surrounded by huge, very beautiful trees. Behind them were well-cared-for flower beds and, in the back, I could see a corner of a vegetable plot.

"Would you like to come in and see my home and meet my mother?" Doris asked.

"I would. By all means!"

Like her husband, Mrs. Leak was courteous, yet

where he showed the casual friendliness of a gentleman, the motherly-looking lady of the house made no effort to hide the anxious appraisal in her eyes as she studied my face and every gesture. I soon left, for I had to get back to New York for a birthday party Constance Hope was giving for me. But first I obtained permission to come again the following day.

Mrs. Leak was reserved and polite as before, and soon left us alone in the living room. But I felt her wary presence linger on and—how often Doris and I laughed about it later—our conversation revolved very properly around the weather.

"Please show me the sights of Larchmont." I resourcefully took advantage of Doris' remark about the beauty of its outskirts in May.

Stopping the car in the first secluded spot I found, I said without any preliminaries, "Will you marry me, Doris?"

"You don't even know me. . . . How can you ask?"

Which launched me on a long tirade about how well I did know her, for I had been courting her for nearly two years. Couldn't she understand, I demanded, that each accidental meeting was a shattering event for me? That every rebuffed invitation to a meal or to a walk had the ardor and the intent of a marriage proposal?

Doris finally did understand, she later told me, but at first she could hardly believe that this was anything more than a superlative bit of acting on the part of Metropolitan's Don Giovanni, who had chanced to come into her life.

All she said then was, "I need time to think."

I, too, needed to think—not because I was having a change of heart, but because, having seen her parents, and having been in her home, it suddenly occurred to me that I had no right to break into the serene, regulated life of a very young girl who, despite her dancing at the Metropolitan, seemed to have her true existence in a world thousands of miles removed from mine.

I searched my soul that night, earnestly, with merciless candor—and drove back to Larchmont the next day.

This time, we both talked a great deal. We could not stop, as a matter of fact, trying to make up for the wordlessness of the day before and for our ignorance of each other.

I told Doris all about my life, including Augusta and Greta, and about my yearning for a quiet domestic life, and of my having become practically penniless overnight, for a cable from Italy had informed me of Augusta's acceptance of my ultimatum. In my desire to be honest with the girl whom I wanted more than anything else in the world, and who was now looking at me with a trusting directness, I sounded almost as though I were trying to talk her out of accepting me. I was forty-eight, and she only twenty-two, I pointed out to her. The divorce would give me the freedom to marry her, but it would also rob me of my savings, leaving only my voice to fall back on, and I'd be lucky if it held out for another five years. "Of course," I quickly added, "I'll support you even if I have to return to carpentry."

Doris, who had said practically nothing so far, smiled. "But I would not marry you for money, Ezio. I love you."

It was in this fashion that she accepted my hand in marriage, brushing aside, with the courage and fearlessness of youth, all preliminaries and apprehensions. Yet, as she went on telling me about herself, I understood that her decision was an even harder one to make than I had realized.

Both her parents were ultra-conservative English Canadians, devout memebrs of the Episcopalian Church, of which Doris, too, was a dutiful member. They appreciated music and the arts, and had arranged for Doris to take piano and dancing lessons early in her life, never dreaming that she might make a career in either field. When she was sixteen, they innocently took her to see the Ballet Russe, with the exquisite Danilova, Baranova and Toumanova. Doris left the theater with a determination to become a ballerina at any price. She persuaded the principal of her school to intensify her studies so that she could graduate with utmost speed, then argued her mother into permitting her to enroll at Finch Junior College in New York, instead of attending an out-of-town university. This enabled Doris to include in her program ballet lessons with the famous Alexei Yakovlev.

Mrs. Leak took a dim view of her daughter's activities, but made no attempt to impede them, upon seeing that Doris cheerfully complied with the one condition laid down by the family—to be home for dinner every evening of the week. After a year she abandoned Finch for the American Academy of Dramatic Arts, while continuing her studies with Yakovlev and with still another teacher, an expert in the Spanish school of dancing.

One evening, Doris proudly announced to her family

that she had been going to auditions, and had been accepted for the Broadway show, *White Horse Inn.* Her mother was horrified. Even the more easygoing Dr. Leak was disturbed by the idea of his daughter in a chorus. A line was drawn: Doris would audition and accept a job nowhere but in an established artistic institution, such as a ballet company or an opera house. Competition there was at its fiercest, Doris knew, but she yielded—and was promptly accepted by the Russian Opera Company for the ballet scenes in *Prince Igor.* This job involved only a few performances, after which she went on studying and dreaming.

Her great opportunity came soon after she had turned twenty, when the Metropolitan Opera undertook to revamp its entire ballet company. All of America's future Pavlovas appeared for the tryouts, keeping the auditions going full blast for three days, at the end of which Doris was one of those offered a contract.

"I was elated," Doris told me, "especially because I was to understudy the prima ballerinas and do small solo parts—until the moment we received instructions to report for the first rehearsal the next day *at seven o'clock in the evening!* What the others took as but a routine order sounded like the voice of doom to me.

"I was home on time for dinner that night and reported my victory as matter-of-factly as I could. All went well until I mentioned the rehearsal time. The silence that followed was fit to cut with a knife. Mother spoke first, urging me to back out and stay home, but in vain. To me, for all my studies in New York, all the people I talked to there, and the sights I saw, the Metropolitan Opera House was a cathedral, and the leading stars in it—including the great, the adored Ezio Pinza—were just short of saints with haloes around their heads.

"My mind had been made up but, fortunately, there was no need for a real showdown, for my father and my two brothers sided with me. Mother had to compromise, which she did after she had wrested a promise from Daddy to call for me each night I had to stay on for a rehearsal or performance. And a promise from me that I would not become romantically involved with anyone connected with the Metropolitan.

"I willingly agreed, for I *knew* it couldn't happen. That is, I knew until that night a few weeks later when you, Ezio, came up to me after the performance of *Lakmé* and introduced yourself. By that time I no longer saw the halo around your head. Instead, I saw the man I loved.

"All the ballet girls had to be slender and graceful, and many were exceedingly attractive. The men in the chorus, the soloists and even the stars paid flattering attention to us, an attention I found easy to ignore or laugh off, until you came along. I tried to fight my feelings because of the agreement I had made with my parents, but actually I lived for our next meeting."

We could not stop talking. There were so many discoveries to make, blanks to fill. My desire to be honest with Doris—about the future no less than about the past —made me, normally reticent, the most talkative man in the world. I wanted no doubts, no misunderstandings later.

I made Doris a promise on that occasion, and she made one to me. Hers was to give up her career as a dancer, to make a home for us. Mine, to allow Doris to bring up the children we might have in the teachings and spirit of her Episcopalian Church. This is an unusual thing for a person baptized as a Catholic to do, but I have never been a good Catholic, I am afraid, at least not in the strict sense of the word. I believe in God and I often pray to Him, but the subtleties of religious denominations escape me. My parents were not churchgoers and had done nothing to instil the habit in their children, while my vagabond life was so hectic as to make regular church attendance an impossibility. Whenever, in the course of my travels, I felt the need of prayer, and this I did often, I would enter the first church I came across—any church—and would pray to Him. I would not be surprised at all to learn that I thus worshiped in churches of every denomination, and I can recall more than one occasion when I said my prayers in a synagogue.

There was happiness all around from that day on. Even Mrs. Leak—whom I soon began to call "Monie," the name her children used—replaced her wariness with warmth and affection. As for "Daddy," Dr. Leak, we had taken a liking to each other on the first day we met, a liking which rapidly developed into an affectionate friendship. The one misgiving he had shared with Monie—that I might decide to return to Italy and remain there, taking Doris away from them and from her native country—was quickly dissipated when I assured them that her country was now mine to the end of my days, and that I had taken steps to become an American citizen.

No sooner did I buy Doris an engagement ring than we got the first taste of what was to plague us for many years thereafter: partings. I had to take a trip to Hollywood, where my agent had arranged interviews for me with some film people, and where I wanted to see the Bruno Walters, to share my happiness with them, for they had become like second parents to me. My father was no longer living by the time Doris and I got married, but Mother and Uncle Gino sent their blessings.

On my return to New York, I took a room at the Larchmont Shore Club for the rest of the summer, spending each day with the Leak family, swimming, boating and picnicking. Doris and I were happy with each other after our long separation, which proved painful despite the daily letters flying back and forth. We invariably signed off with *"Sempre! Sempre! Sempre!"* an Italian word meaning "Always!"—a vow of undying love and undying devotion.

The marriage took place at the home of the Leaks on November 28, 1940, after my return from the San Francisco opera season; and a year had hardly gone by before a twist of Fate subjected Doris' *"Sempre!"* to a merciless test.

CHAPTER TEN

Sempre! Sempre! Sempre!

DORIS AND I were so happy that neither World War II, which made a battlefield out of Europe for the second time in my life, nor the realization that both my homelands were soon to draw swords against each other, could dim our joy. We clung to it—I especially—almost as if in defiance of the sinister world events. Enchanted as my life on the stage was from the very first, there had been little enchantment in my private existence. Now that the very air we breathed was permeated with happiness, I guarded it jealously, finding fulfilment in our daily discoveries of each other and in our mutual love and respect.

Everything was bridged: the difference in age, in religion, cultural background, temperament. Every bit as American in her way as Nellie Forbush in *South Pacific*, and as Mary Martin herself, Doris rejoiced in the unpretentiousness which I preferred in my daily life. Like her mother, she was happily surprised at my visits to the kitchen, whenever we had dinner with the Leaks, to look into every pot on the stove and add a little bit of this and a little bit of that to each dish. Few things pleased Monie more than experiments with my recipes, while Doris delighted in my Italianized English, laughing as heartily at my being "emotioned" and "conversating" as I at her Americanisms, which, now that I was hearing English about me all the time, were coming to life for me in all their imaginativeness and humor.

After the first few months in an apartment on New York's Central Park West, we bought a house in Mamaroneck, an old, reconverted grinding mill on the Sound. With a beautiful motorboat I had acquired and a membership in the Larchmont Horseshoe Harbor Club, we had no vacation problems, and could also see a great deal of Doris' parents and brothers, to whom I became warmly attached. Ideal homemaker that she proved to be, Doris saw to it that in Mamaroneck, and wherever else our life later brought us, I had a little workshop for carpentry and a plot to grow vegetables. After Pearl Harbor, I practically became a professional farmer, cultivating a victory garden and raising chickens.

At one time we had a marvelous Negro couple working for us. The wife was a first-class cook, who quickly learned to prepare the Italian dishes I liked, and the husband was a butler. Not just a butler, but a butler *par excellence*, exquisitely mannered, immaculately dressed in black tie and striped trousers, awe-inspiringly dignified. His elegance, as a matter of fact, tended to embarrass me, but to ask Reuben to wear more plebian clothes was unthinkable. As it was, he did not seem very happy in our service. Indeed, he always looked the very picture of dejection when he approached me in my victory garden to announce that lunch was served. Not one to make food wait, I would quickly wash my hands, put on a clean shirt and join Doris at the table. She worriedly followed Reuben's eyes to my open collar and to my pants and shoes, always soiled from gardening.

Still, even she did not suspect the depth of Reuben's disapproval, until one day he told me with impressive firmness that a jacket and tie, which he would cheerfully lay out for me, were obligatory for lunch, irrespective of the weather.

I was trying to be reasonable. "Is it not enough that I have to worry about my costumes and the changes on the stage? I'm tired of it. Here I like an open shirt collar. Here, in my home, I shall dress as I please."

"I regret it deeply, Mr. Pinza, but under the circumstances I cannot properly perform my duties," Reuben declared with the air of an ambassador delivering a note to an unfriendly power. And he left us, taking his good wife with him.

On August 29, 1941, our first child was born, a daughter we named Clelia in honor of my mother. That was the last joyous event in our life for many months to come.

With the entry of the United States into the war, in December of that year, I was automatically classified as an enemy alien, although I had only four months left before I would be eligible for American citizenship. I understood that this classification was the law of the land, not aimed at me specifically, yet I could not help feeling wronged by it. It was not so much the necessity to obtain

permission to travel for my concerts and opera performances that disturbed me—those permissions were given
readily enough. I was humiliated at the thought that I
might be under suspicion. In principle—let me say it
again—I approved of the law, but the feeling of humiliation persisted, nevertheless.

As it does every spring, the Metropolitan Opera was
planning a tour early in 1942. Along with the many other
Italians in the company, I applied for permission to join
the traveling group. Days passed, weeks, and no answer.
There was no refusal, but no permission, either; whereas
most of my colleagues had received theirs without delay.
It was clear to me that something had gone wrong. I even
had my suspicions of what it was—the fierce jealousy of a
fellow bass—but I could not bring myself to believe that
he would stoop to treachery. Now my thoughts kept drift-
ing to him.

On Thursday, March 12, 1942, at eleven o'clock in
the morning, two well-dressed young men entered my
house through the back door without ringing the bell.
Doris had gone to the village to shop. The seven-month-
old Clelia was in her room with the nurse. I was at my
desk in the living room, writing out some checks. The
two men came in and walked straight up to me.

"Are you Ezio Pinza?" one of them asked sharply.

"Yes, I am. What can I do for you?"

"In the name of the President of the United States,
you are under arrest!"

There was such iron in his voice that I rose involuntarily. For one fleeting moment, I had the illusion of
myself behind bars, handcuffed, condemned, lost to the

world for all eternity. A sound came from Clelia's room. Was she crying or laughing? I don't remember, but the sound brought me back to reality.

"Would you mind waiting until my wife comes back from the village?" I asked. "It won't be long."

"There's plenty of time," one of them said. "We intend to search your place, anyway. Here is the warrant."

"I know who sent you," I suddenly blurted out.

"Who?" one man said.

I named the Met singer. One of the men made a note, without giving any indication of whether he knew the name. Then the two young men systematically set about searching our house. They missed nothing—every closet, every drawer, every scrap of paper was examined—while I sat helpless. After a long while one approached me and asked where I had hidden my ring with the Swastika.

"Do you mean my tortoise-shell ring?" I asked them. "It was brittle and broke up years ago. I threw away the pieces. It was not a German Swastika anyway."

The men made no comment, but wrote down my words and went on with the search. Their function, I understood, was not to interrogate or discuss my case with me, but to search the house and take me away. I was silent from then on.

They were still at it when Doris came home. The two FBI men said that I could talk to her all I wanted and paid no further attention to us.

Young, inexperienced and immature in so many ways, my *Piccola* ("the little one," as I called Doris in Italian) quickly overcame the initial shock and began to ask questions and make suggestions that were calm, direct, realistic. There was nothing except her very, very pale face to show that she was engaged in anything other than the businesslike conversation between husband and wife on the eve of a normal parting. I knew that, as an enemy alien under arrest, I would be able to do next to nothing on my own behalf. This meant that the fight for my release would be completely in Doris' hands, and it braced me to see that those hands, which I thought had been made solely for me to kiss, were steady.

The search finally came to an end. The one thing the FBI men found of sufficient interest to take along with them was the bill of sale for my motorboat. We were about to leave when one of them noticed a framed letter, written in Italian, hanging on a wall alongside autographed photos of some of my friends and colleagues. Pointing at the letter, he said, "What is this?"

"A letter written by Verdi. One of my prize possessions."

"Who?"

The question, coming as it did from an exceedingly keen-looking young man, was so unexpected that Doris and I exchanged glances and smiled. It was a good sign that we smiled, I thought, an omen signifying that I would come back soon, a free man. I did come back, and I was free, but that did not happen soon at all.

The men took me to the Foley Square Courthouse, where I was searched, photographed, fingerprinted and questioned. Then, the same two men took me to Ellis Island on a private boat, to prevent publicity, and there they surrendered me to uniformed guards and said in farewell, "Good luck, Pinza!"

There were one hundred and twenty-six of us, Italians, Germans, Japanese, milling around in the enormous barracklike room on Ellis Island. Most of us were bewildered and frightened, desperate for solace and despairing at our helplessness. Our misery was still further intensified by the untidiness to which we were reduced: all suspenders, belts, shoelaces and other objects that might help a would-be suicide had been taken away from us.

Many of the internees recognized me and wondered why I had been brought in, for I had never taken part in political activity. Whatever the degree of their own guilt, they all were touchingly solicitous of me, especially the Italians. They introduced me to a card game called *scopa* and welcomed me as a partner whenever I wished to play.

The men I was with came from different walks of life: workingmen, professional soldiers and intellectuals. One man was a member of a noble German family, who, far from resenting the incarceration, as most of us did, justified it in conversations with me as a necessity dictated by centuries of experience with enemy espionage. Sophisticated, superior and, I can wager, unhappy in his personal life, he discussed our plight with the detachment of a scientist speaking of insects. Every living cell in my body cried in protest against that approach. Let the guilty be punished, but I—I wanted to go back to my family, the opera house, the daily routine of playing with Clelia, puttering around in my victory garden, rehearsing, facing the audience! Instead, there were the guards, the open latrine, the dull food, the weary monotony of prison life

—a monotony broken by sporadic questionings and by Doris' weekly visits. She had only a few brief minutes each time, into which she crowded news of our child and home, and reported on her efforts to obtain my release— all within the earshot of a guard.

I must confess that I did Doris a great wrong during that period: aside from worrying about my fate and career, I was consumed by jealousy. I had no doubts about her loyalty or the wholeheartedness of her activity on my behalf, but I could not imagine that she, young, beautiful and so desirable, was not being pursued by a host of men. Seeing her during the visits, meeting her direct gaze, I knew that I was being ridiculous, insane; and found within me the strength not to insult her by questioning. But then, she would leave—she had to—and with her would go my sanity, my will power; and I would abandon myself to despair.

At first I thought that mine was a simple case of an anonymous denunciation which could be disproved easily, because I knew I was innocent of any wrongdoing against my adopted country, in thought as well as in deed. A good lawyer, a few affidavits, would turn the trick, I was sure; but the rigidity of legal procedures, the nature of the questionings to which I was subjected and the obstacles Doris kept encountering soon opened my eyes to the magnitude of the blow that had befallen me.

Doris' natural first step was to telephone my friends and associates, Constance Hope, Edward Johnson and Marks Levine. All three were horrified and asserted their confidence in my integrity, and a readiness to anything in their power on my behalf. Just as unanimously, they recommended that Doris retain the services of a reputable lawyer and that the fact of my detention be kept out of the newspapers until the authorities reached a decision.

Easier said than done. Every newspaper in New York carried the story of my arrest under sensational headlines, the very next morning. Even *The New York Times* front-paged it as a "hot" story, with my photo thrown in:

EZIO PINZA SEIZED AS ENEMY ALIEN;
FBI TAKES SINGER TO ELLIS ISLAND

The very thoroughness of the press coverage proved to be the silver lining in the cloud: it won me a powerful ally. Mayor Fiorello LaGuardia, a patient of Dr. Leak's, remarked to him in the course of a telephone conversation, "There's something crooked about this business. Someone was terribly anxious to tip off the papers. Let me know if there's anything I can do for Mr. Pinza."

I heard of this remark the very next day from my father-in-law himself. Luckily, he had been treating my teeth at the time of my arrest, which gave him the right to a pass two or three times a week to complete his job. He was therefore able to keep me in touch with developments far more regularly than Doris could.

The law firm to which she turned for help, on Constance Hope's advice, was that of Greenbaum, Wolff and Ernst, headed by the well-known champion of liberal causes, Morris Ernst. He agreed to represent me, but only on the understanding that, in view of the wartime situation, his ultimate client was the United States government, and that he was free to withdraw from the case at any time he became convinced that my freedom was not thoroughly warranted. This meant, in effect, that he and his associates would sit in judgment of me before wholly identifying themselves with my case, and would continue to sit in judgment throughout its course. Neither Doris nor I hesitated. A lawyer who is convinced of his client's innocence, we knew, is a hundredfold more effective than one who is not. Whatever doubts Ernst entertained at the outset were dissipated by the facts that emerged during his inquiry, and by Bruno Walter's plea for him to undertake my defense. My old friend, himself a foe and victim of totalitarianism, rallied to my side the moment he heard of my arrest.

The decision taken, Ernst assigned one of his firm's brightest young men, Harold Stern, to handle my case— a most happy choice. Tireless, resourceful and a man of integrity, Harold was to become, with the years, a personal friend and a trusted business associate.

By the time he came into the picture, however, it was almost too late. A hearing of my case had been held on March twenty-fourth, twelve days after my arrest, and the decision of the Board was against me.

To understand the full gravity of my situation, you must bear in mind that the Bill of Rights, not always applicable to U.S. citizens in time of war, is nonexistent so far as an enemy alien is concerned. In being summoned to a hearing, he is presumed guilty until he can prove his innocence, and is expected to answer charges of which he is kept in ignorance. It is up to him to refute detractors whose identity and allegations are withheld from him, and to show that his release is not inimical to the best interests of the United States. This, at a time when he has no way of knowing whether the evidence he offers is to the point or is utterly irrelevant. The hearing is held before a Board of three reputable private citizens, from which the defendant's lawyers are barred, unless called in as witnesses. If the Board fails to reach unanimity in clearing the accused, he is sent to a detention camp for the duration.

The Board consisted of Dr. George Schuster, president of Hunter College; Edward Collins of the Fifth Avenue Coach Company; and Dr. Henry Van Dusen, then president of the faculty at Union Theological Seminary. There was never any doubt in my mind that these men, selected to weigh the testimony and reach a verdict, were fair-minded American citizens doing a necessary job, yet how could I, or any other person whose happiness and career depended on the outcome of a hearing conducted under such circumstances, help finding it all strange and forbidding?

Shocked by the arrest, demoralized by the prison-like life in the barracks, and ignorant of the charges against me, I put on the worst show of my life at the hearing. My English, imperfect under the best circumstances, must have been positively murderous as I stuttered, mumbled and repeatedly proclaimed my innocence—the least recommended and most unconvincing method of defense, for who would acknowledge his guilt under those circumstances?

Several days later I was informed of the Board's failure to acquit me. As I learned subsequently, only one of the three judges was not convinced of my innocence, but that was sufficient to condemn me to a camp until the war's end, with no visitors allowed, and only one letter a month from home. That was the end. The end of family, of love, of opera, of sweet life itself. Only a mere formality stood between me and incarceration for God knows how many years: the signature of the United States Attorney General, Francis Biddle, approving the Board's decision. He had, of course, the power to order a second hearing, but thus far, we were told, he had not exercised it in cases involving enemy aliens. I therefore listened without hope or enthusiasm to various plans of carrying on the fight, outlined to me one day by Doris, the next by her father, the third by Harold Stern.

I did not discourage them, naturally. What I did was far worse. Bewildered by the verdict and by the legal processes I did not understand, I yielded to apathy, to a kind of hypnotized listlessness which kept frustrating them at every step.

The strategy, as worked out by Stern, aimed first at obtaining Francis Biddle's order for a second hearing; next, testimonials from unimpeachable character witnesses, that might outweigh the allegations of my slanderers; and finally, finding out the nature of the charges against me in order to enable me to meet them, should we succeed in gaining the hearing. I could help little in connection with Biddle's order or testimonials, but Stern depended almost exclusively on me in his efforts to trace the charges. Yet I was of no help whatsoever.

"Please try!" Stern appealed to me. "Recall the questions you were asked; analyze them. What were they after—the FBI, the Board? What precisely did they want to know?"

The men who had been questioning me since my arrest were cagey, yet I had some vague ideas. All I needed was to make an effort and work it out in my mind, but this seemed beyond my power to do.

"How can you expect me to fight windmills?" Stern would shout in desperation, and turn to Doris for help. She pleaded with me, tears in her eyes, but I was like an ox unresistingly led to slaughter. I behaved as though I had lost all interest in the case. Or in anything, for that matter. Before the hearing, I used to delight in the fruit and cheese which Doris was allowed to bring for me, to supplement the wholesome (lots of meat, milk and butter) but monotonous fare at Ellis Island. Now I hardly touched Doris' food. I listened dutifully to her stories of baby Clelia's intelligence and happy vitality, but they no longer aroused that sharp longing which might have awakened me to alert participation in the struggle for my freedom. Blocked myself, I was blocking those who tried to help. Nothing short of a miracle, it seemed, would turn the trick for me, and a miracle did happen, wrought by none other than my little Clelia.

She was a most cheerful baby, a ready smile on her face at all times and for anyone who might come along. She was also a healthy child, but one morning she woke up vomiting, then lay pale and silent, hardly showing signs of life. Doris immediately called Dr. Elsworth

Smith, an old friend of the Leak family, who had taken
care of Doris herself since she was nine months old, and
who was now our pediatrician. Dr. Smith found Clelia
suffering from intussusception (the telescoping of the
small intestine into the larger one), and rushed her off
with Doris to a New York hospital equipped for an immediate operation. The operation itself, he said, was not
complicated, but there was the danger of shock, which
might be fatal.

While Doris was on her way to New York, her mother
informed the Ellis Island authorities of the emergency,
requesting them to send me to the hospital so that I could
be on hand during the operation. They responded with
utmost sympathy, dispatching me immediately in the
company of a guard. I met Doris in front of the hospital,
took the prostrate child in my arms and carried her in.
Alerted by our doctor, the hospital personnel had everything ready for the operation, but first Clelia was given
barium by enema. Dr. Charles Blakemore, the famous
surgeon, watched the progress of the liquid through a
fluoroscope to find the point of blockage, simultaneously
exerting gentle pressure on Clelia's abdomen with his
fingers. Miraculously, the manipulation unknotted the in-
testines, making the operation unnecessary. Clelia came
to life and started to cry, and soon the sparkle returned
to her eyes, the color to her cheeks. Doris picked up our
daughter and handed her to me. Clelia looked at me and
smiled happily. I cried. Then drew Doris toward me, and
kissed them both. The guard, who had orders to take me
back the moment my presence was no longer needed,

turned to look out the window and waited until I told him I was ready to go.

I leave it to psychologists to explain why the shock of this experience should have proved more effective than Doris' pleas, Harold's logic and my own realization of the danger confronting me. Whatever the reason, the fact remains that my memory and power of analysis began to function from that day on. Alert and co-operative, prodded by Harold at every step, I was able to gather the various clues inherent in the questionings and to pinpoint the following accusations:

1. I owned a ring with the Nazi Swastika on it.
2. I had a boat equipped with a radio that received and sent out secret messages.
3. I was a personal friend of Benito Mussolini.
4. I proudly bore the nickname "Mussolini."
5. I sent coded messages from the stage of the Metropolitan Opera House during the Saturday-matinee radio broadcasts. The code was allegedly based on a system of changed tempi in my singing.
6. In 1935, I had organized a collection of gold and silver for the benefit of the Italian government.

Harold was shaken by the cumulative effect of the implied charges, the deadly intent behind them, and the peril to me, should I be unable to disprove them. The year was 1942, you will recall, when the enemy was riding high, and the military situation was fraught with the gravest danger. The mood of the country was dominated by suspicion and lack of forgiveness.

One by one, Harold went over the accusations against me:

1. The "Nazi" ring referred to was that Pago Pago tortoise-shell ring I have mentioned earlier, with the primitive inverted Swastika.

2. I had sold the boat soon after Pearl Harbor, simply because gasoline was not available for pleasure boats. The common ship-to-shore radio that came with the boat was not functioning, and I did not have it put in order, as any radio mechanic could verify with no difficulty.

3. I had never met Mussolini, and never tried to.

4. No one called me "Mussolini" at any time. That was the nickname of another Metropolitan basso, the distinguished Virgilio Lazzari, who, in fact, resembled the dictator. Harold obtained a photo of the singer, which was shown to the Board.

5. This is the most ridiculous of all charges, considering the fact that it emanated from sources well versed in music. No singer can change tempi of an opera. They are set by the conductor, and the conductor alone.

6. The only charge that had some basis in fact concerned the collection of gold for Italy. I had no hand in organizing the collection, but I did contribute a plain gold ring. However deeply I regret the contribution, the regret is in no way to be interpreted as evidence of Fascist leanings on my part, or as an admission of participation in an act directed against the United States. The time was 1935, the year of Italy's invasion of Ethiopia. Most of us Italians in the U.S.A. saw the conflict as merely a war between

their mother country and a land named Ethiopia. I came to know better, but I did not then.

Among the letters submitted to the Board was one by the assistant conductor at the Metropolitan, Giacomo Spadoni, who, like myself, contributed to the collection. In his letter Spadoni stated:

I have always been anti-Fascist and am now a naturalized citizen of the United States since 1923. . . . Many Italians in 1935 were on the side of Italy as a country against Ethiopia. I think I am fair in saying that all Italian people or people of Italian descent in this country, citizens and non-citizens, in 1935 felt the same way. Fascism or Mussolini or the form of the Italian government had no bearing on the incident. I feel sure that the question of being or not being a Fascist never crossed anyone's thoughts.

I have known Ezio Pinza for many years and am certain that he feels that the United States is his country and that he would do anything he could to help it even against Italy.

Like Morris Ernst, Harold was troubled by the incident of the gold collection, and undertook a thorough investigation to resolve their own doubts in one way or another. As Ernst was to write in a memorandum to the Board on April 25, 1942:

These doubts arose through rumors I had heard, which may have come to the attention of your Board, alleging that Mr. Pinza had organized some kind of a collection of gold for the Italian government. I checked on these rumors to the best of my ability

and I believe they are entirely without any significance. I am convinced he did not organize any such
activity. On the other hand, there is no doubt that he,
together with thousands of other Italians, long before
the United States was involved in the war, made a
contribution of gold in aid of Italy against Ethiopia;
the particular contribution which was the only one
that I have been able to discover, was the result of a
virtual mass meeting of all Italians connected with
the Metropolitan Opera House. Mr. Pinza was one
of the mass. My inquiry indicates that not a single
Italian at the Opera House declined to join this mass,
that many of the contributors were also non-citizens,
and that the effort itself was organized by citizens
of Italian origin whose allegiance to the United
States at this time of war is above suspicion.

It seems unnecessary to burden you with quotations
from the many, many letters and testimonials written at
the time by various people on my behalf. But one brief
note must be cited, for it bears directly on the most dangerous charge against me: activity as an agent of the
enemy. The writer was Carlo Tresca, the most violently
anti-Fascist Italian in the United States. Addressed to the
Attorney General, his letter reads:

> The undersigned, Carlo Tresca, editor of the
> Anti-Fascist publication Il Martello, believes he
> knows all the dangerous agents of Mussolini, all the
> Fascist propagandists and all the potential "Fifth-
> Columnists" of Italian descent.
> The undersigned is of the opinion that Ezio

Pinza never has shown himself to be, directly or indirectly, an agent of Fascism or of Mussolini.

Tirelessly searching through my records, Harold produced evidence of my singing without remuneration for the benefit of organizations above reproach or suspicion, including the U.S. Treasury Department (aiding its Defense Bonds drive), the Red Cross, the International Ladies Garment Workers Union (at a convention which adopted a strongly worded anti-totalitarian resolution), and the Friends of New Music.

Our work on the preparation of my defense was completed with the arrival of a letter signed by Wilfred Engelman and Giacomo Spadoni, pinpointing my main accuser and his motivation:

> We, the undersigned, do hereby testify that on several occasions of recent date we have heard an American bass state that he personally is responsible for exposing to the FBI Ezio Pinza's political conversations of the past three years, adding that he (the American bass) never had an opportunity to sing because Ezio Pinza was the first basso of the Metropolitan.

The slow pace of the bureaucratic machine had hitherto worked in our favor. Now that our defense was as complete as we could possibly make it, time was heavy on our hands, especially mine. You will recall that the Board had made its adverse decision on March twenty-fourth. Attorney General Biddle could, with one stroke of his pen, condemn me to the detention camp or decree a new hearing. On April second, LaGuardia informed Dr. Leak that the necessary papers finally had been forwarded to Washington, and my father-in-law, accompanied by Doris, went there in the hope of prevailing upon Biddle not to close the case. Day after endless day, they sat in the anteroom where the Attorney General's chief assistant, Ugo Carusi, kept informing them that the papers had not reached his desk. When they finally did, at six in the afternoon of April seventh, Carusi assured Doris that he would see to it that Biddle gave his personal attention to the matter. But Doris insisted that the Attorney General receive her and Dr. Leak, so they could present their arguments in favor of a new hearing. Biddle sent word that he could not see them. At this, Doris broke down. The strain of the past weeks and the endless hours in the anteroom had proved to be too much. She insisted hysterically that an American citizen has the right to speak to the Attorney General, and she was determined to exercise that right. Poor Carusi had to make another trip to Biddle's office, only to return with the message that the Attorney General was swamped with work on similar cases and that mine would have to await its turn.

Doris returned home, but she could not rest, fearing that the overworked Biddle might not read the various documents with sufficient care, that some vital detail might escape him, that he might automatically accept the Board's verdict. Bruno Walter wrote a moving letter to Biddle, and also called on LaGuardia with Doris, appealing to the Mayor to help her. LaGuardia wrote a personal message to Biddle. The very next day, on April thirteenth, the Attorney General received Doris and Dr. Leak. There was an icy politeness in his manner, but he listened attentively.

As loyal Americans, they told him, they were not asking for my release—only for another hearing to establish my guilt or innocence. This the Attorney General granted. The hearing was held on April twenty-eighth, at the Federal Court in New York.

The curious thing about the hearing was that I took almost no part in it. Several witnesses were called, including Marks Levine and the Metropolitan Opera singers Thelma Votipka and Wilfred Engelman, all three of whom were exceedingly generous in their remarks about me; but the star of the show was Doris. She spoke for fully an hour and a half, exposing the plot and refuting the charges. She also emphasized my essentially apolitical nature and stressed the Board's responsibility for my destruction as an artist, which was bound to follow a conviction.

"Had I thought there was the smallest grain of truth in the charges against you," she later told me, "I would not have been able to do what I did."

What she did was to effect my release.

We were not informed of it immediately; and, indeed, I was not allowed to return home until June fourth, nearly three months after I had been taken into custody, with instructions to report regularly to a parole officer in my area, and to our physician, Dr. Smith, who would act as sponsor. I was completely free to pursue my profession, except that I still had to apply for permission each time my work involved a trip away from home. After the first flurry of excitement and statements to the press, I settled down to a quiet summer devoted to my family, the victory garden and to the planning of a comeback. Some friends urged me to denounce those at the Met who were known to have had a part in the plot that had caused me so much anguish. My constant reply was, "God will punish them in His own time and way." Unfathomably, He has. I cannot say any more without disclosing the identity of the persons involved, thus adding to their suffering.

I had to resume my career, and as quickly as possible, if only for financial considerations. Everything I had managed to earn since I had given up my life savings to Augusta had gone into the purchase of our house, toward doctors' bills and for my defense. My bank account was almost as bare as the cupboards in our home in Italy after Father's bankruptcy, many years ago. I was thinking of this while planning my comeback, not knowing yet that the reasons for resuming my career were actually far more compelling. This I found out later in the year, when I tried to take out an insurance policy and was rejected as a poor risk because of high blood pressure. This meant that in case of death I would leave my family with nothing except whatever savings I could manage from then on. After the insurance company turned me down, my one thought was to leave Doris protected.

The men who had the power to help me make my comeback could not have been more generous and friendly. Edward Johnson, of whom I always think affectionately, lost no time in informing me that the position of first basso at the Metropolitan was mine again. The San Francisco Opera Company, where I had performed season after season, had held up all decisions on casting and repertoire until my release was official, so that they could include me in their plans. Last, but not least, Marks Levine was eager to move mountains for me in arranging recitals throughout the country.

Such support and confidence were heartening, but what of the ultimate arbiter, the great Public? It was still wartime, after all, and American boys were dying on the battlefields. There were some straws in the wind: letters, telegrams, telephone calls from friends and strangers alike, offering advice, help and apologies for the wrong that had been done me. Still, one never knew.

By way of tryout, I accepted an invitation from a private group of Metropolitan Opera artists to join them in a series of performances in Montreal during the month of September, 1942. Difficulties arose immediately. U.S. immigration officials followed a policy of granting re-entry permits only to those aliens who were sponsored by a reputable American organization. Since the group of which I was a part had not been sent by the Metropolitan Opera, I had to turn elsewhere for sponsorship, and naturally applied to AMGA (the American Guild of Musical Artists). I was a charter member of the organization and had been on its Board of Governors at the time of my arrest. My name was actually on AGMA's official stationery at the time. These facts were well known to the officers of the Guild in 1942. Yet, far from giving me the needed sponsorship, AGMA refused even to acknowledge the fact of my membership. When informed of this,

Mayor LaGuardia exploded with the eloquent indignation that was so typical of him, and assumed personal responsibility for me. Thereupon, the re-entry permit was issued, and I was free to go to Montreal.

Our first performance, *The Barber of Seville,* took place on the evening of September seventeenth. A letter Doris wrote to her parents the next morning, which was touchingly saved by Monie, tells the story of my crucial first encounter with the public after my arrest:

> Ezio received the greatest ovation I have ever heard. At the end of the second act, Defrere sent each artist out to bow alone—everyone had a great applause because it was such a splendid performance all around—but he sent Ezio out last, and the house nearly came down.
>
> Pelletier and the other people who have known him a long time said that never in twenty-five years have they heard Ezio sing so well! And everyone backstage was so happy and so kind. One lady at a party afterwards said it was as though people were saying "forgive us."

Participation in San Francisco's brief opera season followed. The audience in that most beautiful of all American cities was every bit as appreciative and generous as in Montreal, but trouble still dogged me, as you can see from still another letter Doris wrote to her parents. The date is October 2, 1942.

> When we arrived here we found to our amazement that we shall be treated like spies as long as we

remain. Wherever we go and any time during the day whatsoever, a detective is with us; when we are in our room he sits outside our door in the corridor. He goes to rehearsals, performances—everywhere, and is never more than five feet away from Ezio.

Poor Ezio is so terribly hurt and upset by this treatment that he has not slept for two nights. He won't go out of the hotel rooms unless imperative, and at the theatre he is so nervous he can hardly work. It offends him terribly.

It is not the immigration or Justice department —it is the military authorities, and of course, in wartime, in a war zone, they have complete control.

. . . We both have wanted to go right back to New York from the first moment but everyone advises against it.

. . . To look to something more cheerful, Clelia is having the time of her life. Once in a while she got a little bored on the train, but never frightened. I guess it is in her blood—she is a born trouper.

Of course, we could not go back to New York in defeat. Instead, we and the opera company complained to the military and civil authorities. After a few days, the guard was recalled! The rest of our stay was as pleasant as only San Francisco can make it.

Who would have guessed that on July 2, 1945, when 105,000 citizens of the same war zone welcomed home their two great war heros—Generals Patton and Doolittle —I should be asked to sing "The Star-Spangled Banner" in the Los Angeles Coliseum?

New York, with its teeming, diversified population,

was a real cause for worry. To fail there was to lose most, if not all, of the gained ground. We therefore planned my first appearance there with the greatest caution. Edward Johnson and Bruno Walter had the happy idea of reviving *The Magic Flute* on that occasion, to be sung in English for the first time at the Metropolitan, with Walter conducting. To the accompaniment of Mozart's serene, indescribably beautiful music, I made my entrance, dressed as the High Priest Sarastro, walked up to the apron of the stage and sang, enunciating the words with maximum clarity:

> "Within these holy portals revenge remains unknown
> And by all erring mortals their way by love is shown
> And guided forth by friendship's hand
> They journey to a better land
> And guided law is led aright . . ."

Even granted the influence of the atmosphere thus created, I sensed in the ovation accorded me a quality of personal affection I had never felt before.

To make my comeback complete, Marks Levine found the demand for me so great he would not have been able to meet it even had I given him twice the number of dates I had free for concerts.

A letter from Ugo Carusi, written on February 7, 1944, informed me that the Attorney General had just signed my unconditional release. I was gratified, of course, but the letter could not make much of an impression on me at that time. Nothing could, for exactly three weeks earlier, Doris had already made me the happiest man on earth by giving birth to a boy—my son Pietro!

CHAPTER ELEVEN

South Pacific

THE YEARS that followed were crowded with work: operas, concerts, radio guest appearances and, above all, travel. Travel without end. My salary was averaging more than two hundred thousand dollars a year, thus providing the foundation of security for my family; but I saw so little of my wife and children that, in thinking of that period up to 1948, I recall mainly snatches of telephone conversations with Doris, Clelia's bell-like little voice, Pietro's unintelligible babble. Each conversation brought happiness, and with it a sharp longing never to be away from my family. It then occurred to me that if I replaced my concerts with film work, I could live with Doris and the children in New York during the Metropolitan's winter season and also have them with me during summers, while I made motion pictures in California. A film career would definitely solve the problem, I thought.

As in all major decisions affecting one's life and work, more than one factor went into the making of this one.

For all my joy and sense of fulfilment in my opera career, I had become restless, having practically exhausted the repertoire available for my voice and sung in every major opera house and concert hall in the world. I was looking for new fields to conquer, especially in a medium of such unlimited possibilities as the motion pictures, which would not necessarily preclude my continued associa-ation with the Metropolitan.

Then again, there was the long view: Sooner or later, I knew, my voice would start to go, and since existence outside of show business was unthinkable to me, it seemed that for the present I could combine Hollywood with the operatic stage, and in the future with the legiti-mate stage.

My problem was not urgent at the time, for my voice was holding up miraculously. Furthermore, my approach to the opera stage differed sharply from that of some of my colleagues, especially the prima donnas. When Lucre-zia Bori, for instance, was reproached for abandoning opera at the age of forty-seven, she replied, "I do not wish to stop, but since no one can give me back my youth, I must stop."

I had not found the means of regaining my youth, either, but then I had never sought to limit my portrayals to men distinguished for their youthful looks and virility. There are other roles. If one takes a realistic account of one's possibilities and limitations, one can remain on the opera stage for many years after the bloom of youth is gone.

My first gropings in the film world, you will recall, date back to the year 1940, when I was courting Doris.

I so hated the thought of staying away from her that I went to Hollywood most reluctantly, and then only because my agent, Marks Levine, had committed me to some interviews with producers, and because I was looking forward to a reunion with the Bruno Walters. Having seen them, and having obtained their blessings on my forthcoming marriage, I precipitously left Hollywood, soothing Levine's hurt feelings with the following true story.

"The first movie mogul I spoke to, said to me, 'So, you're an opera singer! Well, well, well . . . Let me tell you something, Mr. Pinza, I've never been to an opera. Not interested!' "

But I was not completely honest with my agent, I am afraid. There were other studio chieftains to speak to, and one of them, Boris Morros, was interested in me precisely because I was an opera singer; but all I wanted just then was to see Doris, so I left for the East without pursuing the matter any further.

Sometime in 1945, I went to Los Angeles for a concert at the Hollywood Bowl. At a reception given for me by Atwater Kent, I was introduced to Ida Koverman, executive secretary of Louis B. Mayer, *the* Mayer of M-G-M. Miss Koverman told me I was just the man she had been looking for; her boss wanted me to make a screen test. This I did, and was most agreeably surprised when she telephoned me the next day, "Mayer is crazy about the test! It's simply wonderful! You're in! Come and see it!"

They gave me the full celebrity treatment at the studio, including a grand tour of the lot and introduc-

tions to everyone with a big name who happened to be
there. The only name I remember is José Iturbi. The
test looked good to me, too. All that remained, it seemed,
was to draw up a contract and sign it. When I said that I
had to leave almost immediately for a scheduled concert
in Denver, the studio people did not seem worried.

"We'll find you by long distance the moment the
contract is drawn up," they told me.

They never looked for me in Denver or anywhere
else.

About a year later, while in Mexico City, I answered
a long-distance call from Boris Morros of Paramount, who
offered me twenty-five hundred dollars for two singing
scenes in a film to be called "Carnegie Hall." Assisted by
Marks Levine, I settled for seventy-five hundred, and at
last I stood in front of the cameras for my first moving
picture. It was all over in three days, with such happy
results that Morros signed me up right then and there for
the lead in two films.

The first, based on Victor Herbert's "Babes in Toyland," was to be made in 1947. I so believed in my Hollywood future that we bought a house in Beverly Hills and
settled there with the children.

What followed was fit for a Marx Brothers picture.
My producer, Boris Morros, was telephoning from here,
there and everywhere, setting up arrangements for shooting and screening dates, shifting them, asking me to obtain the score from Fred Waring—who, it turned out, did
not know what I was talking about: no one had even
spoken to him about "Babes in Toyland."

Most exasperating were the sudden postponments

of screening dates, and Morros' equally sudden, mysterious disappearances. My entire concert schedule was so disrupted that at one point my agent and I faced the prospect of being sued to the tune of two hundred thousand dollars by disappointed, angry local concert managers. Marks Levine performed miracles in finding suitable replacements on short notice, thereby avoiding the suit; but he viewed the future darkly indeed, just as I did, until we discovered one morning that we no longer needed to worry: there was to be no future. Boris Morros had vanished altogether, at least as far as we were concerned, leaving our letters and telegrams unanswered, as though "Babes in Toyland" had been only a mirage. In the face of what looked like sheer lunacy, I gave up. If this is Hollywood, I decided, I had better sell the house and go back to New York, to the opera and concert stage, where things may be erratic but are not built on quicksand. It was 1948 by now, and all I had to compensate for lost time and concert fees was ten thousand dollars.

[Had Ezio Pinza lived but several months longer, he would have learned from sensational press reports that Mr. Morros' postponements and disappearances were dictated by his secret activity as an FBI undercover agent within Soviet Russia's espionage network. The activity came to an abrupt end in the summer of 1957 when U.S. intelligence agents discovered that the Russians had learned of Mr. Morros' true allegiance and were planning to destroy him. He then returned to the United States for permanent residence and to his career in the film industry.
—R.M.]

For some four or five years I had given much thought to the legitimate stage, as well as to motion pictures, if only because I had been approached by a number of producers. Dick Kollmar, for instance, sought me for his *Early to Bed;* Jed Harris for *The Play's the Thing;* and Edwin Lester, the head of the Los Angeles Light Opera Association, for *Kismet.* I was not ready for the stage at that point in my career. But when, in 1948, Lester came to talk to me about another play, I listened carefully. I also sought the advice of Bruno Walter, who gave his approval of my plan for eventually establishing myself as a straight actor. Lester came to me with an outline for a Broadway musical to be called *Mr. Ambassador,* rather than with the script itself. That remained to be written. The humor, dash and excitement that permeated the conception of *Mr. Ambassador* appealed to me tremendously, and since I liked and trusted Lester, I signed a contract with him and gave the Metropolitan notice that I would be unavailable for the next season. My final appearance with the company that had been so generous toward me, in good times and bad, took place in Cleveland (where we were on tour), on May 14, 1948. The opera was *Don Giovanni.*

The contract I had with Edwin Lester was excellent, guaranteeing me two thousand dollars per week for a minimum of twelve weeks, with a percentage of the receipts thrown in. That was fine, except that nothing seemed to be happening. The various versions of *Mr. Ambassador* presented to Lester and me satisfied neither of us, and there was no assurance that a script would be ready in time for the production date we had set. Unlike

Mr. Morros, Lester was on hand whenever I wanted to see him, friendly and interested, but having nothing tangible to say about the one subject that interested me most: Would the script be ready in time for our rehearsal schedule?

One day, during a luncheon in Los Angeles, to which he invited Doris and me, Lester was called to the telephone. He was so excited and mysterious when he rejoined us that I sensed that the call had had something to do with me, and I bluntly asked, "What is on your mind?"

"That was a call from New York," he replied. "A certain party made me a proposition in regard to your contract with me."

"What you are trying to say is that someone wants to buy out my contract. If so, who is it and what is the play?"

Instead of replying, Lester said he would send a book to me by messenger, with instructions on what parts of it to read. Then, he promised, he would answer my question. Doris and I read the passages that very same evening, and told Lester that we loved every word of what we had read. The book was James A. Michener's *Tales of the South Pacific*. The men who wanted to buy out my contract, Lester now disclosed, were Rodgers and Hammerstein.

"Sell me right away!" I said.

He did. My new contract retained all the conditions of the one with Lester, including the clause stipulating I was to be the star of the musical.

In the meantime, two other phenomenally successful theater men had joined Rodgers and Hammerstein as associate producers: Leland Hayward and Joshua Logan. The latter was also to write the book of *South Pacific* with Oscar Hammerstein II, and to direct it. The work on the musical was beginning in real earnest, and with it began a series of moves that gradually modified the terms of my contract.

During my first meeting with Rodgers and Hammerstein, they asked me what I thought of the idea of co-starring with Mary Martin. "Magnificent!" I said. "She is a natural for Nellie Forbush." A short while later, the word was passed on to me that Mary Martin was interested, but had asked for first billing. I reacted with something like, "Ladies first," and that was that. But then, as co-star, Mary Martin expected to be paid as much as I was.

"Fine," I said to the producers, "I cannot have any objections. This really is your problem, not mine."

It did not take me long to realize that the problem was mine as well: financially, the musical was unable to sustain two actors on the conditions specified in my contract, even if played to sold-out houses every night. To be able to meet Miss Martin's request, the producers would have to cut a slice off my salary. I did not like the idea at all, but Doris finally convinced me of its essential fairness: Mary Martin was, after all, tops in the musical-comedy field, and was herself accepting less than her usual compensation because she was sharing star billing with me.

"Fine," I told the producers. "Redraw my contract to make it identical with Mary Martin's."

The two future co-stars met for the first time at a Stork Club dinner party, after my Telephone Hour broadcast, which I had been doing regularly for years. Doris, Rodgers, Hammerstein and Mary Martin's husband and manager, Dick Halliday, completed the party. Although I was seated next to the lively, charming Mary, I was reserved and silent most of the time. Whatever conversation did take place between us revolved, oddly enough, around the lofty subject of real estate.

We did not see each other again until November, when the same group, reinforced by Leland Hayward, gathered for a supper party at the Rodgers' apartment, after a concert I gave at Hunter College. Mary had already cropped her hair for the role of Nellie Forbush and looked the part to perfection. She was natural, easygoing, endearing, with her earthy humor, horseplay and wonderful common sense. I was amazed to find that she felt as much identification with her part as I did with mine. She laughed when I remarked on this, for she was about to say the same thing to me. Arm in arm, we walked up to Rodgers and Hammerstein to compliment them on the genius they had shown in the casting. With this, Rodgers played the melodies from *South Pacific* for us, and Mary did song after song at the top of her voice, hardly looking at the score, as though she had known the tunes all her life. Everyone loved her, including myself. But I—I nearly ruined the evening by refusing to join in. Under the spell of the moment, I might have broken my rule of not singing unless I am in rehearsal or on the stage, but, as you know, I needed to put in some hard work on a song before I could sing it.

To make things worse, while everyone else kept raving about the music, I said nothing at all, and Rodgers seemed disturbed by my silence. Had he known me then as he came to know me later, he would have thought nothing of it, for I rarely speak up in a crowd, especially about music. The truth is that I was just as charmed by the songs as everyone else. It simply had not occurred to me that Rodgers would pay any attention to my silence, or attach any significance to it. But he did. And when I failed to comment even after he had played "Some Enchanted Evening," Rodgers looked up at me from behind the piano and said with something of a challenge, "This is going to be the hit song of the show!"

"It's a very lovely song," I countered. "One of the loveliest I know, but it can't compare in popular appeal with 'A Wonderful Guy.'"

Rodgers seemed hurt by my remark, but he has had his sweet revenge, I am happy to say: he proved to be right.

The rehearsals, which started on February 7, 1949, lasted for about a month, the strangest and most trying month of my entire professional life. It was a month of "firsts": my first musical comedy, a form for which I have developed a healthy respect; my first experience in day-to-day, side-by-side work with the playwright and the composer; the first time I had been in a purely American show, the language of which was almost as far removed from the English used in opera as from a foreign tongue. I had expected that I would have to make certain readjustments, but it had never occurred to me that they might be so difficult. After all, I had a perfect role in a perfect musical comedy. The leading male character, Emile de Becque, was a kindred soul into whose shoes I

stepped with the greatest ease. We were both Latins of
about the same age, both of whom fell in love with a
much younger American girl. In each case, the man had
to fight in order to get her, and fight he did. I also sympathized with Emile's enlightened views on problems of
race and color.

As for the show itself, I loved it. It had romantic
charm, the plot was good, the dialogue witty, the music
wonderful and easy to project, and the lyrics had warmth
and poetry. Moreover, the people I was working with
were brimming with talent and inventiveness, and were
more fun than any I had ever known on the opera stage.
And yet, somehow, I was missing fire from the very start.
It was altogether a strange and upsetting experience,
more disturbing in its way than the trial of rehearsing
Don Giovanni.

The source of most of the trouble lay in the unend-
ing changes made both in the script and in the direction.
The words never stood still, while the plot kept shifting all
the time, and with it the scope of some parts, including
mine; the development of character; the intent of the
action. The music itself kept varying, making turn and
turn about until one was no longer sure of anything except that the notes and the words would be reshuffled
once more the next day.

In opera, as you know, everything is hallowed by
tradition. To suggest a change is to commit sacrilege. The
shortcomings of such a system are obvious, but it pos-
sesses a virtue of inestimable value to the performer:
once I mastered a role, I had no further worries about it,

either in rehearsal or in fitting myself into a production of the opera anywhere in the world.

With *South Pacific*, one never was sure. The production was put together right there at the rehearsals; everyone was charged with the hectic, creative atmosphere of a great experience—everyone but myself. I would spend the best part of a night memorizing my lines, enunciating them syllable by syllable, with Doris' help, only to discover the next day that Rodgers, Hammerstein and Logan had been just as busy removing some of those lines, and putting in new ones for me to learn. Mary Martin and the others were like fish in water, swimming along gracefully with the changes, whereas I felt that my goose was cooked—to borrow a phrase from *South Pacific*—one which I had difficulty in understanding and learning, only to find it deleted later. No sooner would I adjust myself to the new changes than still newer ones would come, aglow with creative inventiveness, yet living hell and embarrassment for me.

I worked hard and willingly, but soon began to lose confidence in myself, especially when I noticed that my part was being cut a bit here and a bit there, while Mary's kept expanding. To make matters worse, our director, Joshua Logan, who worked tirelessly and effectively with everyone else in the cast, was paying very little attention to me. Or so it seemed. He was either fatalistically resigned to my failure, I thought, and was pinning his hopes on the others; or he was merely biding his time, waiting for me to step aside when I finally realized that I was not giving out any sparks.

The truth, Logan later told me, was that he had been

an opera fan of mine, and had too much respect for my showmanship to attempt to direct me with too firm a hand. Besides, he felt that I must first win my own battle of readjustment. This achieved, all else would take care of itself. The one thing which had never occurred to Logan was that I might give up trying altogether.

As I was driving with Doris and the children to New Haven for the last few rehearsals and the opening, I suddenly told her that I would leave *South Pacific*—it would be best for everyone concerned. The understudy, I said, could replace me easily, and I had better go back to the Metropolitan and the concert stage, where I knew every inch of the way to the audience's heart.

"If it's the audience you're worried about," Doris responded, "why not let the audience decide for itself?"

I never cease marveling at Doris. Here I was at a crucial point in my career, trying to arrive at a truly agonizing decision, and all she did was to ask a simple question, making no attempt to influence me in any way, yet asking the question in a manner that predetermined my reply! She guessed unerringly that I would accept the challenge, just as she knew that I was always at my best in front of an audience.

In the few days left before *the* night, I worked on my lines with a good friend, Edgar Vincent. Edgar was a former actor who had studied in Germany with Max Reinhardt, and who now handled my press relations in the office of Muriel Francis, my new publicity agent. (Constance Hope had decided to leave the publicity business and join R.C.A.)

Those were exhilarating days of searching with

Edgar for maximum effectiveness and sparkle, and every remark Josh Logan had tactfully made during the preceding weeks fell into its proper place. By the time the opening night had arrived, I felt that I was ready for what Doris called the "test by audience." And so was everyone else connected with the show.

The rest belongs to the history of the American theater. And for me personally *South Pacific* brought the third great professional experience of my life, an equal match for my *Nerone* and *Don Giovanni* debuts. The tryout in New Haven, the opening in Boston and, finally, the first night in New York, at the Majestic Theatre, all added up to a triumph rare in show business, and, incidentally, shattered one of my superstitions: that an extraordinarily successful out-of-town opening is a bad omen for the Broadway run. But if my superstition proved wrong, bless it, what of Josh Logan? He who, of all the men I know in the legitimate theater, most closely approaches my conception of genius, and whose experience on Broadway has been so varied and rich; he so badly misjudged the hushed fascination of the New Haven audience that he ran out of the Shubert Theater just before the ovation and locked himself in his hotel room.

"My whole body," he later told me, "was shaking with despair at the thought of the greatest failure of my career." Only the write-ups the next day and the mobs at the box office convinced him of *South Pacific's* huge success, and of the general appreciation of his creative contributions to the play that was destined to become part of this country's cultural tradition.

I have a special reason for thinking of Oscar Ham-

merstein with particular affection—he proved to be a
fellow believer in superstition. It so happened that he
had left his coat in my dressing room on the unforgettable
opening night on Broadway. The enthusiasm of the audience was so great that people refused to leave their seats,
as though unable to believe that the magic show could
ever end. From that night on, and for as long as I remained in the cast, Oscar desposited his coat in my dressing room whenever he came to the show.

The first days of exaltation had come and gone, replaced by the implacable routine of a successful Broadway run. Rain or shine, heat or frost, there was a
performance every night except Sunday, and matinees
on Wednesdays and Saturdays. I was a seasoned trouper,
but had never had to keep up such a pace. With the Metropolitan, for instance, I had averaged one opera and
two concerts a week. Some of my friends had warned me
of the two dangers that are inherent in the kind of long
run *South Pacific* was bound to have—strain and boredom—and here they were, threatening me for the first
time in my life.

The strain was by far the greater danger, aggravated
in my case by the fact that, on the stage, I had to speak
English (a language I had learned in maturity), as well
as by the need to project the speaking voice. My many
years of training and experience in singing had proved
almost useless in preparing my vocal chords for speaking
on the stage. Before the winter was over, I began to show
fatigue by catching cold easily, and since I was unwill-
ing to stay away from the show for as long a period as the

doctors wanted me to do, I rarely seemed to be really free from nose and throat infection.

The ailment finally went into my ear. My doctor gave me some medicine and a long, pointed metal instrument on which to fashion a cotton swab, with instructions to treat my ear several times a day. Early one morning, while still a bit groggy, I had the instrument with the medication in my ear, when I noticed the little bottle of medicine slipping from the washbasin. Instinctively, I reached for the bottle. My head jerked and the instrument—cotton and all—pushed right through my eardrum. I almost jumped to the ceiling with pain. . . .

The infected ear did not heal, but kept running, making it almost impossible for the jagged edges of the drum to heal. The pain disappeared, only to be succeeded by vocal difficulties. A torn eardrum, as you probably know, does not allow a singer to hear his own voice properly, with the result that I pushed mine until the doctor warned me that nodes were forming on my vocal cords. This is death to a singer. To prevent the formation of nodes, I had to miss many performances and to keep absolute silence when not on the stage.

The press began to go after me, but I gave the reporters no explanation for my repeated absences from the show, and they thought I was not living up to the traditions of the theater. One newspaperwoman actually reported that the real cause of my absences was alcohol, although, with the one exception of the Salzburg incident, I drink nothing but table wine, and very little of that. Another columnist claimed in print that I was under the care of a psychiatrist. I did not have to defend myself on that one, after Jose Ferrer's declaration that "Ezio Pinza is the least complicated person I know. If a psychiatrist ever got him to lie down on a couch, he would fall asleep." I would.

While strain was a clear and ever-present danger, the threatened boredom, I am happy to be able to say, did not materialize. Boredom was never in sight. It could not be—not with a play like *South Pacific*, and with the kind of cast we had. *South Pacific*, one old lady said to me, was a honey of a show. Whatever danger there might have been in our being surfeited with the honey, it vanished in the response of the audience. Much more diversified than at the opera, our public reacted differently each night to the goings-on behind the floodlights, transferring its moods to us. The one constant was the audience's enchantment, which converted each performance into a triumph, and triumph never becomes monotonous to an actor, no matter what anyone says.

Charged by the play, the cast was forever giving its best, each and all of us tirelessly on the lookout for a new twist in manner, tone, communicativeness. This kind of search is no stranger even to the tradition-bound opera; in a musical, the sky is the limit, so long as the new twists work. We were our own watchdogs, and Mary Martin, that restless perfectionist, was the keenest of us all. Giving the utmost of herself, she demanded the utmost from others. At the first sign of sloppiness, she would let the offender know that being bored means boring others. If this admonition produced no effect, she would speak to the stage manager. There was nothing personal in it, for

Mary was most demanding of herself. If she ever had any fears of my showing boredom, they were groundless; even if I had felt a lagging interest in my work after a while, the joyous response of the audience would have revived my enthusiasm.

But Mary and I did have certain matters to attend to. In the first place, there was that long, ardent kiss which so fascinated the columnists that they kept referring to it time and again. My position on that was simple and firm: as Emile de Becque, I had just returned from a mortally dangerous mission, to find that the girl I wanted more than anything else in the world was at last to be mine. It would have been ridiculous for me not to kiss her with all the passion and artistry of that wonderful Frenchman! Later Earl Wilson wrote in his column: "When Ezio Pinza's understudy took over briefly, Mary was overheard telling her husband, Dick Halliday: 'Look, you've got to teach him to get in close in those clinches!' "

The other matters between us were, unfortunately, of a more prosaic nature. In settling down at the Majestic, I discovered that the theater's only commodious dressing room had been given to Mary, while I was shoved into a cubbyhole so small that Oscar Hammerstein's coat, deposited there for good luck, left little room for me or my costumes. This came about because the performer who gets top billing rates the star's dressing room. No one had bothered to tell me this, nor explain the fact that Mary Martin's contract included the privilege of four house seats every night, and a maid paid for by the show; whereas I paid my valet out of my own pocket and had the right to only two house seats.

I had specified that our contracts were to be identical, and had assumed that they were. Nevertheless, I said, Mary, being a charming lady and a wonderful artist, could have her dressing room, providing mine was enlarged. With the authority of a professional carpenter, I showed the producers exactly how it could be done by cutting into the doorman's booth and removing the closet in my room. I also asserted my right to four house seats and to the services of a valet. It took a series of skirmishes to settle all problems to my satisfaction. This accomplished, I was able to direct all my energies to the pursuit of Nellie Forbush, and pursue her I did with a happy tranquility until the winter set in, bringing with it snow and sleet—and the sudden outbreak of the War of the Radiator.

The causes of the war go far, far back to the days of Mary's childhood and mine, when, in defiance of the Fate that was to bring us to stardom in the same play, she developed a hatred of steam heat and radiators, whereas I grew up longing for them. The first thing Mary did when the steam came hissing up in the radiator in her dressing room was to turn it off. I turned mine wide open. Still, we would have gone on being good neighbors ever after, were it not for the hallway we shared, where a large-sized radiator warmed the chilly air blowing in from the outside directly into my dressing room. Mary, whose room was farther away, kept turning the radiator off. I kept turning it on. The contest grew in intensity with every day until it became a veritable war of nerves, inventiveness and audacity. Mary's husband, being also her manager, was a faithful ally, available to reinforce her at all times. As Doris shied away from the battle, I counted on the assistance of my valet, Charles McLaughlin, a faithful soul whose devotion hardened into a do-or-die determination after Mary drafted her maid for sentry duty. An uneasy stalemate had set in when the enemy outmanoeuvred us with one brilliantly conceived operation: they took the knob off the radiator.

Taken by surprise, my valet and I sat silently in our HQ. But then, just as I was about to step into the chilly corridor on the way to the stage for my tender scene with Nellie Forbush, I had a brainstorm and issued a command: "A pair of pliers, or you're fired!"

A pair of pliers was waiting for me as I made my exit after the scene, with a precipitousness not called for in the script. I turned the heat on full blast. The steam whistled a victory song into my ears all evening long. The battle was won, the enemy routed! But when I entered the hallway the next evening, the radiator was gone altogether! Not prepared for total warfare, I appealed to the producers for protection, charging aggression. An extraordinary session was called, speeches were made by both sides, and a resolution was passed to replace the radiator. Mary submitted with a graciousness that made the moral victory hers.

I hasten to explain that Mary knew very little about the difficulties I was beginning to have with my health. Only Doris and my doctors knew. Mary was, in fact, an endearing colleague, a splendid trouper and a first-class showman, with more than a normal share of generosity. I shall be forever grateful to her for the spontaneity with which she ran into my dressing room, following the first performance in New York, and embraced me, shouting, "You are the hit of the show!"

I knew, of course, that this was not so. In a show as magnificent as *South Pacific* there are many "hits": the music, the lyrics, the plot, the staging, the perfection of the ensemble, each of the leading actors. But I was touched by Mary's words, and I recall them whenever I think of her.

As a matter of fact, even at the height of the War of the Radiator, Mary did not display the implacability of Rosa Ponselle, who, in her war against steam heat, took on the entire Metropolitan Opera Company. The radiator in her dressing room was never turned on—that went without saying. On the day of a Ponselle performance, all radiator pipes on the stage had to be turned off from early morning on. She would have been unable to sing, she insisted, if they were not stone cold when she touched them before curtain time. I had not minded particularly, for my roles usually had required elaborate costumes which kept me warm, but not all singers were that lucky. As for the half-clad members of the chorus and ballet, all they had to sustain them was the miraculous warmth of Ponselle's voice.

Now, at last, I was settled in one city, with no traveling to do except between Rye, where we now lived, and the Majestic Theatre. I had more time to spend with my family, to ride my bicycle every morning, to work a little with my tools and play with the elaborate electric train I had bought for the children. Actually, I had less time for them and Doris than I had hoped for, because, you see, I had become a Celebrity with a capital C. What many successful years on the opera and concert stage had failed to achieve in a big way, *South Pacific* accomplished practically overnight. I was now a celebrity in the Broadway sense, in the Hollywood sense!

For weeks and months on end, every day was Christmas in our home, with flowers, champagne, fruit baskets and other gifts, sent to us by friends and strangers alike. The fan mail was unbelievable in its bulk and variety: people asking for photographs, autographs, tickets to *South Pacific,* advice on personal problems, money for charities; and also personal appearances in hospitals, prison wards, schools, at Boy Scout rallies and so on without end.

Americans are overwhelmingly possessive toward the artists they celebrate, and are as childlike in their generosity toward them as in the thoughtlessness with which they invade the artists' privacy. It was wearying at times, I must admit, though I was never annoyed by the attention given me, whether in a restaurant where the orchestra would strike up "Some Enchanted Evening" the moment I was seen, or in the street where people gaped at me and sometimes started conversations. On occasion, a truckman would pull up at the curb, open the door and—you guessed it—greet me with the same "Enchanted Evening." Taxi drivers are a more sophisticated breed. Used to celebrities, they showed recognition by passing on to me gossip about other show people, and voicing their always authoritative opinions on music and the theater. Best of all, police officers about to issue tickets for speeding or double parking would, upon rec-

ognizing me, forget all about the fine and ask for passes
to *South Pacific*.

My earnings were high, although not much higher
than during my opera and concert days, despite the
phenomenal success of the *South Pacific* album and of
my own records, the growing number of radio and television appearances, and various new sources of income.
Those came chiefly from endorsement of various prod-
ucts: beverages, clothes, cigarettes. Manufacturers of
the foods I liked asked me to endorse them. Pinza recipes
were featured in hundreds of newspapers and scores of
magazines. When Harold Stern, my friend and lawyer,
introduced me to baseball, and the papers learned that
I had become an enthusiatic and knowledgeable fan, I
was invited to write a column during the baseball season.
The offer was tempting, but I held out until the 1953
World Series, the year my favorite Dodgers were fighting
the Yankees for the crown. The North American Newspaper Alliance signed me up to cover the Series, with the
help of a professional sports writer, who performed miracles of ingenuity in grafting lines and phrases from
South Pacific onto the lingo of the great national game.

Under the banner "Some Enchanted Baseball," my
ghost writer demanded of my favorites to "get those
Yanks out of the Dodgers' hair." After New York's victory,
"the refrain running through Charley Dressen's weary
brain tonight is 'This Nearly Was Mine,' while Stengel is
probably humming 'There's Nothing Like a Dame,' meaning Dame Fortune." The Pinza fans were happy with this
bit of horseplay, but some of the earnest baseball fans
were indignant. One of them (writing to the Boston

Globe, which carried "Some Enchanted Baseball" along with columns by respectable sports writers) demanded, "Does this mean that you are going to have Ted Williams cover opera for the *Globe?*" To which the editors, in the fullness of their wisdom and sense of humor, replied, "Not a bad idea. Remind us when the Metropolitan comes to town."

Yes, I loved my popularity and enjoyed its fruits, my sole regret being that it had not happened earlier. At thirty-five or forty, my voice certainly had been as good, my acting as accomplished, and my appearance as virile as they were when I reached fifty-eight, and, to my astonishment, was proclaimed with much fanfare one of the most glamorous men in the entire world. But, then, had the stardust fallen on me earlier, I might not have become the savior of the middle-aged man in America, his gallant rescuer from the abyss of neglect, lack of glamour, pity and self-pity!

You can believe me, I trust, that I never would have undertaken the staggering task were it not for the powerful allies I discovered in the columnists, male and female alike. In fact, they deserve all the credit for getting the campaign started, if for no other reason than that I had not suspected that the middle-aged man was considered on the shelf in the U.S.A. My point here is that I have remained thoroughly European in respect to the question of relationships between the sexes. When, as Emile de Becque, I refused to be dominated by Nellie Forbush, I was only doing what came naturally to me.

Things are different in America. Here, the man is impatient with the details of daily life. Having voluntarily abdicated responsibility for smaller things, he has gradually relinquished authority in the bigger things, and bogged down in the stupor of middle age. To believe the columnists, I achieved immortality by opening the eyes of the world (no less!) to the abnormality of a situation which neither sex relishes. I did it, so they say, by serving as a living example of the vigor, spark, authority, sex appeal, humor and glamour that a middle-aged man can have. Does have! In the historic words of Bob Hope, "Ezio Pinza has done more for the middle-aged man than heating pads or adrenalin!" The dean of theatrical critics, George Jean Nathan himself, wrote a humorous article alleging that fully 5,778 men over fifty years of age had been arrested by the police for displaying vigorous interest in young women—and all as a result of having seen Pinza in *South Pacific!* Analyzing this product of his fancy, the venerable critic concluded with the following remarkable lines:

> Pinza has taken the place of Hot Springs, Saratoga and hormone injections for all the other old boys in town. He has given them back their waning faith in themselves and set them to acting as if they were so many Ezios, with the police consequences noted. Men who had hitherto been sitting dejectedly at home and deploring their lost youth have suddenly been converted into wolves of a high and ferocious order, and no girl is longer safe on the boulevards. Doctors, psychiatrists and Swedish masseurs are starving to death. It's wonderful!

It was indeed wonderful! The word winged its way

across the continent—straight to the film captal of the world. Offers began to come in by wire, mail and telephone, reviving the old Hollywood bug in me once more. I signed an agreement with M-G-M and left *South Pacific* on June 1, 1950, the day my contract expired.

We gave our home in Rye to the Damon Runyon Cancer Fund and drove with the children across the continent, making leisurely stops to take in the marvelous sights of this country. I remember most vividly the sunrise we watched from the rim of the Grand Canyon, when I told Clelia and Pietro that, as a child, I had heard a story about the sun being "a knocker on Heaven's gate," which St. Peter polishes every morning to help it retain its radiance. The children laughed with delight and begged for more stories, luxuriating in their monopoly on me. But the center of attention on that trip was Doris, who told the children that there would soon be a new baby in the family.

The little girl, born on December 15, 1950, was named Gloria Adele, in honor of Uncle Gino's wife.

CHAPTER TWELVE

And After . . .

*F*ATE NEVER intended me to be a film star, after all. Having made two films, I parted with Hollywood, to return only once again for "Tonight We Sing," in which I played the role of Chaliapin and sang, at last, some of the arias from *Boris Godunov* in Russian. It was an old dream come true.

It is difficult to say exactly what went wrong with my films. Being human, I shall blame others first, and then myself. The build-up I was given placed me at an extreme disadvantage both as a singer and as an actor. I was Pinza the Great Lover, God's Own Gift to the Aging Man, Mr. Middle-Aged Sex Himself! All that was necessary, the film executives must have thought, was to place me in amorous situations before a camera, with some enticing female—and a terrific success was certain. Lana Turner was chosen for "Mr. Imperium" and Janet Leigh for "Strictly Dishonorable"—lovely choices. But the scripts were without humor or style or the slightest opportunity for acting. The big mistake of the film executives was to order me to generate sex appeal, rather than create character. My mistake was to try to fill the order.

There was another difficulty. I am not at my best, it seems, unless I have an audience out in front; a live, warm, critical audience to conquer anew with each performance—a challenge which I rarely, if ever, fail to meet. In front of the camera, with only the director's instructions to stimulate me, with lights glaring in my eyes and censors crawling all around, measuring the inches and fractions of inches between me and my screen love, I can give no more than a professional performance. This I did, but professionalism is no substitute for that indefinable quality without which there is no spark. I must go back to the living stage, I decided, where I knew I could give creative satisfaction to myself and to my audiences.

Back in the East, we settled down in a beautiful ten-room house in Stamford, built to my specifications. This, Doris and I decided, was to be our home for the rest of our lives, where our children would grow up in a normal environment. We wanted them to go to public schools, and mix with boys and girls from all walks of life. No chauffeurs would drive our children to school. No private showing of films would be given for their amusement. No throwing their weight about as the offsprings of a "celebrity."

Doris and I love our children and we want them to know that love, for security in childhood means inner security in grown-up life. This, I believe, is the chief prerequisite for happiness and success. I am sad these days when Gloria, my youngest, unaware that I am convalescing from a grave illness, asks me at bedtime to sing her beloved *"Fa La Nana Bambin"* ("Go to Sleep, Little Baby"), and I am too weak to oblige. Not wanting her to think that I do not love her well enough to sing for her, I do not say no to Gloria. Instead, I say, "Maybe tomorrow?" with a big question mark in my voice, fearful that she may insist. But no. She gives me a tender, knowing look, this little woman of six, hugs me and says, "Yes, *Babbo*, tomorrow."

I do not believe in punishing children, though heaven knows they can be trying enough at times. Doris, who loves our children every bit as much as I do and devotes considerably more time and attention to them, sometimes resorts to strict measures, even to spanking. When I reproach her, she puts me in my place by reminding me that she cannot make her voice boom out like mine, an expedient which can work miracles—and does, but unfortunately only while the children are small, as Clelia, the oldest, made me understand not long ago. I cannot recall the occasion, but I raised my voice, which frightened Clelia at first. Then, gradually, the fear was replaced by an expression of rapture. No sooner had I finished than she piped, "Your voice is so beautiful, *Babbo*, when you shout!"

My disagreements with Doris in regard to the children have been so rare that I can recall only one. It happened several years ago, when Pietro was five or six. I was working in the garden that day when I caught sight of his face in a window on the second floor. It was a sad little face, indeed.

"Come down and help me!" I shouted.

"I mustn't. Mommy's punishing me."

I immediately went to Doris. "Why are you keeping Pietro upstairs?"

"Your son," she said, with emphasis on the "your," "has been experimenting to find out whether stones can go through glass, and I'm still not certain that he's convinced."

Judging by her tone and the look in her eyes, my usual excuses on behalf of the children would not do, so I looked at her sternly and demanded, "How dare you punish curiosity? Where would we all be without scientific experiments? Where would you get pasteurized milk for your children?"

Doris burst out laughing, hugged me—and left Pietro to languish upstairs, though not for very much longer.

Yet she would be the first to admit that I try not to spoil our children. They must accept discipline, must know the value of money and the preciousness of a piece of bread. Few things exasperate me more than waste, especially the waste of food at a time when so many children all over the world are going hungry. I am appalled by the injustice of it, the blindness; for thoughtless waste tends to weaken the backbones of people who indulge in it. If you take a look at the history of man's achievements, you will be convinced that those who have had to put up a struggle for the blessings of life have made the greatest contribution to progress, especially in the arts. To me, there is no enchantment in life without exertion, self-discipline, hard work. My son, Pietro, might think at times that I go too far in applying these ideas to him, that I am being too hard on him. I hope that one day he will understand that what I am trying to do, out of deep love for him, is to help him grow up, to develop in him a sense of responsibility and of pride in personal achievement.

I used to be afraid that my children might put on airs because their father was in the public eye, but fortunately they do not. As a matter of fact, each one of them has gone through a stage of thinking that everybody else's *Babbo* is a performer, too, and that their own is not necessarily the best. Gloria regards all artists with magnanimous impartiality, but Clelia and Pietro have had their phases. During my *South Pacific* days their favorite was Bill Tabbert, whom they, like everybody else, found irresistible in the role of Lieutenant Cable. Before that their affections were fastened onto that magnificent clown of the opera, Salvatore Baccaloni.

The only "special" thing about me that the children have noticed is my heavily accented English. Doris and I first became aware of it as a possible problem some thirteen years ago, when we overheard the three-year-old Clelia admonish the happily babbling nine-month-old Pietro, "You talk just like *Babbo!*"

At one time or another, each of our children wondered why my English was different from that spoken by everyone else around them. This is a question I let Doris answer.

"Your *Babbo*," she would say to the child, "grew up in a country different from ours, a beautiful land called Italy, where they speak a language that is like music to the ear. *Babbo* speaks it as well as you and I talk English. But you and I know only English, whereas *Babbo* can speak French and Spanish and a little German. Now, isn't it remarkable?"

Please forgive me for saying it, but the most remarkable thing about it is Doris herself.

People often ask me whether any of the children have inherited my gift for music and acting. "I don't know," I answer, "but I hope not." If this sounds like ingratitude to the profession that has given me fame and fortune, let me add that I am thinking first of all as a father. I would not exchange my enchanted years in the opera and on the stage for anything in the world, but in thinking of my children's future, I cannot banish memories of hardships, uncertainties and anxieties, and above all, the loneliness of a player's vagabond existence.

Claudia, the daughter born of my first marriage, has a fine voice and was given a good start at the Metropolitan, yet she soon exchanged the vicissitudes of a stage career for the joys and sorrows of private life. She married John Hall Boller, and presented me with two lovely grandchildren, Johnny and Marina. Clelia is not interested in a singing career. Her ambition is to be an actress, an ambition I am not trying to discourage in any firm manner, although every now and then I say to her, "Oh, you'll change your mind by the time you grow up," fervently hoping in my heart that I am right.

I have been reproached for being old-fashioned in my views on careers for girls. Well, old-fashioned or not, I believe that there is no greater challenge to a young woman than the career of wife and mother. Still, I shall not stand in Clelia's way if she remains determined to go on the stage. She is an extremely intelligent child, with a mind of her own.

I yearned to return to the stage, and read many a script that was sent to me, but after the perfection of *South Pacific*, it seemed both difficult and dangerous to select one.

I had some exciting adventures in television. There was *The Ezio Pinza Show* on N.B.C., in which I sang, acted and played host to such stars as Jane Froman, Beatrice Lillie, Patrice Munsel, Margaret Truman and Ed Wynn. Then there was a serial called *Bonino*, built around the character of a widowed concert singer who interrupts a successful career to bring up his eight children, a charming situation-comedy written by Robert Alan Aurthur. I particularly enjoyed playing Bonino because I had a host of happy, gifted youngsters around me all the time, and I loved every one of them.

To prove to myself that I could do straight drama, I spent the summer of 1953 on the straw-hat circuit, starring in my first straight play, Ferenc Molnar's *The Play's the Thing*. It was a successful, rewarding experience. The vehicle was fine, the cast excellent, and the director, Ezra Stone, exceedingly good. Doris and the children were with me, traveling by car from barn theater to barn theater over most of lovely New England. We were all happy that summer, but no one was happier than myself, for I had already made plans to appear in *Fanny*, a musical based on three plays by Marcel Pagnol. The comedy, written by Joshua Logan and S. N. Berman, with music by Harold Rome, had the humor, the depth, the joy of life to which I responded instantly. "Of course I'll play in it," I said when Joshua Logan asked me if I would play César; "the character is fascinating and it will be a joy to work with you again."

While not as great a musical as was *South Pacific,* *Fanny* survived the inevitable comparisons and settled down for a long, successful run.

For me, the great significance of *Fanny* lay in its being an ideal vehicle for my transition from romantic to character parts. At my age, and with my desire to turn from singing to acting, I needed just such a play, one which required the creation of a solid character. The bartender, César, whom I portrayed, had fascination, humor, liveliness and a hint of romanticism. What helped me to get inside César's character and sympathize with him was his likeness to someone I deeply loved, a man as volatile and exciting as he—my own father, whose name, you will recall, was Cesare.

Most of the critics, as though they themselves had wondered whether I could make the transition from romantic parts to character acting, discussed this aspect of my effort in *Fanny.* Their generous understanding helped me to establish myself in the public mind as an actor rather than as a matinee idol.

[The following excerpts are typical of the press reaction to the "new" Pinza:

> *Variety:* "Pinza reveals great stature as a dramatic actor . . . displays a magnificent command of the stage, gaining the affection of the audience in an increasingly warm and rich performance. He enun-

ciates every word beautifully and carries himself with great distinction."

The New York Times (Brooks Atkinson): "Mr. Pinza is a finer actor than most of us had realized. . . . He gives a relaxed performance full of quizzical humor."

The Journal-American (George Jean Nathan): "It is Pinza of the warm personality, warm acting and grand vocal gift who dominates the occasion just as he did in the memorable *South Pacific*. That man, I truly believe, could break the audience's heart even with something like 'Poopsy Popsy'."

Surveying the press reaction to Pinza in *Fanny,* Sidney Fields of the New York *Daily Mirror* discovered that the critics "had scratched the singer and found a dramatic actor of finished stature who could be warm, funny, tragic and tender at will."

—R.M.]

With an engaging musical play, an excellent cast; with Joshua Logan for director, and an unprecedented advance sale, *Fanny* had all the makings of a hit, and I foresaw a long run ahead. Naturally, I was delighted at the prospect, yet I could not help recalling the many times the curtain had gone up on *South Pacific* with my understudy playing de Becque. Due to ill health, I had missed fifty-three performances in the course of the first twelve months. I therefore consulted my physician, Dr. David Fogel, a professor of medicine at Yale, asking him to do everything in his power to get me in shape for the months ahead. I was particularly concerned with the strenuous first act and wanted to go through it each time in the full confidence that I would have enough reserves left for the less demanding second act.

The task Dr. Fogel faced was not an easy one, for I am an impatient patient who refuses to take medicine—it tends to depress me. A regimen was set up, including a none-too-strict diet, tonics, outdoor activity, rest and regular hours. In addition, Dr. Fogel insisted that I discontinue what he called extravagant expenditure of strength and energy, due to a natural tendency to throw myself wholeheartedly into anything I might be doing. If I avoided nervous strain and excitement, he said, my high blood pressure would be kept down, and my heart would not be overtaxed. I followed Dr. Fogel's instructions, with such excellent results that I did not miss a single performance of *Fanny* for fully eleven months after it opened on November 4, 1954.

My addiction to baseball was the beginning of my undoing.

I religiously followed the games throughout the 1955 season, chiefly by watching them on television. There was even a set in my dressing room at the theater. I would sometimes get so involved in a game, especially when my precious Dodgers were playing, that I would send wires to their dugout, usually to demand the replacement of a pitcher.

One hot, sunny day I took Pietro to a Giants-Dodgers game, and, of course, forgot all about Dr. Fogel's warnings. The game filled me with such excitement that toward the end I felt faint. That night I had difficulty in getting through my performance. The feeling of weakness kept growing with each day, complicated by a shortness of breath and a persistent cough. On top of it, I began to suffer from lack of sleep, because lying in bed aggravated my difficult breathing and the cough.

After two weeks of this, Doris persuaded me to see Dr. Fogel. My heart, he found, was weakened and greatly enlarged, and was beating irregularly; my legs and lungs were beginning to accumulate fluid due to the heart condition. I was a very ill man, Dr. Fogel told me, and ordered me to the hospital immediately. Faced by a firm refusal, Dr. Fogel prescribed medicine to strengthen my heart, and an injection to drain the fluid from my lungs, and sent me off with a warning that I must continue the treatment indefinitely.

It performed something short of a miracle. I felt better and played better than I had in weeks. Indeed, after a month of the heart pills and the injections, I felt so well that I discontinued them without consulting Dr. Fogel, or telling the producers of *Fanny*—or anyone else, for that matter—about my health problem.

One night in October, 1955, I woke up in terror: my chest seemed clasped in irons which tightened each time I tried to breathe. There was no pain, only an insurmountable difficulty in getting my breath, the heart beating madly all the time. I sat up. The irons unclasped and the heart calmed down. Remaining in a sitting position, I fell asleep and was well enough in the morning to call on Dr. Fogel at his office. An examination showed that the old symptons had returned, and with them the absolute need to resume the previous treatment.

One evening I felt too weak to go back to Stamford after the performance, and stayed overnight in my Hotel Delmonico suite, which I kept for such occasions and for resting between performances on matinee days. Doris came down in the morning and took me to see a prominent New York physician, Dr. Stuart Cosgriff, who ordered me to enter Presbyterian Hospital for immediate treatment and tests. When I refused, he said sternly, "You have pneumonia, Mr. Pinza, complicated by a collection of fluid due to a bad heart condition."

Seeing that I was determined not to miss a single performance, Dr. Cosgriff lured me into agreeing to go to the hospital, after the show that night, by promising to allow me to continue in *Fanny* if I reported to the theater from the hospital bed.

At midnight, still tense with the excitement of the performance, I checked in at the Presbyterian Hospital—and collapsed. Or rather, I sank into an endless kind of sleep. I must have taken food, talked to the doctors, undergone tests; but all I remember is sleep, sleep, sleep —and Doris' face each time I opened my eyes, only to fall asleep again. After several days I began to sleep normally and to think of resuming my part in *Fanny*, where Nicola Moscona of the Metropolitan was substituting for me. At this point, Dr. Cosgriff informed me that the X rays showed one dropped kidney, which might be due to a tumor on the adrenal gland. Subsequent tests convinced the doctors there was no tumor.

[Mr. Pinza never knew that the test had not been completed. Under anaesthetic, he sank so far that it

became unsafe to proceed. Various symptoms, however, subsequently convinced the doctors that there
actually was no tumor.   —R.M.]

Supported by the opinion of another heart specialist,
Dr. Fogel and Dr. Cosgriff insisted that I take a year off,
a whole year of complete rest. Ridiculous! I said. I was in
a play I loved, and had a part I enjoyed. I was under contract until June 1, 1956, and I refused to break it.

"Make it six months," the doctors compromised. But
with the heedlessness of a habitually healthy person, I
refused to settle for even three months. I stayed at the
hospital for a total of three weeks, spent one week at
home and then eight glorious days with Doris in Florida.

Sunburned and gay, I returned to *Fanny,* my sense
of well-being heightened by the wonderful reception
given me by the cast, and by get-well-and-stay-well
messages from nineteen members of the Dodgers' team.
I would have been completely happy, were it not for a
conversation I had with Dr. Fogel upon my return from
Florida. Far from being impressed by my bronzed skin
and my boasts of regained health, he repeated with uncharacteristic sternness his earlier demand that I take off
a complete year. When I exploded with "It's ridiculous!"
Dr. Fogel said something that sounded melodramatic,
but was, I could see, his last hope of making me listen to
reason. Pointing at Doris, he said, "This young woman
will be a widow, and quite soon, if you fail to take my
advice. A full year of rest is indicated."

I replied with something that must have sounded
equally theatrical, though I was equally sincere. The

stage was my life, I said, and therefore I could not give up *Fanny*.

After we left the doctor's office, Doris, who had not uttered a word so far, begged me to take the prescribed leave. It was more difficult to refuse her, but I did, though I promised that I would take a long rest after June first, the day my contract expired. Only a few more months were left, and arrangements were being made for Lawrence Tibbett to take over my part. After that I would take a sabbatical. We would go to Italy for the summer, children and all; do some traveling by car; and return to the peace of our home for the remainder of the year's leave. Doris had no choice but to agree.

All went well for a brief period. Then, inch by inch, a feeling of weakness crept over me. Each morning I found it just a little bit harder to get out of bed. Each day I had to wrestle more desperately with the thought that I might not be able to show up at the theater that night. Each evening, as I frolicked on the stage, I encountered an increasing difficulty in fighting off the fear that I might not last out the performance.

But I did, week after trying week.

The New Year had come and gone. Then the winter passed. Spring came at last, and with it my birthday, Friday, May eighteenth. Only thirteen more days remained, only fifteen more performances. The old trouper had pulled through!

So it seemed to me.

On the night of my birthday I was too exhausted to go home after the performance, and I telephoned Doris at nine thirty the next morning, as I always did whenever

I stayed overnight at the Delmonico. Everything was fine at home, Doris reported. I, too, was fine, I said; then hung up and went back to sleep. My next customary telephone call home was to be at one thirty in the afternoon. When I awakened, I felt very weak and, without looking at my watch, I called Doris and said I wondered whether I should go to the theater for the matinee performance. She had already been alarmed, for it was two thirty. She realized that something must be desperately wrong if I was still in bed at curtain time, and not aware of it. Trying to sound casual, she said, "Don't go. I'll phone the theater and come right in. Meanwhile, you stay in bed. Promise me you will. Please, Ezio."

Doris heard me say yes. She also heard the sound of the receiver, which dropped out of my hand and fell to the floor as I lost consciousness. She immediately tried to get in touch with Dr. Fogel, but failed. Anxious to have someone take care of me until she could get to New York, she phoned Edgar Vincent and Gibner King, but neither was at home. Finally, she located Dr. Michael Di Preta, an old Italian friend. He promised to rush over to my bedside. After that she telephoned Joe Marchase, the Delmonico's faithful bell captain, who stayed with me until Dr. Di Preta arrived.

Soon Doris came in, then Dr. William Field, summoned by Dr. Fogel, to whom Doris' message had been relayed. Dr. Field found that I had suffered a stroke. There was a clot in the brain and my right arm and leg were slightly affected. It was imperative that I have the care of both a day and a night nurse.

Lawrence Tibbett had learned my part by then and

was able to step into it immediately. I was out of *Fanny*.

The press was told that I was leaving the cast because of exhaustion. I recovered so quickly that we sailed for Europe on June tenth on the *Andrea Doria,* as planned; and by then I had committed myself to play the leading male role opposite Sylvia Sydney in a late fall production of *A Very Special Baby,* by Robert Alan Aurthur. I was at last to have my chance in a straight play on Broadway —a dream come true.

We were wonderfully happy on the *Andrea Doria,* the beginning of my first long vacation in years. In Europe, I promised the children, I would show them the places that had meant so much to me. But first, there must be rest.

Well, there was no rest. On our arrival in Italy we were besieged by reporters, cameramen and radio correspondents armed with microphones. Some of the newsmen followed us for eight hours—all the way to the villa we had rented at Milano-Marittima, about twenty miles from Ravenna. The villa was spacious and comfortable, but swarming with people at all hours of the day. There were relatives, friends, old schoolmates, and just people who, out of the goodness of their hearts, came with gifts, fruits and flowers, giving generously of themselves and their time, and unable to understand that at times I lacked the strength to come out and see them. There were also those who came to ask for loans and gifts, and scholarships for their talented sons and daughters.

Doris did her best to protect me, but failed with friends and strangers alike. If they could not see me in my house, they would corner me on the beach or while

I was taking a walk, robbing me of the much-needed rest. When August came around, Doris did not even attempt to postpone our scheduled trips by auto. Alas, she had not foreseen that I would insist on doing all the driving along the winding mountain roads. On the way to Salzburg I sat behind the wheel for two straight days, so that we would arrive in time to hear Cesare Siepi in *Don Giovanni*. *Everyman* followed, stirring me as always. After the performance, we went to a café, and when the time came to leave, I felt unable to stand up. Trying to control my panic and not to let Doris and the children notice the terrible effort I was making, I finally got on my feet and made it to the hotel. Doris saw that I was having a bad time of it, and tried to postpone the trip we had scheduled for the following morning. But the stubborn streak I had inherited from my father asserted itself. We left, and again I did all the driving. After only twenty-four hours of rest in Munich, I drove back to our villa in Italy.

Two days later, groggy and unrefreshed, I woke up at dawn and went to the bathroom. As I stood bent over the basin, my right leg suddenly gave way and I fell against the bath, painfully injuring the hip. The doctor summoned to examine me discovered that I had suffered another stroke.

Doris immediately cabled David Susskind, the producer of *A Very Special Baby*, urging him to replace me. He did this, and then something happened which underscores a major weakness in the star system as it is practiced on Broadway. Practically overnight, all of the hundred-odd theater parties that accounted for the fabulous advance ticket sale for the show were canceled or transferred to other plays. It was a staggering blow. The play lost its theater, had to take an interim booking and closed after several performances.

Back in Stamford, convalescing, I reproached myself for having so absurdly abused my injured health, thus missing my first opportunity for a straight play on Broadway. Frequent inquiries by theatrical and television producers gave every indication that there would be other opportunities, but complete recovery had to come first. I gave up smoking and driving, ate and slept regularly and took all the tests and medicines given me, including an anticoagulant drug to prevent further blood clots. Once more I was improving rapidly, and my hopes soared. Even the two unhappy incidents that followed did not dampen my high spirits.

I had had, for many, many years, on the thumb of my left hand, a large wart which I decided to have removed. The operation itself was a minor one, but the wound kept bleeding and refused to heal. I temporarily stopped taking the anticoagulant drug, giving no thought to the possibility that a blood clot might form in some more vulnerable spot.

The second incident involved Doris. A small internal tumor was detected during a routine medical examination she had sometime late in November, 1956. Fearing that the tumor might be cancerous, the doctors advised an operation, which was performed the day after Thanksgiving at the Presbyterian Hospital in New York. Fortunately, the tumor was nonmalignant. Although Doris had engaged a chauffeur to drive me back and forth to the hospital, I was feeling so well, and I so longed to get behind a steering wheel again, that I insisted on driving myself. On the last day of her stay at the hospital, I stopped at a Stamford jeweler's to buy Doris a gift—a gold heart with a sapphire center. Handing me the package, the shopkeeper gave me an anxious look and said, "Excuse me, Mr. Pinza, are you well? Can I help?"

"No, thank you, I'm perfectly all right," I replied.

I actually felt fine, though tired. That was on December 1, 1956.

Two days later, I had breakfast in my bedroom on the second floor as usual, did some reading, watched a television program or two, walked a little. At last the time came to have lunch, our main meal of the day at home. I walked down the stairs and lounged in the living room, waiting to be called. Doris was busy with the cook in the kitchen, a sign that something special was being prepared to please me—an old favorite, perhaps, or some new dish Doris was certain I would enjoy. Her face beaming, the cook announced lunch. I rose with great difficulty and walked slowly toward my chair in the dining room, to join Doris.

As I was sitting down, an excruciating pain stabbed me in the chest. I gasped, "Take care of the children, Doris. . . . I'm dying . . ." And I sank into blackness.

As I learned later, Doris eased me to the floor until I lay flat, following Dr. Fogel's instructions over the phone. She then called the Glenbrook Fire Department for an ambulance and portable oxygen tent. The ambulance arrived in record time, simultaneously with Dr. Fogel, who gave me oxygen and an injection to relieve the pain. As no rooms were available at the Stamford Hospital, arrangements were made to admit me to the Greenwich Hospital. Preceded by a police car, the ambulance rushed through traffic, Dr. Fogel administering oxygen to me en route. The attack was diagnosed as coronary thrombosis, and I was placed on the critical list.

A curious incident took place soon after I was brought to the hospital. In registering me, Doris entered my religion as Catholic. As I have already told you, I am not a good Catholic in the strict sense of the word. (Only once in my entire adult life have I taken Holy Communion—on Easter Sunday, in April, 1957—and even that was at the Episcopal Church in Stamford, which I had been attending for years with Doris and the children whenever time and health permitted.) Nevertheless, because I was baptized a Catholic and have never formally changed my religion, Doris felt it her duty to register me at the hospital as a Catholic. While I was lying under an oxygen tent, still in a state of shock, she heard someone knock on the door. It was a Catholic priest who had seen my name on the critical list, and had come to give me the last rites.

Doris stepped out into the corridor, closed the door behind her and begged the priest not to enter. He indignantly reproached her for having taken it upon herself to stand between her husband and God, and between him, the priest, and the discharge of his duties. Doris explained that despite the many years I had spent in the artistic world, I was still in many ways a peasant at heart, and she had heard me tell on several occasions that, in Italy, a village priest calls on a sick person only when all hope has been abandoned. The doctors had told her that I had a fighting chance, and she herself found it unthinkable that I might not pull through. The sight of a priest, she feared, might weaken my will by implanting in me the thought that I was being given up for dead, especially if I caught sight of him as I was coming out of the shock. The priest returned twice and warned Doris that she was taking a grave responsibility upon herself, but she remained firm. How well she knows me!

Ten days crawled by before the doctors removed the oxygen tent and took me off the critical list. I begged to be taken home, but they stalled for nine more days. These were to me days of misery, worse than the preceding period, when I had been in a haze most of the time. The truth is that I am a terrible patient, and completely impossible in a hospital. I hate the smell of medicine, the deathly whiteness everywhere, the precision of a routine not of my own making. However kind and efficient the nurses, I resented their intrusion upon my privacy and was ungrateful and unco-operative. I even went so far as to refuse the hospital food, and for each meal Doris brought me a tray of food cooked in our own kitchen.

Doris drove me home on Friday, December twenty-first. After another three weeks in bed, I began to return to normal life. At first it was as though I had reverted to early childhood, learning how to get out of bed by myself, how to stand on my feet with no one to support me, how to walk. What a joy it was to be able to take a few steps again! What an adventure to cross the entire width of my bedroom, then its length, and then explore the vast stretches of all four bedrooms on our second floor!

Other prodigious feats followed. One day I descended halfway down the stairs to the first landing—exactly six steps. Exhausted by the effort, I stopped. Besides me, as always, was Doris—frightened, excited and happy. I saw tears in her eyes when they met mine, but they were smiling. Somehow, it was at this moment that I became aware of how pale she was, how fragile and tired. She was too young and too lovely, I thought, for the burden I had become to her. My excitability, exaggerated by the illness, constantly threatened the peace and warmth of our home, however patient Doris and the children were. Standing there, halfway down the stairs, I resolved henceforth to keep myself under control. I said nothing to Doris, but she noticed, I am sure, that I was easier to take care of from that day on. I also began to recover more rapidly, just as Dr. Fogel had said I would if I could only learn to keep calm, with the result that my strength is no longer dissipated by outbursts of ill temper.

I was soon able to walk down the entire flight of stairs without help; to wander from room to room all over the house; to step out on the balcony and look at the brook that runs below it, and the trees that climb the steep bank on the other side, tripping over each other in their scramble toward the sunlight on the hilltop. Only three or four acres of the woodland come within the field of my vision, but on those few acres is concentrated the very essence of our earthly existence: old trees die, and young ones replace them; worms eat wood, and birds eat worms; and beasts hunt birds and each other. There is tragedy in this struggle for survival; yet the thought of it does not

make me sad, for it contains something that transcends
tragedy—life renewing itself over and over again.

Now, as I look up at the hillside from my chair on
the balcony, I feel the warmth and excitement of spring-
time more keenly than ever before in my life. Perhaps it
is because I have been on the very edge of the final cycle
and am moving away from it. A semi-invalid, I am grateful for the sense of renewal that comes from a day spent
in the warmth of a loving family without irritability and
pain, and for the anticipation of work to come.

How terribly I miss my work! I miss the sweat and
creative confusion of rehearsals, and the backstage tangle
of ropes and wires. I miss the glare of the bare light bulbs
around my dressing-room mirror, and the colors and
smells of make-up. I miss the fever and the tension before
a performance. Most of all, I miss the callboy's cry: "Curtain going up, Mr. Pinza!"

Ezio's Last Days

By Doris Pinza

❧

*E*ZIO SEEMED to be recovering steadily. There was life in his eyes once more, and he was beginning to rediscover pleasure in food, in recorded music and television programs. And he was spending more time with the children. That was all to the good, but there still remained many hours of idleness to threaten him with boredom. Ezio's was too spirited a temperament to be satisfied with vicarious participation. He had to be doing something himself, and that which he craved above all—acting and singing—was out of his reach for God alone knew how long. He saw Ceroni once, and Edgar Vincent and Gibner King, and then shut himself off from the world. Friends, he knew, would either make pathetic efforts at speaking about everything under the sun except the theater and music world, or would be bubbling over with talk about their own work; and he would feel even more left out of things.

The only people he was seeing were the members of my family, whose visits he enjoyed. And he looked forward to Dr. Fogel's calls, for the doctor is a music lover who discusses opera with knowledge and profound appreciation.

Seeing how heavily time hung on Ezio's hands, I suggested to him that he resume work on the story of his life. Urged on by publishers and his professional associates, he had attempted an autiography soon after he had left *South Pacific,* but life had been too crowded and exciting for Ezio really to have his heart in it. The effort had never achieved satisfactory results. Now, I thought, was the time to go back to the autobiography, and Ezio agreed with me. Consulted, Dr. Fogel encouraged us, making the condition that my husband spend no more than two hours on each session with his collaborator.

This is how Robert Magidoff came into the picture. Ezio and I had read his biography of Yehudi Menuhin, and felt that its author would be the right person for Ezio to work with. By a felicitous coincidence, on the very day before we invited him to visit us, Mr. Magidoff had completed a play which had taken him over a year to write.

The two men took to each other at the very start, so I was not surprised when Ezio said at the conclusion of the conversation that he would join me in seeing Mr. Magidoff to the station—my husband's first automobile ride since his last attack.

As they shook hands in farewell, Ezio said, "I'm glad you came. I feel . . . how should I say it? You are *simpatico.*"

From that day on, they spent two hours a day, several times a week, assembling the material for the book. I frequently sat in on the sessions, occasionally filling in the details of this or that story, or reminding Ezio of some incidents he had forgotten.

Mr. Magidoff also spent many mornings in the den downstairs, studying Ezio's files, clippings, letters and other mementoes of a long and busy life. He would return to the den after a quiet lunch with us, while Ezio rested until about four. Then they had their two-hour session.

Time was now passing much more quickly and pleasantly for Ezio. Elegant and debonair in his sports clothes, he was businesslike and alert. Occasionally he would tell a story with all his old gusto, his voice rising and falling with the action he described. Before we knew it, we were well into the third week of April, 1957. Mr. Magidoff said he would have his final session with Ezio on the thirtieth of the month; he would then be ready to start writing the book.

I shall never forget that thirtieth of April!

Ezio had had a good morning and participated in the interview with his usual alertness, but after an hour or so his attention began to wander. His right leg was bothering him, and he would occasionally stop in mid-sentence to rub it. Once he rose from his chair and walked the length of the living room several times to stir the circulation in his leg. More alarming, a story that would normally glow with life and laughter in his telling now ran its full course in one limp sentence, whereas a remark deserving nothing more boisterous than a smile would cause him to laugh loudly, and keep on laughing. My anxiety grew. Mr. Magidoff and I exchanged glances. He nodded, cut the session short and left.

"You're tired, Ezio," I said. "You'd better go upstairs and lie down."

"Yes, I'd better lie down." And he started walking up the stairs. Suddenly he staggered, his legs giving under him. I caught him just as he started to fall backward, and with great difficulty helped him up the stairs. The weird thing about that terrible climb was his outbursts of laughter, for which there was no reason. He was light-headed and, as the day was very warm, I led him to Gloria's bedroom, the coolest in the house, where he would be more comfortable.

He lay, breathing heavily, while I put my head out of the door to whisper to Clelia, who had come out of her room when she heard us, to call Dr. Fogel. Ezio kept on talking, but was unable at times to produce the right words for what he wanted to say. Hearing the ridiculous phrases that rolled off his lips, Ezio would laugh at them himself. He wanted to say, for instance, that he did not care for his supper tray, but kept repeating, "I don't want my supper slippers." It was as though he were intoxicated, but aware of it. He did not seem frightened. Nor was he in pain.

Dr. Fogel came within a matter of minutes and confirmed my worst forebodings. It was another stroke, this time affecting the speech center as well as the right leg and arm. The doctor gave Ezio a sedative so that he could relax, and said that for the time being nothing else could be done for the patient.

Ezio slept quietly until about midnight, when he

awoke with a start, gasping for breath. Making a super-
human effort, he managed to sit up and began to breathe
with greater ease, but the big chest was heaving, the
eyes full of suffering as he tried to speak.

Taking my hand in his, he looked at me intently and
began, "I want . . . I want . . ."

Then he closed his eyes and gave up trying. I telephoned Dr. Fogel, who rushed over once more, gave
Ezio an injection and called for an oxygen tent.

By morning Ezio's right arm and leg were completely paralyzed, and his power of speech had gone
altogether. Somehow I managed to make myself talk
constantly whenever Ezio was awake, assuring him that
the voice would return. The doctor had said so. Only I
did not tell my husband that the doctor had also added,
"If the patient recovers."

On May fourth, Dr. Fogel and Dr. Resnik, a renowned
consultant, jointly recommended that Ezio be removed
to a hospital. Knowing his aversion to hospitals, I asked,
"What will be done for him there that cannot be done
right here, in his own home?"

Nothing in terms of care, the doctors replied; the
care I was giving Ezio with the help of Clelia and of a
wonderful visiting nurse, Miss Lee Vargo, had a quality
no hospital could offer. There were, however, several
therapies and tests the hospital could give, for which our
home was not equipped.

"What can this accomplish?" I pressed the doctors,
ready to yield at the slightest encouragement.

They looked at each other gloomily. At the very
best, was the reply, the hospital might save half the man

for a brief time. The chances were slim even for this, as the entire right side was now irrevocably paralyzed.

I must have tried to say something, although I cannot remember what it was, but I could not utter a word. Dr. Fogel mercifully suggested that there was no need to make the decision immediately. He would be in again later in the day.

"Yes," I managed to reply. "I want to consult Ezio."

But first I spoke to my father, whose devotion to Ezio had never wavered from the day they met. As a matter of fact, ever since his release from Ellis Island, my husband had sought Daddy's opinion whenever he had a major decision to make. Under the circumstances, Father told me, it would be best to leave Ezio in the peace and dignity of his own home.

I telephoned Ezio's trusted friend, Harold Stern. Advised of the nature of the problem I faced, he got into his car and drove to Stamford.

"I agree with you," he said after one look at Ezio. "He ought to remain at home."

For a brief moment I had thought of talking to Clelia, our oldest child, who, though not yet sixteen at the time, behaved throughout the ordeal with the maturity and sensitivity of an adult. She carried trays, kept charts, answered the telephone, went out on errands, and performed miracles in coaxing Ezio to take liquids. She took care of me, too, seeing to it that I got some food and rest. Still, I hesitated. She was a child, after all, I thought, and I had no right to ask her or the two younger children to share with me the burden of the tragic decision.

I was, at last, ready to speak to Ezio. He always

knew when I entered the room, even if I made no sound, and would grope for my hand the moment I was near the bed. He was a gentle, undemanding patient during that last illness, insisting on one thing only—holding my hand. I stood or sat beside him almost constantly, and he seldom released my hand, even in his sleep. This was a token of such trust and affection that I allowed no one except Clelia to replace me whenever I left his side for brief periods.

I began talking to my dying husband, talking slowly and clearly, choosing the simplest words to explain the problem. In the end I said, "Try hard to answer me. You can stay home, where we'll all take care of you, lovingly. Or you can go to the hospital, where, possibly, they can do more for you. Try hard, Ezio, and tell me what to do. Take you to the hospital?"

I repeated, "The hospital?"

He shook his head.

"Home? Stay at home?"

He nodded several times.

"My answer is no . . . not yet," I told Dr. Fogel when he called again. "Ezio remains at home."

"Knowing your husband," the doctor said, "I think you've made the right decision. This I say as a friend of Mr. Pinza and as his physician."

Then followed hours, days and nights, the details of which are blurred in my memory. I prayed and hoped, waiting for a miracle, holding Ezio's hand, talking to him and taking care of him. All else became unreal. Thus, until the early hours of May seventh. I remember looking at my watch at three in the morning. I must have dozed off after that, my hand in Ezio's, my head on his mattress, for it was five thirty when I looked at the watch again. I suddenly became aware of dark spots on Ezio's pillow —spots of blood which I traced to his ear. Despite the early hour, I summoned Dr. Fogel.

"It was a hemorrhage," he said. "We'll have to stop the anticoagulant, I'm afraid."

This meant, I knew, that the last chance to prevent further blood clots in the brain was now gone completely. It was at this moment that I gave up hope.

The Reverend Keith Chidester, of St. Francis Episcopal Church in Stamford, telephoned later in the morning to inquire about Ezio's condition. The Reverend said that he would pray for Ezio, as he usually did, at his service of intercession. Clelia, who had taken the call, told me of the conversation and I called back, begging the Reverend to offer all the prayers he could. Alarmed at the despair in my voice, he came to the house and asked whether it would comfort us if he gave Ezio the Absolution.

It would, I said, as Ezio was in a coma.

By early evening, the heavy, tortured breathing bespoke such a struggle that the children and I knelt on the floor beside Ezio's bed and prayed to God to take him in His mercy. Then Gloria, our youngest, was driven to my parents' home, to spend the night with Monie, while the older children remained with me at the bedside. Daddy and my two brothers were in and out of the room.

Although Dr. Fogel had said earlier that Ezio was in a coma, I kept talking to him, caressing him, convinced that he heard me and felt my fingers, and wanted me to be with him. Suddenly his breathing became easier, and, several minutes later, ceased altogether. The drawn expression left his face, replaced by one of complete serenity.

My brother Paul called Dr. Fogel, and by the time he came I had removed the oxygen tent and lowered the hospital bed on which Ezio had been propped up all those days.

"Ezio has finally found his peace," I said when Dr. Fogel came in. He bent over the body and listened to the heart. Then, slowly, he shook his head, straightened up and turned to face me, tears welling up in his eyes.

"Yes," he said, "he has found his peace."

Ezio is buried a few short miles away from his home, in the Putnam Cemetery at Greenwich, Connecticut. I selected the plot primarily because it lies near the playground of a grammar school. Children's voices—always music to Ezio's ears—are heard constantly, shouting, singing and laughing. Three majestic pines stand at the foot of the grave, and right over it hang the sheltering branches of an ancient cherry tree. The burial took place on a windy day, and the tree, which was then in full bloom, rained pink blossoms onto Ezio. The monument is of pure white Italian marble, carved in Italy, representing the face, chest and the extended arms of Christ.

Thousands of people paid their last respects to Ezio,

filing past his bier at the funeral home; and thousands more attended the service in the Cathedral of St. John the Divine, in New York City. Friends and admirers of Ezio telephoned, wrote and wired from all over the United States and from the four corners of the world, voicing their sorrow and expressing their esteem of the man and artist that Ezio was. This tribute was movingly summarized by a *New York Times* editorial of May 10, 1957:

One of the rare qualities of Ezio Pinza was his ability to project himself directly into the life of the persons who heard him and saw him. Somehow he made each one of those persons feel that he, Pinza, was deeply concerned with the personal pleasure of everyone who listened. For that reason literally millions of Americans are now mourning the loss of an artist toward whom they have had a feeling of warm and genuine personal friendship.

Even those who did not know his amazing "success story," which is in the best American tradition, must have felt that he embodied it. There was no aloofness about him. His contacts from the stage, like his contacts in and with life, were direct.

The artistic world was interested in his amazing versatility. At the very height of his career in grand opera he turned to other media and became sensationally successful in a Broadway musical and later in motion pictures and television. Here was a man who lived not merely in the world of the fine arts but in the world of other men and women whom he understood.

He was an honor to his profession. But most of all he was a warm and well-loved friend to millions of persons. A very large number of them will genuinely feel, now, that a member of the family has been lost.

Operatic Repertoire

Ezio Pinza sang many roles abroad (marked below by a question mark), of which no record has been kept, prior to his American debut.

OPERA	COMPOSER	ROLE
Die Entführung aus dem Serail (The Abduction from the Seraglio)	Wolf Amadeus Mozart	Osmin
L'Africaine	Giacomo Meyerbeer	Grand Inquisitor & Grand Brahmin
Aida	Giuseppe Verdi	Ramfis
Andrea Chénier	Umberto Giordano	Roucher
Un Ballo in Maschera (The Masked Ball)	Giuseppe Verdi	Samuel Tom
Il Barbiere di Siviglia (The Barber of Seville)	Gioacchino Rossini	Don Basilio
The Bartered Bride	Bedřich Smetana	Kezal
La Bohème	Giacomo Puccini	Colline
Boris Godunov	Modest Mussorgsky	Tsar Boris Pimenn
La Campana Sommersa	Respighi	Il Pastor
Carmen	Georges Bizet	Escamillo
La Cenerentola (Cinderella)	Gioacchino Rossini	Don Magnifico
Les Contes d'Hoffman (The Tales of Hoffman)	Jacques Offenbach	Doctor Miracle Coppelius

OPERA	COMPOSER	ROLE
Le Coq d'Or (The Golden Cockerel)	Nicholas Rimsky-Korsakov	King Dodon
The Damnation of Faust	Hector Berlioz	Mephistopheles
Debora e Jaele	Ildebrando Pizzetti	?
Dejaice	Alfredo Catalani	?
Don Carlos	Giuseppe Verdi	Philip II
Don Giovanni	Wolfgang Amadeus Mozart	Don Giovanni
Don Pasquale	Gaetano Donizetti	Don Pasquale
Ernani	Giuseppe Verdi	Don Ruy Gomez de Silva
The Fair at Sorochintzy	Modest Mussorgsky	Tcherevick
Falstaff	Giuseppe Verdi	Pistola
Faust	Charles Francis Gounod	Mephistopheles
La Favorita	Gaetano Donizetti	Baldassare
Fedra	Ildebrando Pizzetti	?
Fedora	Umberto Giordano	Grech
Fidelio	Ludwig van Beethoven	Rocco
La Figlia del Regimento (The Daughter of the Regiment)	Gaetano Donizetti	Suppizio
Der Fliegende Höllander	Richard Wagner	Delaud
La Forza del Destino (The Force of Destiny)	Giuseppe Verdi	Padre Guardiano
Fra Gherardo	Ildebrando Pizzetti	Podesta & Old Man

OPERA	COMPOSER	ROLE
Gianni Schicchi	Giacomo Puccini	Simone
La Gioconda	Amilcare Ponchielli	Alvise
Guglielmo Tell (William Tell)	Gioacchino Rossini	Walter Furst
Hamlet	Ambroise Thomas	?
Iris	Pietro Mascagni	Il Cieco
Isabeau	Pietro Mascagni	?
L'Italiana in Algeri (The Italian girl in Algiers)	Gioacchino Rossini	Mustafa
		?
La Juive	Jacques François Halévy	Cardinal de Brogni
Khovanshtchina	Modest Mussorgsky	Dositheus
Lakmé	Léo Delibes	Nilakantha
L'Amore dei Tre Rè (The Love of Three Kings)	Italo Montemezzi	Archibaldo
L'Elisir d'Amore (The Elixir of Love)	Gaetano Donizetti	Dr. Dulcamara
L'Incoronazione di Poppea (The Coronation of Poppea)	Claudio Monteverdi	?
Linda di Chamounix	Gaetano Donizetti	The Prefect
Lohengrin	Richard Wagner	King Henry
Loreley	Alfredo Catalani	Margravio
Louise	Gustave Charpentier	Louise's father
Lucia di Lammermoor	Gaetano Donizetti	Raimondo
Luisa Miller	Giuseppe Verdi	Count Walter
Macbeth	Giuseppe Verdi	Banquo
Manon Lescaut	Giacomo Puccini	Geronte de Ravoir
Mefistofele	Arrigo Boito	Mefistofele
Die Meistersinger	Richard Wagner	Pogner

OPERA	COMPOSER	ROLE
Mignon	Ambroise Thomas	Lothario
Moses	Gioacchino Rossini	Moses
La Navarraise	Jules Massenet	?
Nerone	Arrigo Boito	Tigellino
Norma	Vincenzo Bellini	The Archdruid Oroveso
Le Nozze di Figaro (The Marriage of Figaro)	Wolfgang Amadeus Mozart	Figaro Count Almaviva
Otello	Giuseppe Verdi	Lodovico
Parsifal	Richard Wagner	Gurnemanz
The Pearl Fishers	Georges Bizet	Nourabad
Pelléas et Mélisande	Claude A. Debussy	Arkel & Golaud
Le Prophète	Giacomo Meyerbeer	Matthisen Zacharias
I Puritani	Vincenzo Bellini	Sir George Walton
Rienzi	Richard Wagner	?
Rigoletto	Giuseppe Verdi	Sparafucile
Roméo et Juliette	Charles Francis Gounod	Friar Lawrence
Sacùntala	Franco Alfano	?
Samson et Dalila	Camille Saint-Saëns	The Old Hebrew
Il Signore Bruschino	Gioacchino Rossini	Gaudenzio
Simon Boccanegra	Giuseppe Verdi	Jacopo Fiesco
La Sonnambula	Vincenzo Bellini	Count Rodolfo
The Sunken Bell	Ottorino Respighi	The Parson
Il Tabarro	Giacomo Puccini	Talpa
Tannhäuser	Richard Wagner	Landgraff Hermann
Thäis	Jules Massenet	Palemon
Tristan and Isolde	Richard Wagner	King Mark
Il Trovatore	Giuseppe Verdi	Ferrando
Turandot	Giacomo Puccini	Timur

OPERA	COMPOSER	ROLE
Tsar Saltana	Nicholas Rimsky-Korsakov	Nicholas
La Vestale	Gasparo Spontini	Pontifex Maximus
La Wally	Alfredo Catalani	Stromminger
Die Zauberflöte (The Magic Flute)	Wolfgang Amadeus Mozart	Sarastro

Oratorio and Orchestral Works

Mass in B Minor	Johann Sebastian Bach
Manzoni Requiem	Giuseppe Verdi
Missa Solemnis (in Latin)	Ludwig van Beethoven
Ninth Symphony (in German)	Ludwig van Beethoven

Index

Academy of Music. SEE New York City

Aïda. SEE Verdi, Giuseppe

American Academy of Dramatic Arts. SEE New York City

American Guild of Musical Artists, the (AMGA), 224

Andoga, Victor, 172, 173, 175, 178

Andrea Doria, the, 270

Atkinson, Brooks [Quoted], 263

Atlanta, Georgia, 191

Attorney General of the United States. SEE Biddle, Francis

Aurthur, Robert Alan, 261, 270

Very Special Baby, A, 270, 271

"Babes in Toyland." SEE Herbert, Victor

Baccaloni, Salvatore, 259

Bagnacavallo, Italy, 111, 112

Ballet Russe, 197

Baranova, ———, 197

Barber of Seville, The. SEE Rossini, Gioacchino

Beaumarchais, ———, 163, 165, 166

Beethoven, Ludwig van, 103, 186

"In Questa Tomba Oscura," 186

Ninth Symphony, 103

Bellini, Vincenzo, 61, 64, 153

Norma, 61, 63

Sonnambula, La, 64, 103

Berlioz, Hector, 27

Damnation of Faust, The, 27

"Song of the Roses," 27

Berman, S. N., 261

Beverly Hills, California, 232

Biddle, Francis, 213, 219, 220–221, 222, 227

Blakemore, Dr. Charles, 215

Board, the [Hearing of Ezio Pinza], 212, 213, 217, 218, 220, 222

Bodanzky, Artur, 149

Bohème, La. SEE Puccini, Giacomo

Boito, Arrigo, 108, 109, 111

Nerone, 103, 108

Mefistofele, 109, 111

"Ecco il Mondo," 109, 112

Boller, John Hall, 260

Boller, Mrs. John Hall. SEE Pinza, Claudia

Boller, Johnny, 260
Boller, Marina, 260
Bologna, Italy, 44, 46, 47, 49, 51, 64, 67, 76, 98, 110, 111, 130, 156
Conservatory, 49, 53, 54, 56, 58, 60
Bonino, 261
Bori, Lucrezia, 126–127, 230
Boris Godunov. SEE Mussorgsky, Modest
Boston, Massachusetts, 242
Boston *Globe*, the. SEE *Globe*, the Boston
Brownlee, John, 167
Buenos Aires, Argentina, 107, 115, 176
Teatro Colón, 107, 116, 118, 176
Buffalo Bill's Wild West Show, 36
Burgarelli (family), 3, 6, 7, 9–10, 19, 20, 21, 22, 23, 86
Burgarelli, Adele, 22, 23, 31
Burgarelli, Clelia. SEE Pinza, Mrs. Cesare
Burgarelli, Gino, 20–21, 22, 23, 28, 31, 58, 108, 201
Byron, Lord, 37

"Calunnia, La." SEE Rossini, Gioacchino
Calusio, ———, 99–100, 103

Carmen, 62, 131
"Carnegie Hall," 232
"Caro Mio Ben." SEE Giordani, ———
Carusi, Ugo, 221, 227
Caruso, Enrico, 62, 71, 99, 107
Cassinelli (family), 60, 75, 76, 77, 86, 87, 89, 113
Cassinelli, Alessandra, 59, 75, 85–86, 89
Cassinelli, Augusta, 59, 60, 75, 76, 85–87, 89, 93, 98, 107, 111, 114–116, 117, 141–143, 144, 146–148, 150, 155, 187, 188, 192–193, 196, 223
Cassinelli, Giuseppe, 113
Cathedral of St. John the Divine. SEE New York City
Cavallaro, ———, 67
Ceroni, Otello, 66, 108–109, 144–145, 146, 147, 278
Certago, Italy, 108
Chaliapin, Feodor, 94, 99, 107, 123, 132, 171, 176–178, 179, 186
Chidester, Reverend Keith, 285
Chotzinoff, Samuel [Quoted], 168
Cimara, ———, 186
"Fiocca la Neve," 186
Cleveland, Ohio, 138, 234
Collins, Edward, 212

Condotti Dance Club, 39
"*Cor, Le.*" SEE Flegier, ⸺
Corona, ⸺, 138
Cosgriff, Dr. Stuart, 266, 267
Crooks, Richard, 126
Crosby, Bing, 57

Damnation of Faust, The.
  SEE Berlioz, Hector
D'Andrade, ⸺, 149
D'Angelo, Louis, 167
Danilova, ⸺, 197
Dante, 7, 15–16, 134
  Divine Comedy, 15–16
  Inferno, 134
da Ponte, Lorenzo, 134, 153, 165, 166
Deborah and Jael, 103
Defrere, ⸺, 225
Delibes, Léo, 188
  Lakmé, 188, 199
Dellera, ⸺, 120
Dell'Orefice, ⸺, 134
de Luca, Giuseppe, 135
Denver, Colorado, 232
De Paolis, Alessio, 167, 180
de Reszke, Édouard, 186
de Segurola, Andrès, 62
Didur, Adamo, 176
di Giovanni, Edoardo, 119
  SEE ALSO Johnson, Edward
Di Preta, Dr. Michael, 269
Dolomites, the, 68, 69, 72, 93

Domingo, Dr. ⸺, 116
Donizetti, Gaetano, 65, 153
  Favorita, La, 65, 110, 163
  Lucia di Lammermoor, 103, 123
Doolittle, General James, 226
Dodgers, the (Brooklyn), 251, 264, 267

Eames, ⸺, 132
Early to Bed, 234
"*Ecco il Mondo.*" SEE Boito, Arrigo
Edinburgh Festival, 164
Ellis Island. SEE New York City
Engelman, Wilfred, 222
  [Quoted], 220
Ernani. SEE Verdi, Giuseppe
Ernst, Morris, 210–211
  [Quoted], 218–219
Ezio Pinza Show, The, 261

Faenza, Italy, 109
"*Fa La Nana Bambin,*" 257
Fanny, 261–262, 263, 264, 265, 266, 267, 268, 270
Farell, Marita, 167
Farrar, Geraldine, 103
Faust, 126
Favorita, La. SEE Donizetti, Gaetano
FBI, 206, 207, 220, 233

Federal Court, New York.
    SEE New York City
Ferrer, Jose [Quoted], 245
Field, Dr. William, 269
Fiji Islands, 159
Finch Junior College. SEE
    New York City
"Fiocca la Neve." SEE
    Cimara, ———
Flegier, ———, 186
    "Cor, Le," 186
Fleischer, Editha, 136, 139
Fogel, Dr. David, 263–264,
    265, 267, 269, 274, 276,
    279, 281, 282, 283, 284,
    285, 286
Foley Square Courthouse.
    SEE New York City
Forza del Destino, La. SEE
    Verdi, Giuseppe
Francis, Muriel, 241
Friends of New Music, the,
    220
Froman, Jane, 261

Gadski, ———, 132
Galleria, the. SEE Milan,
    Italy
Gatti-Casazza, Giulio, 107,
    120, 123, 127–129, 130,
    131, 132, 133, 134–135,
    137–138, 140, 162, 163–
    164, 177, 178
Gatti-Casazza, Giulio
    [Quoted], 163, 176

Giannini, Dusolina, 152
Gilman, Lawrence
    [Quoted], 121, 139
Gioconda, La, 123
Giordani, ———, 186
    "Caro Mio Ben," 186
"Girommetta, La." SEE Si-
    bella, ———
Globe, the Boston, 251–252
Golden Cockerel, The. SEE
    Rimsky-Korsakov,
    Nicholas
Graf, Herbert, 167
Grand Canyon, 254
Grand Opera of Paris. SEE
    Paris, France
Greenbaum,   Wolff   and
    Ernst, 210
Greenwich, Connecticut, 286
    hospital at, 274
    Putnam Cemetery, 286
Guarda Batteria, 72, 82
Guarnieri, ———, 103
Guiccioli, Countess, 37

Halliday, Dick, 237, 246, 247
Hamlet (opera), 163
Hammerstein, Oscar, 235,
    236, 237, 240, 242–243,
    246
Harris, Jed, 234
Harris, Ruth, 191
Hayward, Leland, 236, 237
Herald Tribune, The New
    York [Quoted], 121, 139

Herbert, Victor, 232
  "Babes in Toyland," 232, 233
His Master's Voice (HMV), 107, 108
Hollywood, California, 201, 230, 231, 233, 254, 255
Hollywood Bowl, 231
Hope, Bob [Quoted], 253
Hope, Constance, 185, 195, 209, 210, 241
Horseshoe Harbor Club, Larchmont, 203
Hotel Ansonia. SEE New York City
Hotel Delmonico. SEE New York City

"Il Lacerato Spirito." SEE Verdi, Giuseppe
"In Questa Tomba Oscura." SEE Beethoven, Ludwig van
International Ladies Garment Workers Union, the, 220

Johnson, Edward, 119, 164, 166, 178, 209, 223, 227
  SEE ALSO di Giovanni, Edoardo
Jorgulesco, Jonel, 167
Joseph II (Emperor of Austria), 166, 167

Journal-American, the New York [Quoted], 263
Journet, Marcel, 103, 104, 106
Jurinac, Sena, 164

Kent, Atwater, 231
King, Gibner, 57, 187, 269, 278
Kismet, 234
Kollmar, Dick, 234
Kolodin, Irving [Quoted], 129, 180
Koverman, Ida, 231

LaGuardia, Fiorello, 210, 221, 225
Lakmé. SEE Delibes, Léo
L'Arbore di Diana. SEE Solar, Martin y
Larchmont, New York, 189, 190, 194, 196
  Horseshoe Harbor Club, 203
Lauri-Volpi, Giacomo, 110–111, 120
Lawrence, Robert [Quoted], 129–130
Lazzari, Virgilio, 152, 167, 217
Leak, Doris. SEE Pinza, Doris
Leak, Monie. SEE Leak, Mrs. William
Leak, Paul, 286

Leak, Dr. William, 189, 190, 194, 197, 198, 199, 200, 201, 210, 221, 222, 283
Leak, Mrs. William, 194–195, 197, 198, 199, 200, 201, 203, 285
Leigh, Janet, 255
Lester, Edwin, 234–235
Levine, Marks, 184–185, 186, 209, 222, 224, 227, 231, 232, 233
Licia (———), 38, 39, 40, 41, 42, 87, 122
Lillie, Beatrice, 261
Lincoln Square Project. SEE New York City
Logan, Joshua, 236, 240–241, 242, 261, 262, 263
Lohengrin. SEE Wagner, Richard
Los Angeles, California, 231, 235
  Coliseum at, 226
  Light Opera Association, 234
Louise, 103, 104
Love of Three Kings, The. SEE Montemezzi, Italo
Lucia di Lammermoor. SEE Donizetti, Gaetano
Ludikar, Pavel, 135, 136, 137, 138, 141
Lugano, Switzerland, 161

McLaughlin, Charles, 248

Magic Flute, The. SEE Mozart, Wolfgang Amadeus
Magidoff, Robert, 279–280, 281
Magill, Wallace, 187
Mahler, Gustav, 132
Majestic Theatre. SEE New York City
Manon Lescaut. SEE Puccini, Giacomo
Mantua, Italy, 175
Marchase, Joe, 269
Marmaroneck, New York, 203
Marseille, France, 158
Martin, Karlheinz, 148, 152
Martin, Mary, 202, 236, 237, 240, 245–249
Martinelli, Giovanni, 129
Masked Ball, The. SEE Verdi, Giuseppe
Mayer, Louis B., 231
Mefistofele. SEE Boito, Arrigo
Meistersinger, Die. SEE Wagner, Richard
Metropolitan Opera. SEE New York City
M-G-M, 231, 254
Michener, James A., 235
  Tales of the South Pacific, 235
Milan, Italy, 5, 60, 63, 64, 98, 107, 117
  Galleria, the, 61, 107, 117
  Scala, La (Teatro alla

Scala), 5, 61, 98, 99, 101,
103, 104, 106, 107, 108,
114, 118, 119, 162, 172,
176
Milano-Marittima, Italy, 270
Molnar, Ferenc, 261
Play's the Thing, The, 234,
261
Montemezzi, Italo, 170
Love of Three Kings, The,
170
Montreal, Canada, 224, 225
Morros, Boris, 231, 232, 233
Moscona, Nicola, 266
Mozart, Wolfgang Amadeus,
134, 136, 148, 149, 150,
152, 153, 162, 163, 165,
166, 227
Don Giovanni, 132–140,
141, 144, 148, 153–154,
158, 163, 164, 165, 166,
169, 171, 179, 234, 271
"La Ci Darem la Mano,"
132
Magic Flute, The, 62, 227
Marriage of Figaro, The
(*Le Nozze di Figaro*),
148, 162–169, 180, 186
"Non Piu Andrai," 186
Mr. Ambassador, 234
"Mr. Imperium," 255
Munich, Germany, 271
Munsel, Patrice, 261
"Mussolini." SEE Lazzari,
Virgilio

Mussolini, Benito, 216, 217,
219, 220
Mussorgsky, Modest, 170,
173–174, 176
Boris Godunov, 96, 103,
113, 123, 133, 169–180,
255
Mussorgsky, Modest
[Quoted], 173
Muzio, Claudia, 116

Nagliati, Major, ———, 71
Naples, Italy, 87
Nathan, George Jean
[Quoted], 253, 263
National Concert and Artist
Corporation, The
(NCAC), 184
NBC, 184
Nerone. SEE Boito, Arrigo
New Haven, Connecticut,
241, 242
Shubert Theater, 242
New Orleans, Louisiana, 191
New York City, 117, 136, 142,
144, 154, 158, 192, 195,
215, 226, 229, 233, 235,
242, 272
Academy of Music, 118
American Academy of
Dramatic Arts, 197
Cathedral of St. John the
Divine, 287
Ellis Island, 207, 210, 214,
215

New York City (*cont.*)
Federal Court, 222
Finch Junior College, 197
Foley Square Courthouse, 207
Hotel Ansonia, 143, 144
Hotel Delmonico, 266, 269
Lincoln Square Project, 118
Majestic Theatre, 242, 246, 249
Metropolitan Opera, 115, 117–119, 120, 121, 122, 123, 125, 128, 129, 130, 131, 132, 135, 136, 138, 142, 152, 158, 162, 163, 166, 167, 169, 176, 177, 178, 183, 188, 190, 198, 205, 216, 219, 220, 223, 224, 227, 229, 234, 243, 260
Presbyterian Hospital, 266, 272
New York *Herald Tribune,* the. SEE *Herald Tribune,* the New York
New York *Journal American,* the. SEE *Journal American* the New York
New York *Post,* the. SEE *Post,* the New York
New York Times, The [Quoted], 210, 263, 287–288
Niagara Falls, 36, 145

"Non Piu Andrai." SEE Mozart, Wolfgang Amadeus
Norma. SEE Bellini, Vincenzo
North American Newspaper Alliance, The, 251
Novak, Joseph, 179

"O Sole Mio," 43

Padua, Italy, 119
Teatro Verdi, 119
Pagnol, Marcel, 261
Pago Pago, 159, 217
Palermo, Italy, 67
Opera House, 67
Paltrinieri, Giordano, 167
Panizza, Ettore, 167, 179
Paramount, 232
Paris, France, 103, 158, 179
Grand Opera of, 158
Opéra, 179
Théâtre des Champs Élysées, 103
Pasubio, Italy, 77
Patton, General George, 226
Petina, Irra, 167
Pinza, Alfonso, 6, 14, 31
Pinza, Augusta. SEE Cassinelli, Augusta
Pinza, Beniamina, 6, 26, 31, 113
Pinza, Cesare, 3, 4–6, 7–8, 10–13, 14–15, 16–18, 23,

25, 26, 28–29, 30, 31, 32–
33, 39, 41–42, 43, 44, 46,
47–48, 49, 50, 51, 58, 65–
66, 68, 75–76, 89, 108,
110, 111–112, 113, 130,
201, 262

Pinza, Mrs. Cesare, 3, 4, 6–7,
8, 10, 11, 13–14, 31–32,
36, 67–68, 75, 89, 108,
111, 112–113, 201

Pinza, Claudia, 116, 117, 141,
143, 145, 148, 150, 260

Pinza, Clelia (daughter of
Ezio), 12, 204, 205, 206,
214–215, 226, 254, 257,
259, 260–261, 281, 283,
284, 285

Pinza, Doris, 41, 188–192,
193–201, 202, 203, 205,
206–207, 209, 210, 211,
213, 214–215, 221, 222,
223, 228, 229, 231, 236,
237, 241, 254, 256, 257,
258, 259–260, 266, 267,
268, 270, 271, 272–273,
274–275, 276

Pinza, Doris [Quoted], 225–
226, 278–287

Pinza, Gloria, 12, 254, 256–
257, 259, 285

Pinza, Pietro, 12, 228, 254,
257–258, 259, 264

Plançon, Pol, 186

Play's the Thing, The. SEE
Molnar, Ferenc

Polacco,———, 62

Pons, Lily, 126

Ponselle, Rosa, 120, 129, 136,
138, 249

Portinari, Mr.———, 33–34,
58, 70, 78

Portinari, Guido, 19, 33

Post, the New York, 168

Prato, Italy, 63

Presbyterian Hospital. SEE
New York City

Prince Igor, 198

Puccini, Giacomo, 63
Bohème, La, 62, 103
Manon Lescaut, 63

Puta Riva (mountain), 69

Pushkin, Aleksandr, 170

Putnam Cemetery. SEE
Greenwich, Connecti-
cut

Ravenna, Italy, 3, 6, 7, 15–
16, 19, 23, 25, 26, 27, 36,
37, 42, 47, 53, 60, 65, 66,
76
Rotondo, 26, 27, 42
opera house at, 65

Red Cross, the, 220

Reinhardt, Max, 150, 241
Everyman, 150–151, 154,
271

Resnik, Dr. ———, 282

Rethberg, Elisabeth, 127,
167

Reuben (———), 203–204

Rieseman, —— [Quoted], 174

Rigoletto. SEE Verdi, Giuseppe

Rimini, Italy, 89

Rimsky-Korsakov, Nicholas, 64

Golden Cockerel, The (Le Coq d'Or), 62, 64, 126

Rodgers, Richard, 235, 236, 237–238, 240

Rome, Harold, 261

Rome, Italy, 3, 4, 5, 7, 87, 88, 94, 98, 99, 109, 171

Teatro Constanzi (Teatro Reale dell'Opera), 87–88, 95, 98, 99, 109, 171

Rossini, Gioacchino, 153, 162, 163, 186

Barber of Seville, The, 62, 123, 162, 163, 169, 186, 225

"Calunnia, La," 186

Rotondo. SEE Ravenna, Italy

Royal Theatre. SEE Turino, Italy

Ruffo, Titta, 129

Russian Opera Company, the, 198

Ruzza, ——, 50, 51–52, 53, 55

Rye, New York, 249

Sachse, Leopold, 179

St. Francis Episcopal Church. SEE Stamford, Connecticut

Salieri, ——, 134

Tarare, 134

Salzburg, Austria, 136, 148, 150–151, 152, 154, 155, 156, 158, 160, 162, 164, 166, 271

Festival at, 136, 148, 150–151, 152, 154, 155, 156, 158

San Francisco, California, 41, 159, 225, 226

Opera Company, 224

Sayão, Bidù, 167

Scala, La. SEE Milan, Italy

Schuster, Dr. George, 212

Scotti, Antonio, 132, 135

Sembrich, ——, 132

Serafin, Tullio, 98, 103, 107, 116, 131–132, 133, 134, 136, 137

Shubert Theater. SEE New Haven, Connecticut

Sibella, ——, 186

"Girommetta, La," 186

Siena, Italy, 47, 48

Siepi, Cesare, 271

Simon Boccanegra. SEE Verdi, Giuseppe

Smith, Dr. Elsworth, 214–215, 222

Solar, Martin y, 134

L'Arbore di Diana, 134

"Some Enchanted Baseball,"
     251–252
"Some Enchanted Evening."
     SEE *South Pacific*
Soncino, Italy, 62
"Song of the Roses." SEE
     Berlioz, Hector
Sonnambula, La. SEE Bellini,
     Vincenzo
South Pacific, 57, 139, 202,
     236, 237, 238–243, 245,
     249, 250, 251, 253, 254,
     262, 263, 279
     "Some Enchanted Even-
          ing," 238, 250
     "A Wonderful Guy," 238
Spadoni, Giacomo [Quoted],
     218, 220
Spontini, Gasparo, 120
     Vestale, La, 120
Stamford, Connecticut, 256,
     266, 272, 285
     St. Francis Episcopal
          Church, 274, 285
Stanislavsky, Constantine, 97
"Star-Spangled Banner,
     The," 226
Stern, Harold, 211, 213, 214,
     216, 217, 218, 220, 251,
     283
Stevens, Risë, 167
Stone, Ezra, 261
"Strictly Dishonorable," 255
Strnad, ———, 148
Suez Canal, 158–159
Susskind, David, 271

Sydney, Australia, 159
Sydney, Sylvia, 270

Tabbert, Bill, 259
Tales of the South Pacific.
     SEE Michener, James A.
Tarare. SEE Salieri, ———
Teatro Colón. SEE Buenos
     Aires, Argentina
Teatro Constanzi (Teatro
     Reale dell'Opera). SEE
     Rome, Italy
Teatro Verdi. SEE Padua,
     Italy
Telephone Hour, The, 187
Théâtre des Champs Élysées.
     SEE Paris, France
Tibbett, Lawrence, 268, 269–
     270
Times, The New York. SEE
     New York Times, The
"Tonight We Sing," 178, 255
Toscanini, Arturo, 98, 99,
     100–103, 104, 105–106,
     107, 108, 114, 150, 151,
     160, 176
Toscanini, Wally, 160, 161
Toumanova, ———, 197
Treasury Department, U.S.,
     220
Tresca, Carlo [Quoted],
     219–220
Trieste [Austria], 28, 29, 30
Tristan und Isolde. SEE
     Wagner, Richard

Truman, Margaret, 261
Turino, Italy, 98
  Royal Theatre, 98
Turner, Lana, 255

United States Treasury Department, 220

Vanderbilt, William H., 118
Van Dusen, Dr. Henry, 212
Vargo, Lee, 282
Variety [Quoted], 262–263
Verdi, Giuseppe, 49, 53, 63, 95, 103, 129, 153, 169, 186, 207
  Aïda, 103, 116, 123
  Ernani, 49, 63, 129
  Forza del Destino, La, 123
  "Il Lacerato Spirito," 186
  Masked Ball, The, 95
  Requiem, 103
  Rigoletto, 123, 126
  Simon Boccanegra, 53, 88, 186
Very Special Baby, A. SEE Aurthur, Robert Allen
Vestale, La. SEE Spontini, Gasparo
Vezzani, Alessandro, 49–50, 52–56, 60, 61
Vienna Opera, 164
Vincent, Edgar, 241–242, 269, 278
Vorhees, Don, 187

Votipka, Thelma, 126, 222
Votto, ———, 99

Wagner, Richard, 99, 101, 103, 169
  Lohengrin, 103
  Meistersinger, Die, 99, 104
  Tristan und Isolde, 103
Walter, Bruno, 101–102, 140, 148, 150, 151, 152, 153, 154, 155, 158, 160, 161, 162, 164, 166, 168, 169, 201, 211, 221, 227, 231, 234
Walter, Bruno [Quoted], 148–150
Walter, Mrs. Bruno, 160, 161, 201, 231
Walter, Gretel ("Greta"), 154–155, 156, 157–158, 159–161, 196
Walter, Lotte, 154, 157, 160
Waring, Fred, 232
Washington, D.C., 221
White Horse Inn, 198
Wild West Show, Buffalo Bill's, 36
Wilson, Earl [Quoted], 246
World War I, 25, 69–84, 109
World War II, 202
Wynn, Ed, 261

Yakovlev, Alexei, 197

Yankees, the (New York), 251

Zaleski, Sigizmund, 94–95, 96–97, 103–104, 123, 171

Zinetti, Madame ———, 60, 61, 64
Zurich, Switzerland, 155 159, 160